# THE
# DEVELOPMENT
# OF AN EDUCATION
# SERVICE

# THE DEVELOPMENT OF AN EDUCATION SERVICE

## The West Riding 1889–1974

P. H. J. H. Gosden
P. R. Sharp

MARTIN ROBERTSON

44094486

First published in 1978 by Martin Robertson & Co. Ltd.
108 Cowley Road, Oxford OX4 1JF

ISBN 0 85520 150 9

Typeset by Vantage Photosetting Co. Ltd., Southampton.
Printed and bound by Richard Clay (The Chaucer Press) Ltd.,
Bungay, Suffolk.

# *Contents*

# LIST OF TABLES

# Acknowledgements

Many people have contributed to this study. After the closing down of the West Riding Education Authority in 1974, a small 'holding force' remained for a while to arrange access for successor authorities to papers which they required for daily administrative work. We are grateful to the three members of this group, Mr Harry Haigh, Mr Edward Hepworth and Mr Norman Oldroyd for the considerable assistance they gave us in finding our way into the files and source material in the early stages. We wish to express our appreciation of the assistance afforded by Wakefield Metropolitan District Council, which accommodated the researchers for nearly two years while they worked on records held in Wakefield, and of the help given by many of the Council's staff, especially Mr Reginald Eyles, Mr John Chalkley, Mr Horace Kamplay, Miss Joyce Graham and Mr John Goodchild.

We have had ample cause to appreciate the assistance given us by members of staff of the following: the West Yorkshire County Records Office, especially Mrs Elizabeth Berry and Mr Robert Frost; the Brotherton and Institute of Education Libraries in this University, especially Mr J. R. V. Johnston; the Leeds City Reference Library; the Wakefield City Library; the Huddersfield Public Library, and the *Huddersfield Examiner*. Former members of the West Riding Education Committee have helped by providing information, and Mrs Jessie Smith loaned to us the papers she has accumulated since joining the Council in the 1930s. Among those who have worked in the institutions of the West Riding Authority we would particularly wish to thank Mr L. C. G. Gilling and Mr W. Bicknell for the information they have provided. Sir Alec Clegg took the initiative which led to this study being undertaken and has been particularly helpful not only in providing oral evidence but also by making his personal papers available to us.

Perhaps the heaviest obligation we have incurred in writing this book is to Mrs Linda Shepherd and Dr Robert Neville, who worked on this project as research assistants. Their help in working through quantities of material in the files, in drawing attention to the relevant and the useful, and in many other ways has been invaluable. After Dr Neville left to take up another post, Mr Kenneth Dobson took his place and helped in the final stages. We are grateful to Miss Joan Booth, who has shown unfailing patience and understanding in typing from our drafts.

We would like to thank Mr Jim Hogan and Mr George Taylor for reading the text in draft. Their comments have been valuable in many ways, not least in enabling us to avoid some of our grosser errors.

Finally we wish to acknowledge the part played by those bodies which generously funded this study, thereby making it possible: the Social Science Research Council, the West Riding County Council and the Brotherton Trust. The former Institute of Education of this University made provision to assist with the costs of publication.

*School of Education*                                   *P. H. J. H. Gosden*
*Leeds University*                                              *P. R. Sharp*

# Introduction

A consequence of the reorganisation of local government in 1974 was that one of the largest county education authorities was reorganised to the point at which it went completely out of existence. However drastic their changes of boundary or methods of working, other large county authorities survived. The demise of the West Riding therefore presented a unique opportunity to study the life and death of an authority. A similar study of the policy and administration of authorities which have continuing existences is not possible, simply because no authority remaining in the business is in a position to open all of its records.

The extent and variety of conditions which existed in the West Riding would in any case have made it a particularly interesting and useful case to study from the point of view of the education service. The local education system had to meet the needs of the textile communities in the west, of the coalfield communities in the south, of the extensive rural areas in the north and of the prosperous suburban districts which grew up in the county area outside the cities.

Against this background, the West Riding was in many ways a pioneering authority, with a good record of developing new approaches to educational problems dating back to 1891. Proponents of the local education authority system believe that it permits individual authorities to produce solutions to problems within their own areas which can later be adopted on a national scale. We believe that this study shows that this did indeed happen in the case of the West Riding. On the other hand a considerable degree of local autonomy can bring some loss; the remarkable persistence of a traditionally hostile attitude to voluntary schools, for instance, seems to have had the effect of delaying improvements in the quality of the education which such schools could offer.

The perceptive reader may notice a difference in style between the earlier and later chapters. The passage of time enables the student to put events of earlier years more clearly in perspective, and perhaps to discuss them more concisely, than is always possible with more recent developments. Moreover, for the later years, the documentation on which this study is based itself differs.

The principal sources for our work are indicated by the references. While the minutes of the County Council and of the Education Committee and its various sub-committees have been essential, it was the memoranda prepared for committee use, items of correspondence and internal office minutes which frequently served to supply the why and wherefore for policy decisions. We had completely free access to recent papers of a personal and confidential nature and these have provided us with essential information for this study. We have not thought it right at this date to quote from or to make specific references to these papers and we should perhaps add that they are not generally available.

*. . . I must tread tenderly because I go not, as before, on men's graves, but am ready to touch the quick of some yet alive. I know how dangerous it is to follow truth too near to the heels; yet better it is that the the teeth of an historian be struck out of his head for writing the truth than that they remain still and rot in his jaws by feeding too much on the sweetmeats of flattery.*

Thomas Fuller (1608–1661) *The Church History of Britain*

# CHAPTER I

# *The Precursor: the Technical Instruction Committee*

When the West Riding County Council held its first meetings in 1889, it had no powers or responsibilities in the field of education. This situation was rapidly changed, however, by the passing of the Technical Instruction Act in August of that year. This enabled (but did not compel) county councils and urban sanitary authorities to raise a penny rate and spend the proceeds on technical education. The West Riding County Council did not hesitate to take up this measure and soon a committee was appointed 'with a view to giving effect to the Act'.[1]* This committee consisted of the chairman and the vice-chairman of the County Council, three aldermen and seven councillors. The chairman of the County Council and of the newly created Technical Instruction Committee was the Marquis of Ripon, a distinguished statesman of considerable standing who had held office in every Liberal government since 1859. The Marquis, moreover, had a strong interest in education and had served in Gladstone's first ministry as Lord President of the Committee of Council on Education. He was also President of the Yorkshire College, Leeds, a Vice-President of the National Association for the Promotion of Technical and Secondary Education[2] and a prominent member (from 1890 President) of the Yorkshire Union of Mechanics' Institutes. Among the other members of the original committee Alderman John Brigg[3] of Keighley was prominent. Brigg, who secured first place in the aldermanic elections in 1889, was an experienced educationist. He was President of the Keighley Mechanics' Institute and a governor of Giggleswick public school and of several local grammar schools and technical colleges. During November 1889 both Ripon

*All notes and references to sources will be found at the end of the book.

and Brigg worked hard to obtain as much information as possible about the powers given to county councils by the Technical Instruction Act. West Riding delegates were sent to a conference at the Mayor's Parlour, Manchester, held under the auspices of the National Association, to consider technical education. Ripon, moreover, invited Swire Smith,[4] a leading contemporary authority on technical instruction, to spend a weekend at Studley Royal to discuss the implications of the Act.

The first meeting of the Technical Instruction Committee was held on 6 December 1889 – one of the first meetings concerned with education ever held by an English county council. W. V. Dixon, the Deputy Clerk of the Peace in the county, attended and was asked to act as clerk, a service which he performed throughout the Committee's existence. At the meeting it was decided that before action could be taken the Committee needed a clearer notion of its powers, and the clerk was instructed to write to the Science and Art Department and the Local Government Board for guidance.[5] In April 1890 the County Council agreed to make the Technical Instruction Committee into a standing committee, and approved of the co-option of several nonmembers of the County Council, including Swire Smith, J. W. Davis[6] and A. H. D. Acland.[7] In general, however, little progress had been made by the end of April 1890. The replies from the central government departments concerning the Committee's powers were most unhelpful, and the Marquis of Ripon promised to raise these matters in the House of Lords. At this time the Committee did not contemplate asking the full Council to raise a county rate for technical education, and further maintained that it was premature for the County Council itself to provide instruction. Requests for aid were received from Hipperholme Grammar School and Ilkley School of Art, but the applicants were merely informed that if public meetings were held in their respective districts, and willingness to raise money locally was expressed, action might be forthcoming. Such a cumbersome procedure was hardly conducive to action, and by the late spring of 1890 it was clear that the initiative of the Technical Instruction Committee would be extremely limited unless finance could be provided by some method other than out of the rates.

In the summer of 1890 technical education in England received a completely unpredictable windfall. A. H. D. Acland persuaded the Government that the so-called 'whisky money' grants,[8] which were to be paid to the county councils, should be devoted to technical education.[9] This measure put ample financial resources at the disposal of the local authorities. The West Riding's share of the 'whisky money' in 1890–1 amounted to no less than £28,000. The availability of these funds completely transformed the scope of the activities of the Technical Instruction Committee. At its very next meeting the Committee resolved that the West Riding could profitably absorb the whole of these funds for technical instruction and advised the County Council against using them for rate relief. A small sub-committee, consisting of J. D. Dent, vice-chairman of the County Council, J. W. Davis and S. Smith, two co-opted members, was set up to devise a scheme of aid. The clerk was instructed to issue circulars and to insert advertisements in newspapers setting out the Council's powers and requesting information from various sources about existing provisions for technical instruction in the Riding.[10] It was mainly the Technical Instruction Committee's pioneering discussion work over the previous twelve months that made it possible for it to start work earlier than most other authorities, now that resources were available. By this time it was clear that the Council's powers under the 1889 Act were more limited than the Committee desired. In particular, the Committee wished to award its own scholarships, and also wanted the power to aid institutions outside its own administrative area.[11] W.V. Dixon prepared a memorandum on these subjects which was sent to the National Association, whose secretary, A. H. D. Acland, communicated in detail with Dixon about these issues.[12] Soon the West Riding County Council sent a petition to Parliament requesting that the Technical Instruction Act should be amended in these respects.[13] Action was not long delayed, for in March 1891 an amending Bill, sponsored by the National Association, became law.[14] This solved the Committee's legal difficulties; thus, largely because of the pressure from the West Riding, all English local authorities could henceforth broaden educational opportunities by means of awarding scholarships out of public funds.

During the early months of 1891 the membership of the small sub-committee considering a scheme of aid was strengthened, but the influence of Swire Smith on the group's proposals was clearly strong. Smith, more than any other member, had considerable practical experience of technical and secondary education, particularly in relation to Keighley. His work at the Mechanics' Institute there from the late 1860s had instituted progressive educational schemes which presaged future trends. He had firm proposals for changes that were needed in education, and he had written extensively on this subject.[15] As early as 1872 Smith looked forward to the day when 'the poor parents of diligent and gifted children are by modern generosity encouraged to make and helped to bear the sacrifice of their children's wages for a few years beyond the elementary school age, and then at last will there be a ladder of learning let down among our struggling poor, whose top reaches to the highest realms of culture'.[16]

Considering that Smith developed the idea of the 'educational ladder' in almost all his writings, it was hardly surprising that the West Riding's original educational scheme gave considerable prominence to scholarships. Although legal doubts were only cleared up in March 1891, the West Riding Committee worked so hard on this that it proved possible to do all the preparatory work, hold qualifying examinations and implement an extensive scholarship scheme from the beginning of the school year 1891 – 2.[17]

Throughout its existence the West Riding Technical Instruction Committee was under Liberal control and in important respects adhered closely to the classic tenets of nineteenth-century liberalism in its educational policies. Early in its life the Committee resolved that 'any scheme to be successful must be largely and even mainly dependent upon local effort. It is by means of such local effort, encouraged by government aid, that nearly all existing schools and institutions have sprung up, and it must be in the same way, to a large extent, that existing deficiencies must be supplied.'[18]

The Committee came to the conclusion that better results would be attained by relying on the local efforts of existing institutions rather than by attempting to supply instruction itself. Although the Committee agreed in some instances to make grants to central bodies organising special branches of instruction,[19] in general it adopted the principle 'of making its grants to governing bodies, committees and others actually carrying out the work'.[20] The Committee was in the fortunate position of being able to turn to the Yorkshire mechanics' institute movement, which had over fifty years' experience in the field of adult education. For many years the leaders of the mechanics' institute movement had argued for financial support from public funds and now large sums were readily available. In view of the fact that leaders of the movement, such as the Marquis of Ripon, Brigg, Smith and Davis, held such prominent positions on the Technical Instruction Committee, it was hardly surprising that it was agreed that 'such institutions should in general be utilised as a basis for further operations'.[21] The Committee's directory pointed out that the mechanics' institutes had considerable experience in science and art instruction, and that with more money now available they could provide more practical and technical teaching.[22] Between 1890 and 1892 the Marquis of Ripon, Brigg, Smith and Davis all addressed the Yorkshire Union of Mechanics' Institutes, promoted the County Council's schemes of aid and urged members of the Union to take advantage of them.[23] Thus the Committee chose to aid rather than to compete with the county's most important voluntary agencies providing technical education. There was certainly considerable continuity between the pioneering work of the West Riding mechanics' institutes and the later developments of the county's first education authority.

In a rather similar fashion the Committee largely entrusted the provision of technical education for girls and women to the Yorkshire Ladies Council of Education. This well-established private organisation, which specialised in instruction in domestic subjects such as cookery, dressmaking, health and laundry work, had branches in Leeds, Sheffield and Wakefield and was prepared to supply peripatetic teachers to the rest of the county. In 1891 the co-operative relationship between the Ladies Council and the Committee was still tentative, but it developed successfully with some mutual satisfaction. In 1894 the clerk praised the work of the Ladies Council to the Bryce Commissioners, and held that its efforts put the West Riding into 'a very much better position than many other councils'.[24] Although requests to set up technical colleges for females[25] and to add women members to the Committee were refused,[26] the Ladies Council ensured that women's education received an important share of the funds available for technical instruction and in so doing expanded its own activities and its own teaching staff considerably.

Soon after the commencement of its operations the Committee came into close contact with both higher and secondary education. With regard to the former, both the Yorkshire College, Leeds, and Firth College, Sheffield,[27] provided courses and services for the Committee and in consequence received considerable aid.[28] From the outset applications for aid were received from endowed grammar schools as well as from secondary day schools conducted in conjunction with technical institutes. At first there were some doubts about the legality of aiding grammar schools, but the secretary of the Science and Art Department, General Donnelly, soon reassured the clerk that, in his opinion, all secondary schools were eligible to share in the grants as long as they complied with the requirements of the County Council.[29] Later the vice-chairman, John Brigg, told the Bryce Commissioners that the Committee had not tried to draw a dividing line between technical and secondary education.[30] On the same occasion W. V. Dixon, the clerk, stressed:

> We got, in the first instance, a number of applications from all sorts of institutions . . . and some of the technical day schools gave an education practically identical with the education given in some of the grammar schools . . . After carefully considering the claims of the two, it was found that . . . if we gave to the secondary technical day schools we could not exclude the grammar schools: therefore, ultimately, a scheme was drawn up, placing them both on the same footing, subject, however, to safeguards for preventing the grammar schools from attempting to give an undue prominence to grant-earning subjects . . . Subject to that difference, the technical day schools and the grammar schools were placed on absolutely the same basis in the first instance.[31]

This early decision to include grammar schools within the county's scheme of aid under the Technical Instruction Act was of crucial importance, and the

Committee's work in relation to the development of secondary education in the Riding is discussed in some detail in a later chapter.[32]

Technical education soon developed into one of the West Riding County Council's major spheres of interest in the 1890s. There was an increasing desire on the part of members to serve on the Technical Instruction Committee[33] and by 1894 it contained about one-fifth of the membership of the full Council.[34] Total membership of the Committee increased from twelve in 1889 and thirty-six in 1896 to forty-three in 1902. With such large numbers it proved essential to delegate work to sub-committees. In addition to short-term, *ad hoc* sub-committees, several important standing sub-committees were appointed. These included Accounts, Agriculture (with the East and North Ridings) and the Examining Boards (for scholarships). Probably the most important, however, was the Administrative Sub-Committee. This comparatively small group met on a regular basis a few days (sometimes only a few hours) before the meetings of the full Committee. It was normally this sub-committee which initiated and reviewed policy matters. Co-optation to the full Committee was used from 1890. Co-opted members were chosen for their specialist knowledge of educational subjects,[35] and their number increased from five in 1890 to twelve in 1902. The expertise of individual co-opted members proved important at certain crucial stages of development. Swire Smith's knowledge of the mechanics' institutes and of national developments in technical education, for example, was essential to progress in the early years, and Arthur Acland's wide experience in educational administration proved invaluable as preparations were made to implement the 1902 Act. For many years co-opted members were all appointed for their individual talents rather than in a representative capacity, but from 1899 the West Riding Federation of School Boards was allowed to nominate two members of the Committee and in 1900 the Association of Governing Bodies of Secondary Schools in the West Riding was granted a similar privilege.

The main source of income for the work of the Technical Instruction Committee throughout the period was the 'whisky money' grants, and in the West Riding not one penny was lost to rate relief. Between 1890 and 1903 the West Riding received the substantial average annual income of approximately £32,000 from these funds. In proportion to the population this was marginally – but not seriously – less than the national average.[36] According to its clerk, the Committee did not consider using the rates to supplement income in the early 1890s, and in 1894 the clerk maintained that rate aid 'could be very difficult at present, I do not think the public would care for it'.[37] It was not until 1898 that expenditure seriously threatened to exceed income and the vague possibility of aid from the county rate was mentioned by the Committee.[38] The 1898 forecasts proved too pessimistic and the question of rating was successfully shelved until 1901. In that year the Committee felt that its financial revenues were inadequate and that a supplement from the rates was essential to ensure that work then in operation would not be 'most seriously curtailed'.[39] Both the Finance Committee and the full County Council soon agreed that rate funds could be used to aid education on the small scale[40] proposed by the Technical Instruction Committee; thus the West Riding became the first English county council[41] to spend rate funds under the Technical Instruction Act. The National Association for the Promotion of Technical Education described this as 'the most notable event of the year'.[42] At the turn of the century the Committee had either to cut back its educational plans or to use rate funds to maintain its financial equilibrium. It was certainly to its credit that the Authority chose the latter option.

The West Riding was also one of the first English authorities to appoint local inspectors. From the outset the Committee, in accordance with contemporary liberal opinion concerning the distribution of educational grants, made it clear that it rejected payments on results and that it wished to use inspection as its means to check educational efficiency.[43] The Committee asked the Science and Art Department, the Education Department and the City and Guilds of London Institute whether their systems of inspection could be used to provide guidance to the County Council about the distribution of its grants.[44] All the replies were negative and General Donnelly intimated firmly that the Science and Art Department 'would not be able to undertake any systematic inspection which would be available for the purposes of the award of the grants by the County Council'.[45] It was clear that if the Committee wanted the classes it aided to be inspected, it would have to inaugurate its own system. In the summer of 1891 F. N. Cook, an experienced science teacher, was appointed as the Authority's first inspector. In 1893 an assistant, James Graham, was appointed to inspect classes in commercial subjects and modern languages. Considerable use was also made of occasional part-time inspectors, particularly for technological classes. By 1902 two full-time lady inspectors were employed to deal with domestic subjects, and another gentleman devoted his whole time to the inspection of aided secondary schools. From the first it was stressed that inspectors were expected to act as advisers on teaching methods rather than as inquisitors.[46] Their work soon took West Riding inspectors into institutions aided by the Committee in the neighbouring county boroughs. The effects of this inspection so impressed Leeds City Council, which had no inspectorate of its own, that it requested the West Riding to inspect classes receiving aid from Leeds. From 1897, therefore, for an agreed annual sum, West Riding inspectors had oversight not only of county classes but also of those of one of the most important county boroughs in the area. Periodic conferences were held, moreover, between the West Riding inspectorate and Her Majesty's Inspectors (HMIs) for the Yorkshire districts from 1895 to discuss common problems and approaches to evening continuation schools.[47] The West Riding attached considerable importance, and devoted important resources, to the development of a comprehensive inspectorate at the local level. A strong and active inspectorate was essential to the Committee's scheme of aid, which involved the broad dissemination of educational policies administered centrally from Wakefield.

Although in general the Committee tried to avoid setting up its own county classes, this certainly did not imply that the Committee wished to opt out of its responsibility for the development of technical education in the West Riding. On the contrary, the Committee felt that its decision to rely largely on schools and classes managed locally not only made it essential to create a county inspectorate, but also necessitated the publication of comprehensive annual directories setting out the detailed regulations governing its scheme of aid. This brought some criticism from detractors who claimed that the Committee had created 'a little South Kensington'.[48] A. P. Laurie, the Assistant Royal Commissioner for Yorkshire, commented that this was hardly fair, but added that its system of regulations was too complex.[49] Although the rules prescribed by the Committee were meticulous, detailed and perhaps cumbersome, it is important that the reason for their existence should not be misunderstood. From its inception the Committee sought to bring about the co-ordination of the various educational forces at work in the West Riding. Its primary aim was to develop a county educational service which was systematic and continuous from the elementary school upwards. At all costs it wanted to avoid a situation in which there was a vast conglomeration of disparate, unrelated classes which led nowhere in particular. With this in mind, the regulations were consistently framed so that each stage in the educational process dovetailed into the next. At the most elementary level, aid to evening continuation schools was so organised that pupils were encouraged to prepare for more advanced work. In the same way, local evening science classes were expected to prepare their students for further work in technological subjects in the neighbouring district technical schools.[50] Small institutions were discouraged from attempting isolated pieces of advanced work, and in later years special establishment grants were given to encourage large centres to provide advanced facilities. From 1897 the grants system was reorganised, so that schools which persuaded students to take integrated courses in a number of related subjects fared better than those which enrolled a large number of students who each attended only a single subject.[51] In 1899 the system of instituting comparatively few advanced centres with contributory feeder classes, which had operated in science and technology from the start, was extended to modern languages and commercial subjects.[52] The Committee, moreover, prescribed the accommodation, facilities and equipment which had to be provided before aid would be supplied to classes in any practical subjects. If inspectors or district committees[53] reported shortcomings in this area, prompt action was normally taken to improve the situation.[54] Some influence was also exercised over syllabuses. These had to be submitted to Wakefield before the commencement of the session. In some areas of the curriculum, particularly commerce and domestic subjects, the Committee's inspectors produced specimen syllabuses which were published in the annual directories. It was stressed, however, that these were only suggestions and that individual teachers could produce their own if they so desired. In a rather similar fashion, the Committee soon began to publish pamphlets of suggestions on teaching methods and approaches for several subject areas. Although this material was usually prepared by the local inspectors, a pamphlet entitled *Lines for the Guidance of Teachers in Elementary Schools who take up Science*[55] was written by five of her Majesty's Inspectors at the instigation of the West Riding Committee. The Technical Instruction Committee did not issue its complex regulations or its suggestions for teachers because it wanted to promote standardisation or revelled in unnecessary bureaucracy; its main aim was to ensure that teachers and students engaged in the educational process had the maximum opportunity to act as purposefully as possible. In this respect the West Riding was considerably more successful in the 1890s than some other authorities.[56]

The development of an effective system of local organisation was of paramount importance to the progress of education in a large area such as the West Riding. In the 1890s the county councils received no guidance about this issue from either legislation or central government departments. They had no experience of educational administration, but they were given complete freedom to devise their own systems of local control. Parliament gave the county councils permissive powers to pay over all or some of their 'whisky money' grants to the non-county boroughs and urban districts in their areas if they so desired. Unlike several other authorities, the West Riding decided that it did not wish to do this and preferred to devise an educational scheme for the county as a whole. This crucial decision was made originally by the small sub-committee[57] consisting of J. D. Dent, J. W. Davis and S. Smith, and was later ratified by the full Committee and the County Council. Swire Smith and the clerk, Dixon, were both strongly opposed to dividing the grant between the minor local authorities in the area. As Deputy Clerk to the county, Dixon was determined that his authority's influence should be paramount throughout the West Riding, and memoranda drawn up on his initiative[58] and his evidence to the Royal Commission on Secondary Education show clearly how very strongly he was opposed to paying out such doles. Swire Smith took a very similar view. His experience had convinced him that it would be unwise to cut off the surrounding countryside from the towns, for at Keighley some of the best pupils were drawn from outlying villages on the moors. He wanted the county to develop a relatively small number of well-equipped district technical schools which would provide advanced instruction in technological subjects. Smith had visited continental countries which operated such systems and he probably foresaw that his particular brain-child, the technical departments at Keighley Mechanics' Institute, would develop into a leading district technical school and hence qualify for large grants from the County Council. He felt that only if these district technical schools were situated in central towns and served large populations would they be able to attract a sufficient number of advanced students to merit the large expenditure involved. A few years later the Committee justified its original decision thus:

> After careful consideration it was decided that no portion of the funds should be distributed among urban authorities, but the control of the expenditure should be retained by the County Council. The reasons are apparent. The urban districts include 124 local government districts and thirteen non-county boroughs. As regards the local government districts it was apparent that the division of funds among so large a number of authorities without means of effective combination would entail a loss of efficiency and waste of resources. While as regards the boroughs not only would there have been a lack of co-ordination in the work, but it would have been impracticable to carry out effectively the scheme that was contemplated whereby the schools and institutions in the boroughs should serve as centres for the surrounding districts.[59]

The Authority's view on this issue did not go unchallenged at the national level. In both 1892 and 1893 the Association of Municipal Corporations led by its President, Sir Albert Rollit, tried to amend the law so as to compel county councils to pay a proportion of the 'whisky money' grants over to the minor local authorities. On both these occasions the West Riding, prompted by Dixon, acted swiftly and petitioned Parliament against these proposals. Pressure was also brought to bear through the County Councils Association (CCA), and the *status quo* was preserved. Apart from a dispute with Rotherham[60] between 1899 and 1901, which reflected little credit on either the County Council or Rotherham Corporation, the relations between the Technical Instruction Committee and the minor local authorities were generally cordial. Once the county's scheme came into operation there was little disposition on the part of the minor authorities to break away from it,[61] and because of the work which they undertook for the surrounding districts, institutions situated in the non-county boroughs and large urban districts received more in grants than their populations strictly justified.[62] By contrast, in Lancashire a large proportion of the available funds was throughout paid over to the large number of minor authorities in that county, and there was continual friction between these bodies and the Lancashire Technical Instruction Committee.[63] The West Riding was fortunate, in that both the County Council and the larger, more important minor authorities were Liberal in their political sympathies, whereas in Lancashire there was political divergence between the largely independent and Conservative County Council and the predominantly Liberal non-county boroughs. Nonetheless, the West Riding's decision to develop a co-ordinated scheme for its whole administrative area proved a wise one. By the end of the nineteenth century some authorities were still struggling to deal with a multiplicity of unconnected educational provisions, whereas the West Riding Committee was already providing an integrated system of post-elementary educational services throughout the county.

The Committee realised that it was essential to keep in touch with developments at the local level. In the early years there were many places in the West Riding where there were no agents of educational administration whatsoever, and in many instances the need for further instruction had to be impressed on these districts.[64] So that close contacts could be developed with the localities, the Technical Instruction Committee set up twenty-two district committees in 1891, which between them covered the whole of the county. Each district was based roughly on a Poor Law union and each had a central town which could be used as 'a nucleus for grouping districts for the purpose of technical instruction'.[65] The size of these districts varied considerably; Dewsbury was the largest with a population of over 160,000 and Selby the smallest with 12,000.

The district committees consisted of (1) the County Councillors representing the electoral divisions comprised in the district, (2) County Aldermen resident therein, and (3) such other persons (including, if thought fit, women) as might be nominated by the West Riding Technical Instruction Committee.[66] The main duties of the district committees were:

To report to the Technical Instruction Committee from time to time as to the schools and institutions in each part of the district, with particulars as to the need for the instruction given thereat, having regard to the work of other institutions; the suitability of instruction, having regard to the industries of the district and other circumstances; the suitability of the fees, having regard to the classes to be benefited and the character of the instruction; the general work of the schools in the district; to report as to the requirements in the way of scholarships; the special subjects most suited to the district ... generally to see that no portion of the district is without means of obtaining technical instruction, that the various local institutions and schools are performing their allotted part of the work, and in other ways to see that the district is satisfactorily provided for.[67]

District committees were not expected to act as managers of schools or classes themselves. They were not empowered to spend funds and they were in no sense executive bodies. Their functions were advisory, and they formed a bridgehead between the county committee and the localities. The scope of their work is shown clearly by a summary of reports from twelve district committees for 1893.[68] A large number of institutions were visited and any deficiencies in accommodation, apparatus or fittings, or in the qualifications of teachers, were reported in detail. Recommendations were also made to amalgamate certain classes and to commence new work in specified subjects in specified areas. As long as the district committees were active, and they usually were, they provided essential advice and information for the County Committee, but they had no power to go their own way and develop plans which might ultimately have undermined the Technical Instruction Committee's county scheme.

In the 1890s the West Riding Technical Instruction Committee soon developed into one of the leading education authorities in Yorkshire. The Technical Instruction Committees of the five West Yorkshire county boroughs[69] were consistently less active than the county committee, and in those towns the school boards retained their positions as the paramount education authorities. In the administrative county itself there were nine boroughs and 169 parishes with school boards and four boroughs and 472 parishes without them.[70] The attitude of the Liberal-controlled West Riding Technical Instruction Committee towards its potential rivals, the larger West Yorkshire school boards (which were also usually dominated by the Liberals), was interesting. Throughout the Technical Instruction Committee maintained that it should be the local authority for all the technical and secondary education in the administrative county[71] and was thus prepared to resist very strongly any ambitions displayed by the school boards in the fields of secondary or adult education.[72] On the other hand, both the Committee and the County Council were quite adamant that they did not want to take over the administration of elementary education.[73] It was paradoxical that the Liberal West Riding Technical Instruction Committee, by developing such successful educational schemes,[74] and by proving at the same time that it was a viable unit for educational administration, provided the Conservative Government in 1902 with very good arguments for making county councils into local authorities for elementary as well as technical and secondary education.

# CHAPTER II

# *The Administrative Structure*

The Education Act of 1902, which imposed duties on and gave powers to counties and county boroughs over most of the elementary and secondary schools, technical colleges and evening classes and over teacher training, could only be put into effect in some counties by creating a new administrative structure, but in the West Riding the task was in one sense far simpler, for in the Technical Instruction Committee and its officers the county already possessed a well-run and efficient administrative system. The implementation of the Balfour Act, therefore, required no more than the adaptation and further development of an existing committee structure and department in order to allow the county to undertake responsibility for the vastly increased number of pupils, teachers and schools for which the County Council became responsible, and to enable it to handle its new relationships with many minor authorities and with voluntary bodies. Yet the very size of the West Riding, the county borough 'islands' embedded in it, the considerable number of non-county boroughs and urban districts granted elementary education powers under Part III of the new Act and, above all, the great variety of local, social and political influences in the remaining urban and rural districts were bound to produce a much more complex administrative picture than almost any other local education authority (LEA) was to have.

Throughout the period that Balfour's Bill was before Parliament, the West Riding County Council vociferously opposed Part III.[1] This was designed to abolish the school boards – which Liberals and Non-conformists so vehemently upheld – and to make the new LEAs responsible for maintaining voluntary and board elementary schools. As late as 8 October 1902 the Council 'reaffirmed' that it would be impossible for it to exercise effective control over elementary schools and called on the Government to withdraw Part III of the Bill. It formally agreed that if the Bill became law, 'any attempt by the Council to satisfactorily administer its provisions would be futile and hopeless'.[2] In taking this attitude, the Council differed from the majority of county councils. All but seven had indicated that they were willing to undertake the duties which Part III of the Bill would impose with regard to elementary education.[3] On the other hand, the predominant Liberal and Non-conformist tradition in the West Riding was obviously of great importance in keeping the Council firmly in line with the Liberal opposition at Westminster to this aspect of the Conservative Education Bill.

It should also be noted that some of those who had done a great deal to forward secondary and technical education under the West Riding Technical Instruction Committee were fearful lest the additional responsibility of elementary education might have the effect of importing religious controversy into County Council affairs and thereby interfering with the work already being undertaken in the secondary and technical fields.[4] The anxiety felt in the West Riding for the future of secondary and technical education was also shown in the efforts made by the two Members of Parliament – Alderman J. H. Duncan (Otley) and Alderman J. Brigg (Keighley) – who expressed the County Council's views vigorously in the Commons. The Technical Instruction Committee was concerned at the limit of a two-penny rate, the most that a County Council would be able to raise for higher education (a term that included everything beyond the elementary school at that time). Both Duncan and Brigg spoke in support of an amendment increasing the limit from two pence to four pence. County boroughs were not thus limited, and it was argued that it was wrong to subject counties to this constraint and particularly oppressive in the case of a county with such a large variety of interests demanding support – 'agricultural work, which was making continual new demands upon the public purse, textile work, mechanical engineering, coal mining, leather tanning; and, in the last few years there had been a demand for instruction in foreign languages and all classes of commerce'.[5] The Government did not accept the amendment but did simplify the arrangements for authorising a County Council to levy a rate of more than two pence. As it foresaw, the West Riding was soon driven to seek such special authority.[6]

Once the Balfour Bill was enacted, the task of working out how it should be implemented in the county fell to the Technical Instruction Committee which, in its turn, appointed a special sub-committee. As early as January 1903 the Technical Instruction Committee sent forward to the County Council a memorandum outlining the steps which needed to be taken to bring the Act into operation at as early a date as possible. Among other considerations, a scheme for constituting the Education Committee would need to be agreed by the County Council and approved by the Board of Education, machinery would need to be established at the local level for the management of schools, possibly utilising the services of minor authorities to manage schools in their districts, above all a complete survey of all schools, board and voluntary, for which the county would be responsible needed to be prepared, so that the extent of the liabilities, financial and other, might be estimated.[7] The minor local government authorities within the West Riding administrative county are shown in Table 2.1 and the number of elementary schools in Table 2.2. The complexity of the situation was aggravated by the existence of six county boroughs which were embedded in the administrative county and to which some West Riding pupils travelled to school. These were Bradford (279,767), Halifax (104,936), Huddersfield (95,047), Leeds (428,968), Rotherham (54,349), Sheffield (398,242); their total population (1,361,309) was almost equal to that of the administrative county.

The Technical Instruction Committee appointed a special sub-committee to undertake the necessary preparations to implement the requirements of the new Act.[8] By the end of January the sub-committee had drafted a scheme for the constitution of the Education Committee and had arranged for it to be considered by the County Council. A meeting was arranged with representatives of the Part III authorities in the county and circulars were issued to school boards and voluntary school managers outlining future arrangements. Inquiries were authorised to ascertain the necessary details concerning school finance, attendance, trust deeds and the like. The sub-committee decided that the 'appointed day' for taking over duties under the Act should be the day on which the new Education Committee first met for Part II (education other than elementary) and 31 March 1904 for Part III (elementary). The later date for elementary education was made inevitable by the need to collect information, set up entirely new machinery and appoint staff. Finally, members of the County Council were to be asked to state their experience in 'school management' before names were put forward for the new Education Committee.[9]

The arrangements were accepted by the County Council at its meeting in March. There were to be thirty-six persons elected from the Council itself to the Education Committee and nine to be appointed from outside – usually the two groups were referred to as 'representative' and 'added' members. Not more than six representative members could be councillors from areas where there were local Part III authorities for elementary education.[10] The Board of Education had issued guidelines which indicated the broad principles on which education committees were to be constituted and the West Riding's proportion of 'added' members was probably as small as the Board would have agreed to accept. Although the scheme stated that various types of education – university, secondary, technical, elementary – were to be rep-

TABLE 2.1

*Part III (elementary only) education authorities*

| | | | | | |
|---|---|---|---|---|---|
| (a) 13 municipal boroughs with a population over 10,000 | | | | | |
| | Barnsley | 41,086 | Harrogate | 28,423 | Pontefract | 13,427 |
| | Batley | 30,321 | Keighley | 41,564 | Pudsey | 14,907 |
| | Brighouse | 21,735 | Morley | 23,636 | Todmorden | 25,418 |
| | Dewsbury | 28,060 | Ossett | 12,903 | Wakefield | 41,413 |
| | Doncaster | 28,932 | | | | |

(b)  1 urban district with a population over 20,000
     Shipley    25,573

                                                          377,398

Remainder of the administrative area

|  | |
|---|---|
|  1 municipal borough (Ripon) | 8,230 |
| 116 urban districts | 680,285 |
|  29 rural districts (including 512 parishes) | 323,271 |

                                                        1,011,786

        Total population of administrative county        1,389,184

TABLE 2.2

*Elementary schools in the West Riding (WR) county administrative area in 1901*

| | Part III only authorities | Remainder | Total for WR area |
|---|---|---|---|
| Number of schools | | | |
| voluntary | 97 | 592 | 689 |
| board | 85 | 264 | 349 |
| Number of pupils in average attendance | | | |
| voluntary | 29,944 | 83,483 | 113,427 |
| board | 31,493 | 71,843 | 103,336 |
| Number of teachers | 2,040 | 5,200 | 7,240 |
| Average cost per pupil in elementary schools in WR | | | |
| voluntary | | | £2. 7s. 2d. (£2.36) |
| board | | | £2. 13s. 3d. (£2.66) |

resented among either the 'representative' or the 'added' members, no outside bodies were to be invited to nominate 'added' members as was done in many other education authorities.[11] One group which was frequently accorded representation by LEAs and, indeed, a group for which the Board's circular encouraged representation, was the Churches, which in the West Riding, as elsewhere, had provided the majority of elementary schools.

Although the Churches sought such representation, it was not agreed.[12] Given the strength of anti-Church feeling among the controlling political group, this was hardly surprising. A smaller number of LEAs accorded some representation to teachers, but not usually to teachers' unions. While teachers' associations sought representation in the West Riding, it was refused on the grounds that those in receipt of emoluments ultimately paid by the Authority ought to be barred from the Council's committees.[13]

A meeting of the special sub-committee was held in June to consider names for the new Education Committee. The sub-committee had before it details of councillors' experience of school management and the new Education Committee naturally included nearly all the members of the Technical Instruction Committee, since they were in any case the most experienced in this field. Among the nine 'added' members were the Rt. Hon. A. H. D. Acland, John Brigg, MP, and William Briggs, who had been very active in Technical Instruction Committee days. Two women were added to meet the Board of Education's requirement for 'at least' two women members, Mrs Ella Armitage of Rawdon, Leeds, and Mrs Annie Eddison of Headingley, Leeds. The chairman of the Finance Committee of Firth College, Sheffield, G. Franklin, and the chairman of the Council of the Yorkshire College, Leeds, A. G. Lupton, were also among the 'added' members.[14] At its first meeting the new Education Committee decided to set up three main sub-committees, one for elementary and another for higher education, and a third for finance and general purposes. It was also decided that the small and very experienced group of active members of the special sub-committee for bringing the Act into operation should now meet again to report on the composition and duties of these three sub-committees. Alderman Anderton, also from the former Technical Instruction Committee, was appointed chairman of the Education Committee.[15]

The Elementary sub-committee was formed with thirty-two members, of whom four were 'added'; Higher Education and Finance and General Purposes both had twenty-two members – six of the former were 'added' and three of the latter. The members of the special sub-committee put themselves on the new Finance and General Purposes Committee without exception, and most of the remainder were from the former Technical Instruction Committee. The new members of the Education Committee were nominated to one or other (occasionally to both) of the Higher or Elementary sub-committees, although these also had many former Technical Instruction Committee members. Acland became chairman of the Higher Education Sub-Committee, while Anderton took the chairmanship of the other two. Five members served on all three sub-committees and four of these had been active in technical instruction – Acland, Anderton, Dunn and Chappell; the fifth person was a comparative newcomer, J. J. Brigg. There is little doubt but that these men between them played a decisive role in setting up the post-1902 education authority in the West Riding and in formulating its policies in the early years. The absence of a Director of Education – or perhaps their unwillingness to have an effective one – established a system under which the influence of leading members of the authority, both on policy and in day-to-day business, was rather more direct and less 'filtered' than tended to be the case with most of the larger LEAs.

The only Director of Education to hold office during the first quarter-century of the Authority's existence was William Loring, who was appointed in 1903 and went the next year. When the Technical Instruction Committee first considered the steps to be taken to implement the Act of 1902, it did not recommend the creation of the post of Director or Education Officer. It recommended an additional post of inspector for higher education, the holder to be 'of good scholastic attainments and possessed of business ability'. In the elementary area it initially recommended the appointment of a 'managing clerk' and other clerical staff.[16] This seems to have reflected the local way of conducting business that had grown up in the 1890s. Professional 'educational' matters had been the business of County Council inspectors; the clerk to the Technical Instruction Committee, Vibart Dixon, had handled legal and clerical matters (besides his position as Deputy Clerk of the Peace he was also Deputy Clerk of the County Council). The West Riding had not appointed an organising secretary or director as such, although many other counties had done so, and in 1891 the Association of Organising Secretaries and Directors – the lineal ancestor of the Association of Education Officers – had been set up with the Director for Surrey, Macan, as its convener. Consideration of the local position led the Technical Instruction Committee to establish a group of four members to look further at the position in April and the group – which included Acland and Anderton – recommended that a Director of Education, 'who should be the head of the Education Department', should be appointed and that a sub-committee should be set up to report on what should be 'the duties of the Director and of the Clerk respectively'. Dixon made it clear that he did not in any case wish to give up his post as deputy clerk to the County Council and become more fully immersed in the Education Department. The duties of the Director and clerk were not in fact clearly defined.[17]

At its meeting in May the County Council confirmed the appointment of an 'assistant secretary and inspector' for secondary education, a similar appointment for technical instruction and evening schools and two such appointments for elementary education. The recommendation to advertise and seek a Director ran into opposition, but eventually it was agreed that the appointment should be made, and on 6 July two candidates were interviewed, William Loring, Acting Senior Examiner at the Board of Education, being appointed.[18] At its meeting on 31 May 1904, less than a year later, the Education Committee accepted Loring's resignation. No statement of the reasons why he wanted to go, or of why the Authority wanted him to go, was ever made public. But it is clear that the first holder of the post of Director, whoever it had been, would have had a difficult time establishing his position, when Vibart Dixon (continuing as clerk to the Education Committee), the senior inspectors and three or four very active members of the Committee were all to some extent occupying part of the ground which a Director would expect to occupy. During the winter of 1903–4, for instance, some of the sub-committees received memoranda and reports not just from the Director but also from the clerk to the Education Committee.[19] If the circumstances of the appointment were inauspicious and the post needed delicate handling on both sides to make it work, the attitudes of those involved made it virtually certain that there would not be that necessary measure of tolerance and understanding. The West Riding Education Authority remained the leading opponent of the new system of aiding voluntary schools and was prepared to make life as difficult as possible for those schools it was required to aid by the Act of 1902. Loring had come directly from the very department which had fostered that legislation and was hardly likely to see the duties of his post as devising or carrying out ways of frustrating its application. Alderman Dunn, who was in the chair at the meeting of the Education Committee when Loring's resignation was accepted, told a newspaper reporter who pressed him for an explanation of the affair:

> Mr Loring has an austere manner, and this, combined with his intimate knowledge of educational matters arising from his former connection with the Board of Education, his firmness of character, the clear ideas of his own which he holds on educational matters, may have been obtruded more than has proved acceptable to some members of the committee, and also to several members of the inspectoral staff.[20]

The special sub-committee set up to deal with the resignation of the Director invited A. V. Houghton, F. N. Cook and W. H. Brown, county inspectors for secondary, technical and elementary education respectively, to attend, and after discussion resolved that the work of the Education Department should be apportioned between these three, adding that in matters of urgency 'Mr Houghton and Mr Cook will confer with County Alderman Acland, and, similarly, Mr Brown will confer with County Alderman Dunn and County Councillor Talbot.'[21]

Initially this was seen as a temporary arrangement to cover current business while consideration was given to the future administration of the Education Department. Eventually the Education Committee adopted proposals from a special sub-committee to seek a successor to Loring, to be known as the Secretary for Education, at the same salary, £1,000 per annum. In addition Houghton, Cook, Brown and J. W. Horne were to be appointed assistant secretaries and inspectors for the different fields of education. 'In the interests of good organisation' a standing sub-committee was to be set up to confer and to give instructions to the Secretary and other officers. When the Education Committee's proposals came before the County Council on 10 May 1905, the opposition to appointing a successor to Loring was so strong that the Education Committee's recommendation was rejected and there was no chief officer for education until 1929.[22]

The boroughs which had sufficiently large populations to enable them to claim the right to operate their own elementary school systems under Part III of the 1902 Act were all anxious to do so, and each of them went its own way as an independent authority for elementary education until the Butler Act of 1944. There was, however, bound to be close contact with the West Riding, which was responsible for the provision of all other forms of education in these towns. Early in 1903 the county called a meeting of representatives of the non-county boroughs and of Shipley Urban District to discuss possible future arrangements. From the county side it was pointed out that if the local education committees were constituted so as to include county representatives, then they might be regarded as responsible for managing evening classes, technical schools and pupil-teacher centres in the boroughs on behalf of the West Riding. School boards had often financed these activities out of the elementary rate. The new Part III authorities could not do so under the new legislation, so if these activities were to continue, they would have to get County Council finance. Representatives from the boroughs expressed a variety of views. Some agreed with Todmorden's attitude: 'They wanted all the control locally; they wanted the County Council to pay all that was to be paid.' Others sought a definite lead from the county itself.[23]

The county maintained its view that if non-county borough elementary education committees were to be recognised for anything more than elementary work as defined in Part III of the Act, they must accept some county nominees. Most of the non-county boroughs accepted this without difficulty. Todmorden, however, formally requested that the borough Education Committee should be recognised 'for all the purposes of the School of Science, of

Evening Continuation Schools, Science and Art, Technical and Technological Classes for the Borough'. The county refused the request, reiterated its
policy on representation and replied that the furthest it could go would be to
agree to the appointment of a sub-committee of Todmorden Education
Committee for the purpose of dealing with Part II of the Education Act to
which the County Council itself would appoint representatives.[24]

Before the 1902 education measure was enacted, the West Riding Technical Instruction Committee had consistently maintained that it did not wish to
see counties take over elementary education from the existing school boards.
When the county actually found itself with direct responsibility for elementary education outside the larger non-county boroughs and Shipley Urban
District, it sought to establish a network of district sub-committees which
might act as a channel for local interest, rather as the school boards had been
doing in many areas. The existing 148 school boards were to be replaced by
eighty-eight district sub-committees. Forty-eight of the proposed new districts corresponded exactly with single-school-board districts. The other
districts included more than one board area and localities which had an
adequate number of voluntary schools and therefore no school boards.
District sub-committees were also managers for all provided elementary
schools in their area. Their constitution, therefore, had to follow that laid
down in the Act for managing bodies and had to consist of persons representing the county and the minor authorities. In practice the county came to
appoint its representatives largely on the nomination of the minor authorities,
although there had to be at least one member of the county Education
Committee on each district sub-committee for the latter to be constituted a
sub-committee of the Education Committee.[25] The districts were grouped
into twenty-eight divisions and a clerk was appointed by the county to each of
these to act for all the district sub-committees contained in it. The clerks –
some of whom were former school board clerks – controlled the work of school
attendance officers in their districts and brought to the notice of the sub-
committee all cases of irregular attendance requiring intervention.[26]

The sub-committees dealt with a wide variety of matters, including the
enforcement of school attendance. They had the usual powers of managers of
provided schools; they controlled the letting of provided school premises and
appointed caretakers and cleaners. The sub-committees also appointed
assistant teachers in provided schools, subject to the approval of the Education Committee. Since many of the members of the sub-committees were
former members of school boards, and the strength of the school board
tradition had considerable influence on the pattern of devolution adopted, it
was not surprising that a meeting of their representatives resolved in 1905

that they should be given 'complete control of all matters governing educa-tion, except laying a rate, as the school boards had'. Since elementary education was now maintained through county financial support, the Educa-tion Committee could not possibly concede so much. A special sub-committee, which was set up to study the matter in 1905, experienced pressure in the other direction from the National Union of Teachers (NUT), which preferred appointments to be handled at county level. A deputation from the Union urged the county to see that the method of appointing teachers should be such as to encourage the flow of movement for promotion over the Riding as a whole and that nothing should be done which might limit it to a smaller area. The appointment of head teachers of elementary schools was in fact kept at county level.[27] The West Riding put forward a scheme by which voluntary schools could have grouped managing bodies with powers similar to those of district sub-committees and which would become sub-committees of the Education Committee, but this was not adopted by voluntary schools in any area. Under the 1902 Act two-thirds of the managers were to be appointed by the voluntary body and only one-third by local authorities. Under the West Riding scheme the voluntary bodies would appoint only one-third of grouped managers, while the county and minor authorities appointed the other two-thirds. In other words, control would pass from the founding body. Moreover, religious instruction in accordance with the foundation deeds was to be restricted to two days a week, with instruction according to the County Council's 'approved syllabus' on other days. It was hardly surprising that the scheme was not adopted and each voluntary, non-provided school kept its own body of managers, with en-trenched powers conferred by the 1902 Act. The Education Committee decided that managers of individual voluntary schools should be subjected to the administrative disqualification of not being 'entrusted with any advances of money for Petty Cash'.[28]

The main features of this administrative system established after 1902 underwent no structural change until the Butler Act of 1944. There were, however, some significant modifications in the prevailing attitudes and arrangements in the years between the two wars. Possibly the most influential individual in West Riding education during these two decades was Sir Percy Jackson. He had become a member of the County Council in 1904 and had joined the Education Committee the next year. From 1917 until his retire-ment from local government affairs in 1937 he was chairman of the Education Committee. Jackson was by origin very much a typical West Riding local government man. His business interests lay in the textile industry and he was a member of the Methodist Church. But while he began by making his way in educational affairs in the West Riding and was steeped in the local traditions and attitudes, he grew into a national figure. In 1919 he became a member of the first Burnham Committee on teachers' salaries and in the twenties served as a member of the Consultative Committee of the Board of Education at a time when it produced its first report of major significance, *The Education of the Adolescent*. Among other national activities he was President of the Association of Education Committees and a member of the Royal Commission on the Civil Service.

The two distinctly unusual characteristics of the county's educational structure which Jackson was largely responsible for bringing closer to the national position were the relationship between the Authority and non-provided schools and the position of county Education Officer. His wide experience undoubtedly helped him to bring a broader and less suspicious attitude to bear on affairs in Wakefield. According to Sir Charles McGrath, clerk to the Council, after Jackson's election to the chairmanship of the Education Committee 'many of the defects which had unfortunately marred relations with the non-provided schools . . . disappeared, and a saner and more generous policy was introduced in the West Riding'.[29]

The suspicion of the over-mighty bureaucrat which lay behind the refusal to have another county Education Officer after the departure of Loring was eventually overcome in 1928, when the Education Committee agreed to the appointment of J. H. Hallam to that post to take charge of the whole department, on a salary scale rising to a maximum of £1,500. Hallam had been serving as a County Council inspector in charge of the secondary branch since 1910 and his appointment to the new post led to the reorganisation of administrative posts in the Education Department. There were to be two chief assistants for elementary and another for higher education, at salaries of up to £900 per annum. There were also to be an assistant for secondary and another for technical education, along with an inspector for elementary schools, at salaries ranging up to £700 per annum.[30] Hallam never, perhaps, became a national figure in the way that his successors, A. L. Binns, and later A. B. Clegg, were to be, but during his eight years as Chief Education Officer he did a great deal to build up the secondary school system in the county. When Hallam retired through illness in 1936, his successor moved to Wakefield from the post of Director of Education for a Middlesex Part III authority, Ealing. Jackson had come to know Binns over a period of fifteen years or so in national affairs and believed that his appointment would give the county a 'first-rate Director'. The regard which other education officers had for the new Chief Education Officer was made manifest two years later when Binns was elected honorary secretary of the Association of Directors of

Education.[31] He remained secretary of the Association during the war and he was consulted a good deal both formally and informally, by officers of the Board of Education when they were putting together the Butler Education Act of 1944. His opinions were highly regarded at the Board[32] and he served as a member of the Fleming Committee on the public schools. In the West Riding it fell to Binns to meet both the emergencies and the difficulties produced by wartime conditions and to handle the discussions and planning for reconstruction, which was taken very seriously by the Education Committee. The publication of various schemes for reconstructing the education system led the Committee to consider appointing a special sub-committee in 1942 to consider the plans which were being put forward. There was some difficulty over the question of entrusting a small group with this task and in March 1943 the Education Committee resolved that all of its members should 'be constituted a special sub-committee to consider proposals with regard to post-war education'.

The Second World War stimulated very strong pressure in society generally for the reform, improvement and extension of the educational system. There was a great deal of criticism of pre-war arrangements and the administrative structure which had sustained them could not expect to be exempt from the process of criticism and review. There seemed to be two main obstacles to the reform of education in the way which was widely desired – the dual system and the arrangements for local authority administration, especially the Part III (elementary only) authorities and the smaller Part II authorities. The question of Church schools and the reform of the dual system is discussed elsewhere.[33] Any proposals to change the administrative structure were bound to have a marked effect in the West Riding, with its high concentration of Part III authorities and quite complex local government arrangements. The more radical proposals did not, in the event, see the light of day outside Whitehall. The Ministry of Health, which was then the Ministry responsible for local government, wanted to constitute new local authorities administering areas much larger than the existing Part II counties. It argued that many counties and county boroughs were financially weak and too small to support adequate hospital services. Fearing that public indifference and low polls would be inevitable if new, very large authorities were confined to health matters, the Ministry proposed that police, education, highways, planning and the fire service should also be made the responsibility of these new authorities. The Board of Education resisted these proposals, believing that very large authorities would be unsuitable as units of educational administration for political and historical reasons as well as on functional grounds.[34]

Within the Board of Education thinking centred on abolishing the Part III authorities and recognising only counties and county boroughs as local authorities which might exercise powers in education. From the purely political angle Butler was anxious to avoid a major local government dispute on educational administration. He sought to do this by making it possible for counties to delegate certain functions to the larger ex-Part III authorities. The Board did not want to give too much away, however, in case the new structures were weakened. In the event the Education Act permitted counties to establish divisional executives in parts of their areas which would act as foci for local interests and to which certain powers might be delegated. Where an existing district or borough had a population in excess of 60,000, or more than 7,000 pupils on the school registers, it might claim to be constituted as a divisional executive in its own right as an 'excepted district'. This particular figure of 7,000 was regarded by the Government as the minimum school population which would support a viable secondary school system.[35]

Nationally the Federation of Part III Education Committees and the Association of Education Committees (AEC) – which had many Part III authorities among its membership – opposed the abolition of these authorities and sought to widen their base, urging that they be given control of secondary education. Where they were too small for this to be done, they should be enlarged by having surrounding county areas added to them.[36] The London suburban areas, Lancashire and the West Riding were the three parts of the country which had large numbers of these authorities; there was indeed a West Riding Association of Part III Education Authorities, which had represented the interests of its members energetically over the years. After the publication of the Hadow Committee's report, *The Education of the Adolescent*, at the end of 1926 this Association had reacted strongly against the Committee's suggestion that Part III authorities below a certain population should be abolished and that administration should be entrusted to fewer and larger authorities, and sent their protest to the President of the Board of Education and to the AEC.[37] Over the years the Association emphasised the advantages of making educational administration as local as possible and tended to stress the danger of large administrative units becoming unwieldy, time-wasting and unresponsive to local needs. Part III Education Committees in the West Riding fully supported their national association's stand against the Government's proposals in the war years and made their position very clear at a meeting in York in November 1943, at which R. A. Butler discussed his administrative proposals with representatives of the authorities. When the 1944 Act abolished them, those which thought they had any chance at all of becoming excepted districts made a bid to do so, rather than become absorbed in a scheme of divisional executives which were seen locally as no more than a replacement for the district committees of the county-administered areas.

Boroughs and urban districts which sought excepted-district status were required to lodge their claims with the Ministry of Education before 1 October 1944.[38] Keighley, Harrogate, Pudsey, Todmorden, Batley, Morley and Spenborough did so. None of these had either a population in excess of 60,000 or more than 7,000 pupils in the school registers; consequently each had to set out some other special grounds on which to base its claim. Todmorden, for instance, with a population of less than 21,000 in 1939, based its claim on its 'geographical location and character'. It was 'situated in the heart of the Pennine Chain at the extreme end of the West Riding on the Lancashire border' and was cut off from the remainder of the West Riding by moorland. The Borough Council believed that its past record showed that it was 'sufficiently experienced and progressive' to become an excepted district. The county wished to include Todmorden along with Hebden Royd Urban District and Hepton Rural District in a divisional executive, believing that it was 'imperative in the true interests of education', both in Todmorden and in the adjacent areas, that excepted-district status should not be granted.[39] The borough of Pudsey, with a population of 28,000, based its claim largely on its 'record of progress over a long number of years'. Again the county authority opposed the granting of the claim on the grounds that the 'true interests of education' would be served by the inclusion of Pudsey in the general pattern of local administration.[40] In a minute to the clerk of the County Council, Binns doubted whether the Ministry would give excepted-district status to Todmorden and Pudsey 'even if we asked them to'. He felt the two applications which would have to be taken seriously were those of Harrogate and Keighley. In his reply Bernard Kenyon, the clerk, set out fully the points he thought should be made in opposing claims for excepted-district status. While inadequate population was an important point, it should be supplemented in each case by facts showing that self-contained services in the areas were not reasonably attainable. Careful consideration should also be given to the question of 'whether anything is known concerning the past record' of a claiming authority which might throw doubt on its ability to administer primary and secondary education; finally any claim to special circumstances should be rebutted with the necessary detail.[41]

Harrogate's population in 1939 was 44,270 but its elementary school population was under 4,000. An interesting aspect of its claim to excepted–district status lay in the reference to the town's financial strength. The product of a penny rate was said to exceed that of five Yorkshire county boroughs, while over the last five years the average rate needed by Harrogate Education Committee had been 18.34d. (7.8p) while the West Riding had needed 52.14d. (21.6p) to meet its elementary education costs. There was in fact little in the claim for excepted-district status which was likely to make it succeed. There was a considerable flow of children to and from the Harrogate borough area for attendance at grammar, junior technical and junior art schools, and it was not difficult for the county to refute Harrogate's claim that its exemption from the general scheme for divisional administration 'should not give rise to any complications or inconvenience in County Council administration'.[42]

The only claim to succeed in this exercise was that submitted by Keighley Borough Council. Its population was also below the requisite minimum of 60,000. It had been steadily declining in the 1920s and 1930s and stood at 55,000 in 1939. The elementary school population was about 1,000 below the prescribed minimum figure. There was certainly a stronger tradition of technical education in the town than in many comparable places but again there was a good deal of movement to the grammar and technical facilities by pupils from outside the borough's boundaries. When he sent the claim forward the Town Clerk of Keighley made a point of addressing it to the Minister, not to the Secretary, and of enclosing a letter reminding Butler that at the York meeting in 1943 he had made a statement which indicated that Keighley would be given 'much greater powers' than those it already possessed as a Part III authority.[43] In the event, the claim was successful and Keighley became the only excepted district in the West Riding, the other claimants being included in the general divisional arrangements made by the county under the 1944 Act.

Apart from the seven Part III authorities mentioned above, Brighouse, Ossett, Pontefract and Shipley[44] exercised powers as Part III authorities until 1 April 1945. The disappearance of the eleven elementary education authorities, leaving the West Riding as the only education authority throughout the administrative area, meant that a considerable amount of technical work had to be dealt with by the county Education Office in taking over the duties and responsibilities formerly exercised by the eleven. Lists of all existing schools, their age ranges, numbers of pupils and details of their buildings and of the teachers who were to be transferred were needed for both provided and non-provided schools. Full particulars were needed of any commitments entered into under the 1936 Act with regard to non-provided schools. Details of administrative staff, of the duties they were carrying out, of possible dates of retirement and of any compensation which might arise would also be required. In all Binns suggested twenty main headings under which information would be needed, quite apart from purely financial matters, if the necessary arrangements were to be made for taking over and running the eleven elementary school systems which were added to the West Riding's administration from April 1945. Although good progress was made, the amount of work to be undertaken in creating the new system of divisional executives and the little time available made it inevitable that interim arrangements would be required. In the former Part III areas the existing education officer continued to deal locally with routine matters in accordance with precedents and, where there were no precedents, to seek the guidance of the chairman of the former Part III education committee.[45]

The specific power which Keighley gained as a result of the acceptance of its claim for excepted-district status was the right to draw up and submit to the Ministry its own scheme for delegation of powers from the county. The West Riding set up twenty other divisional executives. Eighteen of these included more than one district or borough council area within it, the two exceptions being Batley and Morley, each of which was thought large enough to stand on its own. Some parts of the county indicated a desire to stay outside the divisional arrangements and were not covered by the new schemes. In considering both the membership and the functions of divisional executives, the West Riding was guided not only by the arrangements suggested by the Ministry in Circular 5 but also by its long experience of working through the district committee system. In the second week of November 1944 a series of meetings was held at County Hall with representatives of the district councils whose areas were to be included in the areas of divisional executives. A conference was also held with the Yorkshire Association of Part III Education Committees, the West Riding Urban District Councils Association and the West Riding Non-County Boroughs Association to discuss a number of recommendations which these associations had put forward.[46]

The county scheme for divisional administration gave executives the task of keeping under review, and advising the county on, the provision of primary and secondary education. Executive functions as such had to be undertaken within the general lines of policy and finance as determined by the County Council. This was necessary since the provision of finance had to remain a county matter, therefore budgetary guidelines, conditions and terms of employment of various grades of staff, capitation allowances for pupils, limits on maintenance costs for buildings and property and the like all needed to be determined at county level. Thus while executives could order repairs and decorations to school premises, they could only do so within the annual estimates approved by the County Council. The appointment of teachers to schools within divisions was delegated up to a point, but appointment to the post of head teacher was to be made by the County Council, following an interviewing committee which would include representatives of the divisional executive and of the governors or managers. To some extent the West Riding arrangements left rather less authority with bodies of managers and governors than the Ministry suggested and placed more emphasis on the role of the divisional executives and the county itself.[47] Divisional education officers were county officials and their qualifications, salaries and terms of office were decided by the Authority but they were appointed by joint committees consisting of four representatives of the executive and four from the county, with a chairman nominated by the county.

Membership of the divisional executives consisted of three groups of persons – representatives of the county districts constituting the division, members nominated by the county and a number of co-opted or 'added' members. The usual arrangement was for the representatives of the district councils to have a slight majority over the other two groups of members. Thus, typically, in Division 12 Featherstone Urban District Council (UDC) nominated five members, Knottingley UDC nominated four and Pontefract Borough Council six, while the county nominated seven members and a further seven were 'added', so that the district councils nominated fifteen out of a total of twenty-nine members of the executive. The choice of 'added' members was left to each divisional executive to determine. In a number of other large county authorities the scheme adopted made provision for the inclusion of co-opted members drawn from the teaching body and from representatives of the bodies providing voluntary schools. There was pressure from both the teachers' associations and the Churches to follow this practice in the West Riding but the Authority refused to do so, claiming that if any of the divisional executives wanted to have representatives of those interests they could make their own arrangements within their 'added' member total.[48]

In January 1945 the Borough of Keighley exercised its right as an excepted district to submit its own scheme of divisional administration to the Minister. The scheme was naturally drawn up in such a way as to ensure the Borough gained all the powers it could. For primary and secondary education it stated quite simply that Keighley Council might 'exercise all the functions of the Authority [the West Riding] in relation to primary and secondary education' other than borrowing money, raising a rate and preparing an agreed syllabus of religious instruction. The West Riding's objections were quite extensive and the approval of the Minister to a modified scheme was eventually given in December 1945. One of the most important rights which Keighley gained as an excepted district was that the members of its Borough Council became the Committee for Education, and as such had a cohesion and identity which clearly distinguished it from other divisional executives. The staff of the schools and of the education service as a whole, including the borough Education Officer, were, of course, subject to the normal terms and conditions of service of the West Riding. Throughout the period of its existence as an excepted district, Keighley Committee for Education was jealous of the rights which it possessed and showed a natural anxiety to arrange its affairs in its own way, even if this did not always please Wakefield.

The abolition of Part III education authorities meant that the West Riding Education Committee itself needed to be reconstituted from 1 April 1945 so as to cover the whole of the administrative area for all purposes. The new arrangements were, in fact, very similar to the existing provisions – there were still to be thirty-six members from the Council and nine co-opted members – but the new scheme had to be submitted to the Minister for approval so that it might come into operation on the appointed day. From the time the West Riding Education Committee was first established under the Act of 1902, the Authority had refused to follow the general practice and co-opt members to represent the interests of those who provided the voluntary schools. It also refused to have any representatives from the teachers' associations among the co-opted members. The Churches and the teachers' associations now pressed their case for such representation as part of the post-war reconstruction. The Education Committee eventually agreed to meet a deputation from the NUT on 16 January 1945. Its two members – Alice Bacon, then President of the county association and H. Player, its secretary – failed to persuade the Committee to change its attitude.[49] The Ministry was anxious to see that both of these groups were accorded some measure of representation, and only three weeks before the new Committee would need to function wrote asking whether the Authority had considered 'the desirability of including on the Committee representatives of the teachers and of the voluntary school interests'. The Ministry pointed out that since the success of the new Act would ultimately depend on the teachers in the schools, it would seem appropriate that they should be represented on the body responsible for securing the effective administration of the Act. In view of the responsibilities of the Churches and of the large number of voluntary schools in the West Riding, it was also appropriate that these interests should be represented. A week later a further letter invited the county to forward 'satisfactory revised arrangements to this Office at an early date', so that the Minister could take steps to authorise the County Council to constitute its Education Committee by 1 April.[50]

Telephone discussions followed with the Ministry. Neither the clerk nor the Education Officer believed that the Authority would change its mind on this issue. On 20 March the clerk wrote to the Ministry to report that the West Riding Education Committee had now reconsidered the matter and by a large majority refused to include representatives of either the religious bodies or the teachers, since 'such appointments would not be in the interests of education in the county'. This reaffirmation of the West Riding's traditional and very local view on the representation of voluntary bodies, and of its longstanding and more widely shared attitude to teacher representation, was accepted by the Ministry. 'In all the circumstances' the Minister was prepared to approve the arrangements and authorised the County Council to establish an Education Committee on the lines it had proposed.[51]

TABLE 2.3

*Committee structure, 1945*

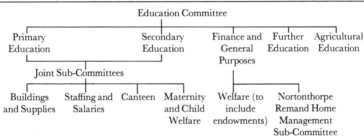

The County Youth Committee to report and submit its financial recommendations to the Finance and General Purposes Sub-Committee

The sub-committee structure for the Education Committee in its new constitution was reformed in the manner set out in Table 2.3. The abolition of the divisions of elementary and higher education in the Act of 1944 and their replacement by primary, secondary and further education meant that the sub-committee structure had to be brought in line. The basic structure of the Elementary, Higher and Finance and General Purposes sub-committees could no longer meet the position. Just as all the members of the Education Committee had been members of the Elementary and Higher Education sub-committees, so it was now decided that the full committee should serve on the Primary, Secondary and Further Education committees. The membership of the Finance and General Purposes Sub-Committee also continued to consist of the full Committee. Perhaps the most important new departure in the Sub-Committee structure followed a little later, with the establishment of a Policy Sub-Committee – to become in due course the Policy and Finance

Sub-Committee. This new sub-committee was designed to serve as the key committee in the structure, the forum in which all the major decisions concerning the education service in the West Riding could be taken. This powerful new sub-committee consisted of all the members of the Education Committee and was established in the summer of 1946. The concentration of most decision-taking in the one body resulted primarily from the desire of the new Chief Education Officer, Alec Clegg, and the chairman of the Education Committee, Walter Hyman, to simplify the policy-making process and make it less diffuse. Sir Alec Clegg later recalled that his task had been made easier since matters of policy and finance were decided in this sub-committee, which he had always attended, while other members of staff of the Education Department had been responsible for the work of the sub-committees 'which ran the service'. He felt that an important advantage of this was that he had been able to spend more time in the schools and colleges and to keep himself more fully acquainted with their development.[52]

The situation which has confronted education authorities nationally since the Second World War has involved them in a great deal more administration and committee activity than before. Some indication of the increased work which the education system found itself undertaking is given by the rise in educational expenditure from 2 to 6 per cent of the gross national product in the quarter-century following the Butler Act of 1944. Thus the simplification of the decision-making process for main policy matters proved to be of even greater value than seemed likely when the new Policy Sub-Committee was set up. The pressure from the Ministry of Education for authorities to produce their development plans by an early date meant that important decisions covering most aspects of the West Riding Education Committee's work for many years ahead needed to be taken as a matter of some urgency.[53] Throughout the last thirty years of its existence the increasing amount of administrative work led to some growth of staff. This growth was strictly limited and from time to time there were outbreaks of complaints that the business was unduly delayed and that letters were not being answered. In 1947 the Education Officer prepared a memorandum on this matter for the Policy Sub-Committee. He found no evidence of undue delay in dealing with day-to-day correspondence but there were delays caused by the necessity to purchase through the county Supplies Department under Section 86 of the Local Government Act of 1933, and by the incidence of the dates for meetings of the various committees of the County Council where matters arose concerning other departments in some way. In the School Meals Service there were no fewer than fourteen bodies outside the Education Department who had to be consulted before a kitchen or dining-hall could be built.[54]

In considering the decision-making and administrative processes in the county during its last thirty years, the degree of involvement of members of the Education Committee, divisional executives, governors and managers should be noted. Just as in the early years elected members were determined to manage things in their own way and declined to have a chief officer, so this strong local tradition of active participation could still be seen at work in recent years. In 1968 the Education Officer pointed out to members that it was common practice in many other county authorities for education committees and their major sub-committees to meet quarterly – in time for each meeting of the County Council – whereas such meetings were held on a monthly cycle in the Riding. He commented: 'The extraordinary intensity of meetings that occurs in the West Riding is due to the determination of the Committee to reserve to elected members decisions which might fittingly be dealt with by a member of staff.'[55] A calculation which attempted to quantify this effort by local people appeared in *West Riding Education: Ten Years of Change*, which recorded that in order to administer the education service some 600 committees consisting of 9,000 members met on approximately 3,700 occasions each year.[56]

While it is not possible, for reasons of space, to follow in detail changes in

TABLE 2.4

*Arrangement of sub-committees in the later 1960s*

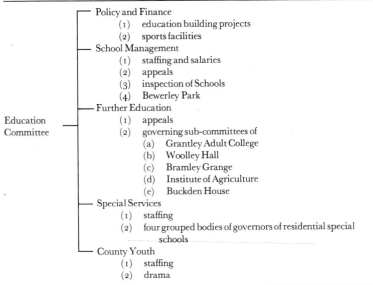

Education Committee

- Policy and Finance
  - (1) education building projects
  - (2) sports facilities
- School Management
  - (1) staffing and salaries
  - (2) appeals
  - (3) inspection of Schools
  - (4) Bewerley Park
- Further Education
  - (1) appeals
  - (2) governing sub-committees of
    - (a) Grantley Adult College
    - (b) Woolley Hall
    - (c) Bramley Grange
    - (d) Institute of Agriculture
    - (e) Buckden House
- Special Services
  - (1) staffing
  - (2) four grouped bodies of governors of residential special schools
- County Youth
  - (1) staffing
  - (2) drama

the pattern of sub-committees and of administrative and other posts in the Education Office, Tables 2.4 and 2.5 set out the position in the later 1960s. Even before the Second World War the Education Department had been obliged to occupy premises other than the rooms allotted in County Hall to house its staff, and by 1953 the central office staff were using nine different buildings and coping with all the difficulties which this situation produced. In April 1962 the Department moved into new offices, built on six floors above the staff canteen and club in Bond Street, and for the first time for many years nearly all the central office was housed under one roof.

TABLE 2.5
*Staff of the Education Department in the later 1960s*

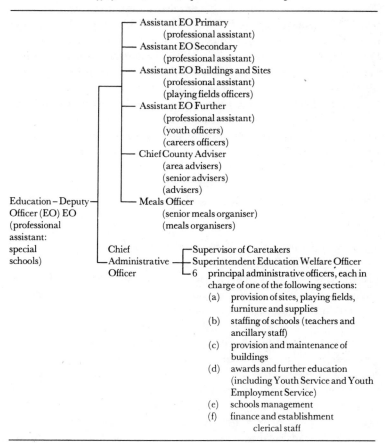

Education – Deputy Officer (EO) EO (professional assistant: special schools)

- Assistant EO Primary
  (professional assistant)
- Assistant EO Secondary
  (professional assistant)
- Assistant EO Buildings and Sites
  (professional assistant)
  (playing fields officers)
- Assistant EO Further
  (professional assistant)
  (youth officers)
  (careers officers)
- Chief County Adviser
  (area advisers)
  (senior advisers)
  (advisers)
- Meals Officer
  (senior meals organiser)
  (meals organisers)

Chief Administrative Officer
- Supervisor of Caretakers
- Superintendent Education Welfare Officer
- 6 principal administrative officers, each in charge of one of the following sections:
  - (a) provision of sites, playing fields, furniture and supplies
  - (b) staffing of schools (teachers and ancillary staff)
  - (c) provision and maintenance of buildings
  - (d) awards and further education (including Youth Service and Youth Employment Service)
  - (e) schools management
  - (f) finance and establishment clerical staff

The only change which was made in the membership of the Education Committee during these years was the addition of one teacher representative. The County Council accepted this departure from the constitution as first laid down in 1903 at its meeting on 16 July 1952. Teachers' associations had not let the matter rest when they failed to secure representation on the Education Committee in 1945 but had continued to raise the issue when it was opportune to do so. In 1949 the West Yorkshire Association of the NUT requested representation on the Committee and on each of the divisional executives. The Headmasters' Association was at the same time pressing the case for the Joint Four Secondary Associations (Headmasters, Headmistresses, Assistant Masters, Assistant Mistresses) to be represented on divisional executives. The matter was further considered by the Policy Sub-Committee but it was decided to make no change in the constitutional arrangements agreed four years earlier.[57] When the number of added members was increased from nine to ten to permit the addition of a teacher representative, the qualification was made that he could not be appointed a member of the Staffing and Salaries Sub-Committee.[58]

The teacher representative was to be chosen by the teachers on the Consultative Committee, where the numerical strength of the NUT led to the filling of the one place on the Education Committee by that Union's nominee. This immediately produced dissatisfaction among members of other teachers' associations and the heads of grammar schools asked that the nomination of the teacher representative should be made alternately by the NUT and the Joint Four Secondary Associations. The Education Committee refused to accede to this request and accepted the nomination of H. J. Adshead as the first teacher representative. Both the Joint Four Secondary Associations and the National Association of Schoolmasters (NAS) continued to seek some form of representation for their members but without success. In 1957 the Education Committee refused to grant representation to the NAS and three months later refused to meet a delegation of three from the Association to discuss various questions affecting the Association's relationship with the Authority.[59] While it had always been possible for individual divisional executives to co-opt teachers if they so desired, it was not until 1962 that the general scheme of divisional administration was amended in such a way as to ensure one teacher representative on each divisional executive, the representative being chosen through the teachers' organisations. This produced a somewhat similar situation to that which had existed at county level since 1952, in that teachers belonging to organisations other than the NUT saw themselves as excluded from representation. In 1965, for instance, the West Riding branch of the Joint Four asked that two teacher representatives be co-opted to the Education Committee and to each executive, one to be a nominee of the NUT and the other of the remaining teachers' organisations, but the request was refused.[60] The Consultative Committee itself was for many years one possible channel through which teachers might make their views known on educational issues, but it really never became a continuously active body influencing the Authority to promote or repress policies. In 1937, when its constitution was revised between the two wars, it consisted of ten members chosen by certificated and uncertificated teachers, four to be chosen by secondary school teachers, four from technical and art institutions, nine members of the Education Committee and up to four other persons with suitable knowledge and experience. This constitution was not revised in line with the changes brought about by the 1944 Act until 1950, when the representation of teachers was changed to give ten places to the NUT, four to the Joint Four Associations and two to the Association of Technical Training Instructors (ATTI). The increasing size of the NAS led to that Association's pressing for representation and this was eventually agreed in 1966, when after a mass lobby by its members at Wakefield it was given one place on the Committee.[61]

There was some questioning of the wisdom of operating a system which consisted of three tiers – county, division and governors or managers – at a time when the pressure of business was heavy and constantly increasing. In an effort to find potential economies during a financial crisis in 1949, the Ministry suggested in a circular that schemes of divisional administration might be reviewed so as to cut administrative costs. A number of counties, including Dorset where John Haynes had gone from the West Riding as County Education Officer, proposed the abolition or reduction in number of their executives, but little came of any of this except in Lancashire, which was able to abolish some of the small divisions which it had created in 1945.[62] There was some pressure to undertake an exercise on these lines in the West Riding but it did not get very far at the time. A few years later the Policy and Finance Committee approved proposals in general terms as a basis of discussion with divisional executives to merge a number of divisions, thereby achieving a saving on administrative costs of about £10,000. At the same meeting the Committee set up a sub-committee to consider the reorganisation of divisional administration generally. This sub-committee produced proposals to reduce the number of divisions from twenty to ten, saving up to £50,000 annually. The proposals were to be fully discussed with divisional executives but proved unacceptable.[63] At the same time it was possible to make financial savings of about £40,000 by amalgamating divisional education offices and by reducing the actual number of divisional education officers following the introduction of joint administrative arrangements for executives in a few areas.[64] In the late forties and fifties there was a strong desire in some parts of the Education Department and among some members of the Education Committee to manage with one fewer layers of administration. It was argued that in some counties the work of providing, equipping, maintaining and staffing the schools was shared very satisfactorily between local committees of managers or governors and the county committee. The interposition of a layer between the schools and the county simply meant that in order to provide the divisional executives with adequate business, some functions had to be withdrawn from governors and managers and others from the county committees. The result seemed to be that governors resented the existence of executives and the diminution of their powers, and the executives – especially in former Part III areas – resented the control of the county. At county level there was a tendency in departments other than Education to have little patience with the claims of the executives who seemed to wish to trespass on terrain which they regarded as their own. In view of this the question arises of how it was that no more determined effort was made to get rid of, or at least to reduce, the number and authority of the executives. The answer to this clearly lay in the strength of the executives in their own localities and in the recognition of this by members of the county Authority, who themselves were elected by and represented those very localities.[65]

The limited reorganisation in local government permitted by the Local Government Act of 1958[66] allowed boroughs and urban districts where the populations had grown to 60,000 or more to take up excepted-district status as of right, while those with a smaller population could seek to persuade the Minister of Education that there were special circumstances justifying such a status. Although there were no places in the county which had grown enough to be able to claim excepted-district status as of right, the prospect was sufficiently attractive for a number of towns to seek to show that special circumstances obtained to justify the status. Batley, Castleford, Harrogate and Spenborough Borough Councils and Wortley Rural District Council applied to the Ministry for excepted-district status, but their applications were rejected.[67]

Divisional executives and excepted districts were both to disappear from the system when arrangements for the local administration of education were overtaken by the general reorganisation of local government which took effect in 1974 and replaced the pattern first set up by the County Councils Act of 1888. Up to 1974 local educational administration had been grafted on to the 1888 county and county borough system by various specific education measures, starting with the Technical Instruction Act of 1889, but principally by the Education Act of 1902 as modified later by the Education Act of 1944. The Board of Education had then had to move on its own again, because any general agreement on a new shape for local government which would also meet education's needs was politically unattainable. Although the reorganisation of local government in 1974 is usually said to have taken the needs of the education service fully into account,[68] clearly this view would not command universal assent among those actually concerned with that service.

As the largest local authority in the country after the London and Lancashire County Councils, the West Riding had experienced at different times the various pressures and problems which the 1888 local government system generated. From the earliest years the Authority had a number of large boroughs – such as Bradford, Leeds and Sheffield – which were geographically within its borders but were themselves possessed of county as well as borough powers and therefore formed quite separate enclaves. The lure of county borough status acted as something of a stimulant to medium-sized towns within the county to seek to grow by enlarging their boundaries and possibly thus to qualify for 'independence' from the county in their turn. The commercial, industrial and social interrelationship of the bigger county boroughs with the county areas immediately surrounding them, and the spread of their suburban dormitories in these districts, produced a strong desire on the part of the county boroughs to extend their boundaries at the expense of the county. Proposals from the boroughs on these lines were most in evidence before the First World War and between the two wars. (From the Second World War there were a number of attempts to achieve a general review of local government and there was a feeling that piecemeal changes and boundary alterations were no longer likely to provide adequate and lasting answers to the problems involved.)

In almost every case where boroughs sought to extend their boundaries the West Riding opposed the move. In 1904 the county and a number of minor authorities successfully resisted an attempt by Leeds County Borough to enlarge its boundaries; five years later the attempt by the then non-county boroughs of Wakefield, Dewsbury and Batley to extend their boundaries were also resisted. In 1911 the county opposed Sheffield's attempt to extend its boundaries; the West Riding lost, but the subsequent financial settlement caused further difficulties and the county petitioned the House of Lords on the issue.[69] In 1912 Barnsley applied for county borough status and the West Riding 'urged that an order should not be made until a suitable arrangement is come to with regard to the future administration of schools for higher education in the Borough and adjacent townships'. Dewsbury's application for county borough status was also opposed in the same year.[70] When

Wakefield applied for county borough status the West Riding did not initially oppose this, but at the national level the Government had by now concluded that the time had come to determine more closely the general principles which should apply in deciding whether a town qualified for county borough status, and Wakefield's application had to wait until a Select Committee had completed its examination of the general principles which should guide the Local Government Board. When the matter had been further examined the county opposed the confirmation of the Order granting Wakefield county borough status. In the next year, 1914, the West Riding was confronted with proposals from Doncaster and Dewsbury to extend their boundaries and resisted both.[71]

After the First World War the conflicts between counties and boroughs again assumed sufficient importance for the Government to appoint a Royal Commission in 1923. The West Riding had sought such an inquiry as a means of defending itself against apparently endless incursions into its terrain. When Sir James Hinchliffe was again elected chairman of the Council in 1922, 'he delivered a trenchant attack on the county boroughs and called for the appointment of a Royal Commission'.[72] The county had come to fear that there was to be no end to attempts to dismember it. Eighteen months later Hinchliffe, in evidence to the Royal Commission, pointed out that the West Riding contained nine county boroughs, of which Barnsley, Dewsbury and Wakefield had been created since 1912. Doncaster had extended its municipal boundaries so as to acquire the requisite population to qualify for county borough status. By a similar process of extension schemes for other county boroughs could be easily formulated in the future. Moreover, the county boroughs already in existence were nourishing ambitious claims, so that minor authorities near them and the county itself were 'subject to constant danger of attack on their areas and disturbance of their administration'. The actual proposals from Leeds, Bradford and Sheffield included large tracts of agricultural land and moorland. These were 'ambitious schemes for forming a Borough which possesses the character of a large County area'.[73] The chairman of the Education Committee, Percy Jackson, was in no doubt as to the superiority of county over county borough administrative practice in education. As a member of the Executive of the AEC and chairman of the Education Committee of the CCA he was in close touch with county boroughs and he defined the difference as one of bureaucracy against local interest: 'The bureaucracy of the towns is quite different from the local government of the counties as far as education is concerned . . . A County Borough school is ruled by the Director of Education and a County school is ruled by the governing body.'[74] Although Doncaster's application for county borough status was finally approved, that was in fact the last county borough to be created from the West Riding and the proposals for the extension of existing boroughs became fewer and less extensive. The Royal Commission did have a stabilising effect on the pattern of local government.

Immediately after the Second World War the Local Government Boundary Commission undertook a review of local government areas as part of the nation's reconstruction planning. It felt the West Riding was too large and recommended its division into two counties, York South and York West. The West Riding county boroughs were to be included, with the exception of Leeds, Bradford and Sheffield, which were to remain as one-tier counties in themselves. The following year, 1948, the Government put the Commission's proposals on one side and the matter was taken no further at the time, but the suggestion that the West Riding should be divided or, to put it another way, that the southern area should be hived off to form a South Riding was revived in 1958, when it was suggested that the northernmost areas of the new South Riding should be the rural districts of Goole, Osgoldcross, Hemsworth, Wakefield and Penistone. The effect of this would have been to produce a southern county containing about one-third of the population (estimated at 582,281 in 1955); the new West Yorkshire would have had a population of 1,028,019. This revival of the Local Government Boundary Commission's scheme now did not, of course, include any county boroughs. The proposal gained the support of the majority of members of the County Council. It was given detailed study and the county got as far as agreeing to submit the proposal for the division of the existing administrative area to the Minister of Housing and Local Government.[75] In the report of the Law and Parliamentary Committee, on whose recommendation the Council acted, the advantages and disadvantages for education were examined in some detail. It was said that neither new county would command the national standing of the large existing West Riding, which gained from its economic and geographical variety; moreover, the various specialist services such as youth employment or agricultural education would be less efficient in smaller counties than in the larger. The smaller southern county might suffer from 'the predatory demands of Barnsley, Doncaster, Sheffield and Rotherham'; it would become known as the coal county, 'seat of a dying industry'; it would not be able to support a well-balanced advisory staff, and most of the special facilities such as the art schools and special schools were in the area designated for West Yorkshire. On the other hand, there would be less travelling and closer contact between schools and the central authority, and 'there would also presumably be very much greater political stability in each of the two new counties, and, therefore, the Education Service would not be subjected to the three-yearly alarms and threats from which it has suffered recently'.[76] The implication of this last point was presumably that South Riding would be permanently Labour and West Yorkshire non-Labour. In the 1950s and 1960s both Labour and Conservative parties enjoyed strong and steady support in some areas but there were sufficient marginal seats to lead to an alternation of party control at the triennial elections – a welcome development provided that there was no serious clash on fundamental strategy, but such fundamental difficulties had arisen over the future organisation of secondary education and at one time it looked as though it might be necessary to change the development plan fairly frequently.

In fact nothing came of the proposals to reshape the West Riding in the 1950s, but the next decade saw the publication of the report of another Royal Commission on Local Government, which was to lead directly to the breaking-up of the Authority. In September 1969, just after the report was published, the Education Officer pointed out in a series of comments to the Policy and Finance Sub-Committee that if the Commission's report were put into operation it would mean that 'every school in the West Riding would eventually be placed in an authority drawing on more meagre resources than those which the present County Council command'.[77] Although the Wilson Government broadly accepted the Commission's recommendations, it did not last long enough to legislate. After the General Election of 1970 the succeeding Heath Government prepared legislation largely on the basis of the report, but it increased the number of metropolitan counties to include West and South Yorkshire and it placed education with the district councils in metropolitan counties. The effect of this was to put the services in the charge of many authorities with populations well under a quarter of a million. In spite of the evidence of the Department of Education and Science to the Royal Commission favouring a minimum population of half a million, and the pressure and advice from various experienced figures in the world of education, the Government would make no change. The Education Officer made no secret of his belief that this was a bad plan and argued that many of the new and small districts showed all the conditions necessary for them to become the new educational priority (and possibly disaster) areas.[78]

A full paper on the effect that the Government's proposed legislation would have on the education service in the West Riding was submitted to the Policy and Finance Sub-Committee in March 1971. The Education Officer pointed out that the insulation of grey industrial areas in small metropolitan districts would impoverish education: 'There will be none of the districts below a quarter of a million in the South, two in the Midlands and nine in the North. Of these nine, three, including the two smallest of all, will be in the West

Riding.' If the West Riding were to disappear, the only kind of arrangement that could offer the schools the supporting services they currently enjoyed would be the creation of three counties centred on Leeds, Bradford and Sheffield.

TABLE 2.6

*Population of the new local authorities, 1974*

|  | Total population | WR county element | |
|---|---|---|---|
| Leeds | 737,110 | 242,560 | 32.9% |
| Sheffield | 571,935 | 52,280 | 9.1% |
| Bradford | 460,995 | 167,305 | 36.3% |
| Huddersfield (Kirklees) | 368,840 | 186,550 | 50.6% |
| Wakefield | 303,000 | 232,860 | 76.9% |
| Doncaster | 281,330 | 196,265 | 69.8% |
| Rotherham | 243,015 | 158,230 | 65.1% |
| Barnsley | 225,355 | 150,040 | 66.6% |
| Halifax (Calderdale) | 194,865 | 103,710 | 53.2% |

The actual proposal was to disperse among thirteen new authorities the Riding's population of 1,786,000. Disregarding the transfers to North Yorkshire, Humberside, Lancashire and Oldham, there would be nine successor authorities, as set out in Table 2.6. Of the ten future education authorities with the lowest rateable value per thousand population in England, five were here – Barnsley, Halifax, Huddersfield, Wakefield and Rotherham – the first three being the lowest in England. These five, along with Doncaster, would include an existing West Riding population of 1,047,000 and would be among the smallest and poorest in the country. The major point, as the Education Officer saw it, was that children born into culturally impoverished homes, and with parents of a low level of aspiration, were among the most severely educationally handicapped of all children in the country. Many lived in 'the grey areas of industrial England which enjoy neither the attractions of the town nor the charm of the country'. Their need was above all for educational enrichment and this the West Riding had striven successfully to provide in the schools in such areas, but in future the schools would be administered by authorities which would be unable to offer any of the supporting services and resources which had in the past contributed to make them what they were.[79]

The last few years up to 1974 were occupied in attempting to make the best arrangements that could be achieved to effect the smooth transfer of schools and services to successor authorities. The success of the arrangements was in itself, in purely technical terms, a considerable administrative achievement.

It was in any case a unique task, for the West Riding was the only major authority in England which had to bring about its own total disbandment with no continuing, even if reshaped, corporate body to succeed it after April 1974. There was a final date by which everything had to be achieved. Although the great majority of institutions simply passed to the successor authority in whose area they were situated, the facilities offered by Woolley Hall, Bramley Grange, the Schools Museum Service and the like were too specialised to be exploited fully by a single successor authority. They were therefore taken over by the new authority for their area on an agency basis, so that all the main successor authorities could make use of them and would contribute to their costs. Some institutions offering rather special facilities were simply taken over by a different successor authority from the one in whose area it was situated. One instance of this was Buckden House; since this had been associated with Bingley College of Education, it was taken over by Bradford, even though it was in the new North Yorkshire.[80]

In this discussion of the administration of education in the West Riding there has been little mention of party political factors as such. The parties were obviously important in making their distinctive contributions to policy formulations in controversial matters and reference is made to these in other parts of this book.

TABLE 2.7

*Chairmen of the Education Committee 1903–74*

| 1903–5 | A. Anderton | (Liberal) |
|---|---|---|
| 1905–18 | Henry Dunn | (Liberal) |
| 1918–37 | Percy Jackson | (Liberal) |
| 1937–49 | Walter Hyman | (Labour) |
| 1949–51 | W. J. Johns | (Liberal) |
| 1951–2 | J. Fuller Smith | (Conservative) |
| 1952–5 | Walter Hyman | (Labour) |
| 1955–8 | J. Fuller Smith | (Conservative) |
| 1958–9 | Walter Hyman | (Labour) |
| 1959–67 | C. T. Broughton | (Labour) |
| 1967–72 | Mrs Laura Fitzpatrick | (Conservative) |
| 1972–4 | G. N. Bott | (Conservative) |

A glance at Table 2.7, which lists the chairmen of the Education Committee, makes it clear that the political stability of the early years gave way, from about the time of the Second World War, to a far greater propensity for change. In its early days the county had been vigorously, indeed abrasively, Liberal. In the inter-war years, under the chairmanship of Sir Percy Jackson, much of this abrasiveness certainly became a thing of the past; a new phenomenon was the emergence of the Labour Party as the single largest group on the County Council in the later 1930s, and from 1937 a Labour member, Walter Hyman, became chairman of the Education Committee. From 1905 to 1937 there had been only one change in the chairmanship. During the Second World War elections and party campaigning in the normal sense were set aside, but from the first post-war election in 1946 a fierce struggle for control developed between the Labour and Conservative parties. In 1949 a Liberal, W. J. Johns, became chairman, with the support of Conservative and Independent members, following the triennial election. Three years later the Labour Party was back in office, with Hyman in the chair. After the 1955 election a Conservative, J. Fuller Smith, became chairman for three years, to be replaced by Hyman when the Labour Party won the 1958 election, and by C. T. Broughton from 1959 to 1967. The electorate favoured the Conservative-led group from 1967 until the end in 1974 – Mrs Laura Fitzpatrick was chairman until 1972 and after her death G. N. Bott occupied the chair for the remaining period.

The very varied social and political composition of the West Riding administrative area has ensured that it has been highly marginal for the last thirty years. So often in local government the party which is out of office at Westminster has found itself favoured in county elections, and there is evidence that in recent years that has happened here. The possibility of electoral reverse and change is a good deal healthier for public life than a situation in which one party is always in the ascendant and is confident of being returned at the next election, almost regardless of its record. Under the post-1974 arrangements this latter position does, of course, prevail in some of the successor authorities. Party differences in the West Riding do not appear to have frustrated development. The fact that while the majority party has taken the chairmanship, the vice-chairman has been drawn from the other party has served to enable the officers to see that all the relevant information has reached both sides. It has also helped the Committee to work as a body and to avoid becoming no more than a place where the majority side announces its decisions while the minority makes its ritual protests.

TABLE 2.8

*Divisional executives, managers and governors – powers and responsibilities*

| Powers and duties | Divisional executive areas | | | Other areas | |
|---|---|---|---|---|---|
| | Managers | Governors | Divisional executive | Governors | District sub-committee |
| *Primary schools* | | | | | |
| Premises – maintenance | Recommend | — | Decide | — | Decide |
| use of premises | Approve subject to direction of Executive | — | Confirm | — | Decide |
| Equipment and supplies | Recommend | — | Decide | — | Decide |
| Estimates of expenditure | — | — | Prepare | — | Prepare |
| Expenditure within estimates | — | — | Incur | — | Incur |
| Appointment of staff: | | | | | |
| head teacher | Appoint 2 representatives to appointing committee | — | Appoint 2 representatives to appointing committee | — | Appoint 4 representatives to appointing committee |
| assistant teachers | Appoint 2 representatives to consult with Divisional executives when appointing | — | Appoint | — | Appoint |
| non-teaching staff | Recommend | — | Appoint | — | Appoint |
| Dismissal of staff: | | | | | |
| head teacher | Recommend | — | Report to County Council | — | Recommend |
| assistant teachers | Recommend | — | Report to County Council | — | Recommend |
| non-teaching staff | Recommend | — | Dismiss | — | Recommend |
| Secular instruction outside school premises | Recommend | — | Decide | — | Decide |
| Religious instruction (special arrangements) | Recommend | — | Decide | — | Decide |
| Holidays | Recommend | — | Decide | — | Decide |
| Admission and transfer of pupils | — | — | Arrange | — | Arrange |
| Enforcement of attendance | Recommend | — | Decide | — | Decide |
| *Secondary schools* | | | | | |
| Premises – maintenance | — | Decide | — | Decide | — |
| use of premises | — | Decide subject to direction of divisional executive | Have power of directing governors in this matter | Decide | — |
| Equipment and supplies other than capitation allowances | — | Decide | — | Decide | — |

| | | | | | |
|---|---|---|---|---|---|
| Estimates of expenditure | — | Prepare | Pass to county with comments | Prepare | — |
| Expenditure within estimates | — | Incur | — | Incur | — |
| Appointment of staff: head teacher | — | Appoint 2 persons to joint appointing committee | Appoint 2 persons to joint appointing committee | Appoint 4 persons to joint appointing committee | Appoint 4 persons to joint appointing committee |
| assistant teacher | — | Appoint | Confirm but to consult County Council if propose to withhold consent | Appoint | — |
| non-teaching staff | — | Appoint | Confirm | Appoint | — |
| Dismissal of staff: head teacher | — | Recommend | Report to County Council | Recommend | — |
| assistant teachers | — | Recommend | Report to County Council | Recommend | — |
| non-teaching staff | — | Recommend | Dismiss | Recommend | — |
| Secular instruction outside school premises | — | Recommend | Decide | Decide | — |
| Religious instruction (special arrangements) | — | Recommend | Decide | Decide | — |
| Holidays | — | Recommend | Decide | Decide | — |
| Admission and transfer of pupils | — | Recommend | Arrange | Arrange | — |
| Enforcement of attendance | — | Recommend | Decide | Decide | — |
| *Other matters* | | | | | |
| School provision | — | — | Review | — | Review |
| Transport of pupils | — | — | Arrange | — | Arrange |
| Medical inspection and treatment | — | — | Arrange through County Medical Officer | — | Arrange through County Medical Officer |
| Meals and milk | — | — | Decide | Decide | Decide |
| Supply of clothing | — | — | Decide | — | Decide |
| Maintenance allowance | — | — | Award | — | Dealt with by Divisional Officer |
| Handicapped children | — | — | Report cases to County Council | — | Report cases to County Council |
| Evening and technical institutes | — | — | Act as managers of such institutes as is decided by the County Council | — | Act as managers of such institutes as is decided by the County Council |

*Note:* Powers and duties were subject to the general regulations of the County Council.

## CHAPTER III

# Elementary Schools 1902−39

On 1 April 1904 the West Riding Education Committee reluctantly took over responsibility for 879 elementary schools (287 provided and 592 non-provided). About 6,000 teachers were employed in these schools and they educated over 200,000 pupils.[1] The religious controversies in English education, which had built up to a climax during the passage of the 1902 Act, did not die down quickly in the West Riding and continued to dog elementary education in this area for many years. Politically the Progressives (Liberals) had a comfortable majority over the Moderates (Independents and Conservatives) on the West Riding County Council and were often supported by a small group of Labour members. But there were deep differences amongst the Progressive members about how far opposition to the 1902 Act should be taken. In the years before the outbreak of the First World War it was this issue which largely dominated elementary education in the West Riding.

Many Liberal members of the County Council who were strongly opposed to rate aid for non-provided schools felt that a solution would be found to the religious difficulty if large numbers of these schools were transferred to the LEA. Accordingly, even before the appointed day, detailed conditions for transfer were approved by the County Council and a conference was arranged with the Yorkshire diocesan authorities to discuss these matters. At the conference both the Roman Catholic and Church of England authorities expressed complete opposition to transfers,[2] and comparatively little use was made of these facilities.

In March 1904 the West Riding County Council had to decide whether it would carry out its duties under the 1902 Act or not. Councillor P. H. Booth, who served as chairman of the Elementary Education Sub-Committee between 1906 and 1920 and who was still described as a 'passive resister'[3] as late as 1913, brought the matter to a head. He informed Alderman C. G. Milnes-Gaskell, chairman of the County Council, that he intended to move a resolution before the next meeting of the Council to deny rate aid to non-provided schools. Milnes-Gaskell replied that he regarded this motion as both illegal and out of order and warned Booth that if he was re-elected chairman he would be unable to put it.[4] At the Council meeting on 17 March Booth accepted Milnes-Gaskell's ruling, but moved that the proposed salary scale for elementary teachers should not be paid to the staff of non-provided schools. This made it possible to discuss the religious issue fully. Predictably, Booth's motion was opposed by the Moderates, but several leading Progressives, including Milnes-Gaskell and Alderman A. Anderton, chairman of the Education Committee, also roundly condemned it. Milnes-Gaskell stressed that he did not wish to see the West Riding 'dragged at the tail of Wales', where several non-conformist Liberal LEAs were refusing to operate Part III of the Act, and asked whether the game was worth the candle. The radical, non-conformist wing of the Progressive group pointed out that they had fared well in the recent local elections and claimed that passive resistance was on the increase. After a lengthy discussion Booth's motion was defeated by fifty-one votes to twenty-three.[5] The matter was not allowed to rest, for in May another passive resister, Councillor W. Clough, moved that the education rate be reduced by the amount that non-provided schools benefited from it, but this resolution was defeated in a division.[6] The following year Alderman J. C. Horsfall, chairman of the Finance Committee, in presenting his annual budget proposed that the West Riding should cease to take responsibility for non-provided schools after 1905. He explained that he had been encouraged by the resistance of the Welsh authorities and claimed: 'We only want the revolt of the West Riding to kill the Act.'[7] Horsfall's suggestion was discussed at length by a special sub-committee, but eventually the Education Committee resolved by fourteen votes to ten not to act on the recommendation.[8] The same issue, however, was raised again at the next meeting of the County Council, when seventeen members signed a motion which would have had the same effect as Horsfall's proposal. Milnes-Gaskell was clearly angered by this and said that he had considered resignation.[9] He had taken legal opinion from Sir Robert Reed as to whether he should allow the motion to be put. Reed had advised him that the motion was illegal. Milnes-Gaskell refused to take the motion but informed the Council that 'there was a way to get rid of a stiff-necked chairman who was perhaps not sufficiently a political partisan to please some of his colleagues – that was by a vote of censure'. As no censure motion was moved the matter rested there, but Milnes-Gaskell had made it amply clear that if he remained chairman threats of open defiance to the 1902 Act must cease. Although in October 1905 Clough persuaded the Council to make a token reduction in the education rate, Horsfall explained that this would merely put finances into a muddle and would not threaten the existence of the voluntary schools.[10] After the summer of 1905 the radical members concentrated on more indirect forms of opposition to the 1902 Act.

The West Riding chose to interpret some of the provisions in the 1902 Act in an unconventional manner. The most famous example of this was the West Riding's contention that it was not required to pay teachers in non-provided schools for time spent in imparting denominational religious instruction. The origins of this contention are to be found in a letter from a lawyer to the *County Council Times* in December 1903.[11] The attention of the Council was drawn to this letter and it was agreed, without a division, that teachers' salaries should be reduced in proportion to the time spent in giving denominational instruction.[12] It was suggested that the school managers should make up the salaries to the full amount. Within a few months over fifty protests were made by school managers to the Board of Education against this decision.[13] The Board of Education instructed the Authority to pay the salaries in full, and after an inquiry a writ of mandamus was issued against the County Council. It was clear that the matter would go before the High Court unless the West Riding capitulated. Moderate members urged the Council to change its mind, and Labour members, with NUT support, argued that the teachers and not the Board of Education were suffering. These appeals proved of no avail, for a substantial majority were in favour of the West Riding's solicitor defending any legal proceedings.[14]

By mid-April 1906, however, it seemed possible that legal action might be avoided after all. The Elementary Education Sub-Committee resolved that 'in view of existing circumstances'[15] the deductions in salaries should not be enforced.[16] This course was urged by Milnes-Gaskell, who took the unusual step of attending this sub-committee meeting. Milnes-Gaskell argued that in view of pending legislation it was not worth incurring legal expenses and annoying teachers. Booth and Clough were unimpressed by the argument that they should not oppose the Board of Education, which was now led by a Liberal President, and even the moderate Alderman H. Dunn, chairman of the Education Committee, wanted to go on at this stage.[17] Consequently, the full Education Committee, by thirteen votes to eleven, reversed the decision of its sub-committee.[18]

The High Court decision went against the West Riding, and the Education Committee soon recommended that no appeal should be made. Dunn insisted firmly that 'the judgement given was entirely erroneous'[19] but felt that it was time to bring the matter to a close. Milnes-Gaskell stressed the expense, and said that 'he was always in favour of the West Riding County Council being a terror to its foes, but he did not think it was wise to make itself a terror to its friends'.[20] Even Clough, the militant 'passive resister', urged the Council not to appeal. He stated that 'there had been frequent allusion made in the House of Commons to pig-headed local authorities, and the allusion always seemed to be to the West Riding County Council'.[21] Despite these pleas the Council decided by the narrow margin of twenty-one votes to nineteen to take the case to the Court of Appeal.

To the satisfaction of the radicals the Court of Appeal found in the West Riding's favour. Their joy was short-lived, however, as the Board of Education went to the House of Lords, which reversed the Appeal Court's decision. The radicals reluctantly accepted the situation, although twelve members still voted against paying the teachers.[22] Briefly it appeared as if the situation might be changed yet again, as the Liberal President of the Board introduced a one-clause bill to negate the House of Lords ruling.[23] Later, however, the Prime Minister announced that this measure was to be dropped and that the Government intended to introduce major educational legislation during the next session.[24] This came to nothing and thenceforth this issue, which had aroused such high passions, received little further attention either inside or outside the West Riding.

In the early years of the twentieth century the friction between the Authority and the non-provided schools was not restricted to the well-known dispute over payments for denominational instruction. One regular bone of contention concerned the right of non-provided schools to close on saints' days and other special occasions. The Committee insisted that the schools should obtain permission from Wakefield for special holidays and this was by no means granted automatically. It was not at first unusual for schools to disregard these rulings from the central office. The dispute which was, perhaps, potentially the most serious occurred in 1904 over the closing of the Silkstone National Infants' School. The local vicar, who was correspondent for the managers, arranged the annual church bazaar in school time and proposed to close the school. This was forbidden by County Hall. The vicar protested that as a band had been engaged and Countess Fitzwilliam was to perform the opening ceremony, the arrangements could not be changed. Later the Council found out that the bazaar had been held and the school closed. It promptly resolved to cease to maintain the school, as regulations had been disobeyed. The managers appealed to the Board of Education against this decision, and it was only after lengthy negotiations, a special conference in London, the removal of the vicar from his position as correspondent and profuse apologies that the Authority agreed to resume to maintain the school. While trivial in itself, this affair was typical of the sour relations of this period.

Another incident which attracted public attention was the Authority's refusal to ratify Mr O. Milnes' appointment as headmaster of Royston National School. A majority of the managers wished to appoint Milnes, but a minority informed the Staffing and Salaries Sub-Committee of their doubts.[25] Consequently a small deputation[26] interviewed Milnes and questioned the pupils at his school. The deputation recommended that Milnes should not be appointed on 'educational grounds'.[27] Later the Authority explained that Milnes was not regarded as a bad teacher, but it was felt that he was unsuitable for the particular post. The managers appealed to the Board of Education, which sent HMI Marvin to report on Milnes. Marvin's report was favourable and the Board asked the Authority to reconsider its decision.[28] The Committee refused to change its mind, and eventually the Board admitted that it could not intervene as the Authority insisted that it had made its decision on 'educational grounds'.[29] The NUT took up Milnes' case and soon the affair was reported in the national Press. Questions were asked in both Houses of Parliament and a debate ensued in the Lords. It was hinted both in Parliament and in the Press that the real reason for Milnes's rejection was that he was 'a Conservative and a good Churchman'.[30] Nonetheless, the West Riding held its ground, despite the rather obvious embarrassment caused to the Liberal President of the Board of Education. Eventually, in 1908, Milnes was appointed head of a bigger school in the West Riding on a larger salary than that paid at Royston. Both the Press and Conservative politicians were quick to point out that the Authority found no 'educational' objections to this appointment.

Another interesting and informative episode concerning conflict over the religious issue involved the elementary schools in Garforth. In February 1907 a new council school was opened in the village, and consequently it was proposed by the Authority, with the agreement of HMI Marvin, that there should be a rationalisation of elementary schooling in Garforth. The Authority suggested that Garforth Parochial School should be used as an infants' and junior school and the new council school as a senior school for upper standards only. The managers of the Parochial School objected, largely on the grounds that children above Standard III would not receive denominational instruction. The dispute was referred to the Board, and an Assistant Secretary soon informed both parties that the Board regarded the managers' objections as legitimate.[31] At this juncture a West Riding Member of Parliament wrote privately to the President of the Board, drawing his attention to this decision. McKenna, the President, was angry about the whole affair, as he sympathised with the Authority's position but had not been consulted. The President brought the attention of Morant, the Permanent Secretary, who had also been ignorant of what was happening, to the affair rather abruptly. Morant sharply reprimanded the official involved, and warned, 'generally speaking it does not do to apply general precedents settled under the late Government to cases of controversy between a local authority and voluntary school managers.'[32] Despite Morant's objections McKenna was determined to find a pretext for reversing this decision, and a fortnight later the parties concerned were informed that the reorganisation could go ahead. This change of mind prompted some awkward questions for McKenna in Parliament, and the managers of the Parochial School resolved to take the matter to law. The case was heard in January 1908, and Judge Channell found in the managers' favour. After its earlier experiences, the Authority decided not to appeal unless the Board agreed to meet costs.[33] Not surprisingly this was refused, and the Garforth elementary schools remained as they were.

After 1908 there were no further attempts to test the religious controversies in the courts, but severe differences of opinion persisted. The Roman Catholic community, which was the only voluntary group really interested in opening new elementary schools in this period, was particularly annoyed by the opposition of the Education Committee to so many of its projects.[34] It would be tedious to give accounts of the details of the many disputes between the Catholics and the Committee concerning the provision of new schools, but it was often left to the Board of Education to hold public inquiries and then to adjudicate between the two. At the same time the Committee came under attack, both in the Council chamber and the Press, from Moderates led by Councillor Claude Leatham for the extravagant provision of new council schools. Leatham maintained that the Committee's bias against voluntary schools was so strong that council schools were built in areas where provision in non-provided schools was ample. On one occasion a motion to make it compulsory to hold a public inquiry when the erection of a new council school was contemplated was defeated by only two votes in full Council.[35] Leatham made much of the fact that there were more school places in the county than there were children to fill them. The Progressives replied that school places at Settle were no use for children who lived near Doncaster.[36] On one occasion Leatham responded to this argument by suggesting that it might be a good thing if the Committee built schools on wheels.[37] Nonetheless, Leatham could not deny that about two-thirds of the new school places provided in this period were for the rapidly developing villages of the Yorkshire coalfield.[38] Another continual bone of contention between Leatham's friends and the Progressives was the relative costs of voluntary and council schools. Statistics were frequently cited by both sides, and on one occasion Leatham even employed a Leeds firm of chartered accountants to prepare figures he wished to quote in the Council Chamber.[39] Both sides, however, merely manipulated the presentation of the statistics to suit their own ends and little of a balanced nature about comparative costings can be gleaned from this lengthy controversy. Instead of concentrating on the most salient fact concerning the financing of elementary education in this period, which was that the proportion of funds contributed by central government was declining sharply,[40] the two factions persisted in fighting a phoney war over which type of school was the more expensive.

Although wrangling over religious issues took up considerable time, it did not prevent the Committee from getting on with its real work of providing facilities for the education of the children of the West Riding. In 1903 the County Architect was instructed to inspect and report on all the elementary schools in the area. In each report the architect gave a general description of the school and assessed the state of the buildings, heating, ventilation, lighting, sanitary conveniences and playgrounds. These reports make instructive reading. Many of the schools were not purpose-built and included one converted toll bar.[41] It was revealed that 413 of the 881 schools surveyed had midden-privy closets, and the architect pointed out that many of these midden-privies were 'continually to be seen full, very filthy and foul-smelling and in a shocking state generally'.[42] Nearly half of the schools had neither gas nor electric light[43] and many were not connected to a public water supply. The Committee concluded that in general the inquiry had revealed 'a very serious state of things in the buildings in use as non-provided schools. Dismal, insanitary schoolrooms are far too common, and striking defects, such as insufficient and unsuitable classroom accommodation, defective heating and ventilation, absence of adequate cloakroom and lavatory provision, insanitary offices and drainage, playgrounds which are quagmires in winter and dust heaps in summer, are found in nearly every part of the Riding.'[44] It was not always easy to get the managers of non-provided schools to put their school premises in order.[45] Sometimes they simply did not have the necessary funds but, according to Booth, chairman of the Elementary Education Sub-Committee, some managers made themselves 'as obnoxious as possible in resisting our requests to make their schools sanitary'.[46] In 1913 Booth wrote: 'In one case I have before me it took us three years to obtain doors to closets, and the managers actually appealed to the Board of Education against our request, and, in another, where the closets were so near the school windows as to be offensive, there was much correspondence and many visits. Time, patience and pressure have effected wonders, but much remains to be done.'[47] Although the premises in the worst condition were generally non-provided schools, the Committee acknowledged in 1905 that some of the schools inherited from the school boards were also in a bad state of repair.[48] There is little evidence to suggest that the elementary schools of the West Riding were in a worse state than those in other parts of the country, but dissatisfaction in this respect stemmed from expectations of higher standards from the new LEAs.

As well as having some jurisdiction over the standards of school buildings, the new LEAs had certain discretionary powers in the field of compulsory school attendance. The law prescribed that in general children should attend school between the ages of five and fourteen. The Factory Act of 1901, however, provided that children over twelve who could find employment in a factory (as defined in the Act) could work part-time and attend school on a half-time basis. Local authorities, in addition, could pass by-laws (within prescribed limits) offering further exemptions from attendance. The West Riding County Council passed a by-law to allow any child over twelve, whether in employment covered by the Factory Act or not, to take advantage of the half-time system as long as he had reached the Fifth Standard or had made 300 or more attendances in each of five school years. In such cases it had to be shown to the satisfaction of the district sub-committee that the child was 'benificially employed'.[49] Later it was stressed that 'the beneficial employment of any child below the statutory school age of fourteen should be regarded as applying to exceptional and not to ordinary circumstances',[50] but the evidence suggests that this was not always taken seriously by district sub-committees.[51] The County Council also allowed total exemption from school attendance to children over twelve who had reached Standard VII or who had registered at least 350 attendances in each of five school years, as long as they could show they had obtained 'beneficial employment'.

At a national level exemptions from school attendance, especially the half-time system, were controversial issues. Progressive educational opinion condemned the half-time system, and legislation to outlaw it was widely expected from the Liberal Government of 1906. Half-timers were much more numerous in Lancashire than in the West Riding, but in the textile areas in the west of the county the system was still widely regarded as essential to the prosperity of both local industry and working-class families. Numbers of half-timers fluctuated somewhat according to the conditions of trade, but in 1911 there were 5,257 half-timers in employment covered by the Factory Act and 1,137 who qualified under the West Riding by-law.[52] In that year the Council amended its by-laws so that from the beginning of 1912 children under fourteen were prevented from taking part-time employment in trades excluded from the 1901 Act.[53] At the same time the Council ceased to allow children over twelve with good attendance records to leave school, but continued to permit those who had reached the Seventh Standard to take up 'beneficial employment'. These changes went through Council without arousing much opposition, but when they were implemented in 1912 objections were raised in many quarters.[54] Petitions were signed by over 6,000 people and several district sub-committees registered protests. In full Council, J. P. Hinchliffe, the Progressive vice-chairman, proposed and P. R. Jackson seconded that total exemption for children over thirteen with good attendance records should be restored.[55] After a long debate, in which various hardships were attributed to the change in the by-laws, Hinchliffe's suggestion was accepted by thirty-six votes to sixteen. There can be little doubt that the public outcry surprised the Progressives and soon caused a division in their ranks. It was interesting that Liberal leaders such as Hinchliffe and Jackson argued that as a democratic body the Council should give way to the wishes of the majority, as it was clear that the ideals of the Authority, as expressed in the new by-laws, were in advance of the desires of the ordinary people of the West Riding. Although the Council reversed its decision on total exemptions, it retained the provision which reduced partial exemptions. From 1912 over 90 per cent of the half-timers in the county were employed in textile mills. Another decade passed, however, before the system was abolished completely.[56]

From the outset the West Riding was well aware of the special needs of the large numbers of older and more intelligent pupils who had passed rapidly through the standards but were not going on to secondary schools. In the Committee's first annual report it was stated:

> Children in the upper standards of an elementary school, more especially those in the Seventh Standard, do not spend their final years at school to the best advantage. It should now be possible to organise in suitable districts central classes for upper-standard children where they may have opportunities for practical work, and the advantage of coming into contact with children of similar age and attainments to themselves.[57]

In 1907 the Authority drew the attention of district sub-committees, managers and teachers to the fact that in many schools all pupils in the top two or three standards had to be taught simultaneously by the same teacher. This led to wasteful repetition of work for the older scholars and gave them the impression that they had already learnt all that school could offer and they were just marking time.[58] The Committee encouraged teachers to divide these top standards into separate sections and to provide different schemes of work for the various sections.[59] It was also suggested that more pupils could be put into these higher standards rather earlier in their educational careers than hitherto.

In 1911 a letter from Caernarvonshire Education Committee directed the attention of the West Riding to the facilities and grants available for the education of older pupils in Scotland.[60] This matter was taken up with interest and a deputation of leading Committee members and administrators was dispatched north of the border.[61] The deputation was so impressed that it was decided to experiment on Scottish lines[62] when the new attendance by-laws came into force.[63] It was also agreed to impress the need for further grants for advanced courses, such as those which existed in Scotland, upon the Board of Education. Although the CCA, as well as individual authorities, took up this question, the Board was unable to offer grants on the lines proposed. In a few selected schools in the Riding reorganisation on Scottish lines took place, but large-scale projects were prohibited by financial constraints.

Instruction in practical subjects was one part of the elementary school curriculum which grew, particularly for older children, between 1904 and 1914. The Committee realised that facilities could not be provided in all elementary schools, and hence encouraged district sub-committees to set up centres for subjects such as cookery and handicraft which could serve the needs of several schools in a locality. Table 3.1 shows the growth in this field.

TABLE 3.1

*Teaching of practical subjects in 1905 and 1914*[64]

|  | Number of children receiving instruction | |
| --- | --- | --- |
|  | 1905 | 1914 |
| Cookery | 3,050 | 6,222 |
| Laundry | 107 | 2,420 |
| Housewifery | – | 1,855 |
| Domestic subjects (combined) | – | 155 |
| Handicraft | 966 | 3,267 |
| Light woodwork | – | 175 |
| Gardening | 88 | 1,866 |

Greater progress was made with the extension of facilities for practical instruction than with the reorganisation of school work generally for older scholars. The Authority was acutely aware of the need to avoid situations in which pupils marked time, but before 1914 comparatively few schools experienced radical changes. Finance was the major barrier, but at least this period gave opportunities to several influential personalities in the Authority to consider what could be attempted with older scholars. Prominent among these personalities was Percy Jackson, who took a strong interest in extending opportunities for children in elementary schools. He was a member of the deputation which visited the Scottish schools and served on sub-committees dealing with this question. When Jackson was elected chairman of the Education Committee in 1918, he was able to ensure that this area of activity played a prominent part in the Authority's educational programme.

The First World War had a temporary rather than a permanent impact on elementary education. The shortage of male teachers tended to slow down the pace of curricular changes, and a number of handicraft centres had to be closed down temporarily.[65] Strict controls on capital developments were imposed, and grants for repairs, furniture and equipment were all subjected to stringent economies. After considering numerous applications from farmers, the Committee agreed to relax the school attendance by-laws and permit children over twelve years of age to leave school and work on the land.[66] There was some opposition to this from trade unionists[67] and Labour members of the Council, who maintained that the country could hardly claim to be short of workers when so many people were still engaged in domestic service.[68] Nonetheless, a large majority of the Committee remained in favour of allowing this practice to continue until the end of hostilities, although the wishes of one district sub-committee to permit boys over twelve to work in coal mines were overruled.[69]

Difficulty was soon experienced, however, with the provision in the 1921 Act which stated that any child attaining the age of fourteen during a school term had to remain at school until the end of that term. Many parents resented this addition to their children's schooling[70] and some district sub-committees were reluctant to prosecute for non-attendance in such cases.[71] In order to meet these difficulties it was proposed to increase the number of terms from four to six per annum. This proposal was favoured by Sir James Hinchliffe, chairman of the County Council; Alderman J. J. Brigg, chairman of the Elementary Education Sub-Committee and other members.[72] In contrast, Percy Jackson wanted to postpone consideration of this issue, as he knew that the President of the Board had still to make up his mind on the question and that the Board's officials favoured no more than four terms.[73] Jackson failed to get his way in Committee, but the Board, after discussing the matter with a deputation, refused to sanction six terms. At a further meeting at the Board it was agreed that the difficulties might be met if a child, on reaching his fourteenth birthday, could be exempted from further attendance if his case met certain conditions.[74] These conditions were that the child had a definite offer of employment, which would be lost if not taken up immediately, and that, owing to poor financial circumstances, the earnings of the child would make an appreciable difference to the family income. The power to grant these exemptions was delegated to the district sub-committees.

To the consternation of both the Committee and the Board of Education, the district sub-committees chose to grant these exemptions rather liberally[75] and resented having any decisions overruled.[76] Between 1925 and 1931 about sixteen per cent of the total of school leavers were released prematurely.[77] Most authorities did not allow this practice at all and by the late 1920s none of the counties bordering on the West Riding had significant numbers of premature leavers.[78] Of other authorities in the geographical area of West Yorkshire only Ossett (twelve per cent) and Huddersfield (ten per cent) approached the proportion attained by the West Riding.[79]

The Board of Education urged the Committee to improve this situation.[80] At an interview with officials of the Board it was pointed out to Hinchliffe and Jackson that the West Riding was the only large authority in England which granted numerous exemptions.[81] The Board rejected the claim that the law was not enforced because of the economic depression and pointed out that other areas equally badly affected managed to enforce the law. It was also urged that the smaller authorities in West Yorkshire were annoyed by the action of the West Riding, as children from their areas had to face unfair competition in finding employment from premature leavers educated in the county area. District sub-committees were asked for their views on this subject; over half wanted to retain the existing system.[82] Despite this opposition the Committee followed the Board's advice and resolved to abolish exemption at the end of 1931–2.[83] Even this was not the close of the matter, for in the summer of 1932 Alderman W. Clough attempted to reopen the whole issue,[84] but after discussion it was agreed to adhere to the decision of July 1931.[85]

There can be little doubt that exemptions were granted in the West Riding in the 1920s to children whose circumstances did not really comply with the Board's conditions. Members of the Committee, such as Jackson, who wanted the West Riding to have a reputation as a progressive education authority, were both annoyed and embarrassed by the situation. Once the control of exemptions had been delegated to the district sub-committees, however, the Committee could not abolish them quickly without consultation, as this would have been represented by opponents as undemocratic and contrary to the wishes of parents. Although this issue did not involve party political differences, it was sufficiently sensitive to prevent speedy solution. Later, when the Government contemplated increasing the school leaving age to fifteen with exemptions for fourteen-year-olds who could obtain 'beneficial employment', Jackson wrote to the President of the Board, Oliver Stanley, and tried to persuade him to drop the exemption clauses: '[In the West Riding] the exemptions would have to be granted by district sub-committees each with views of their own, pulling in opposite ways . . . I wonder what cannot be considered beneficial employment.'[86] Stanley did not heed Jackson's advice, but it is clear that Jackson was strongly opposed to the reintroduction of the type of school attendance regulations which had consistently posed problems for the Committee between 1904 and 1932.

At the end of the First World War the Education Act of 1918 imposed important new duties on LEAs. They were required to prepare schemes to provide continuation schools for adolescents, and for the first time legislation laid down that there should be special provisions (including practical instruction) for the older and more intelligent pupils in elementary schools. The West Riding had made some progress with the latter before 1914,[87] but there was little enthusiasm for compulsory continuation schools. In 1913 Jackson had written that he was sceptical about them, pointing out that many adolescents would be reluctant attenders and learners, that the cost would be tremendous and that there would be difficulties in staffing.[88] Early in 1917, however, the County Council decided to recommend their establishment to the departmental Committee on Juvenile Employment after the war,[89] but at this stage there was still considerable opposition, led by the influential chairman of the Elementary Education Sub-Committee.[90] Once the 1918 Act was passed, the West Riding set up a special sub-committee, with Jackson as chairman, to consider its implications. Unfortunately the memoranda submitted to this sub-committee have not survived and consequently it is not possible to assess its work fully. Nonetheless, it is clear that schemes for continuation schools were prepared by the local inspectorate[91] and HMIs were consulted.[92] Jackson and Hinchliffe, who had served on the departmental Committee on Juvenile Employment, kept in contact with H. A. L. Fisher about this matter.[93] Eventually, however, Jackson proposed that the Authority should drop the idea of continuation schools and concentrate on providing advanced instruction in central schools and classes for all children up to fifteen years of age.[94] In proposing this to the County Council Jackson explained that he did not expect the leaving age to be raised to fifteen for some time.[95] He stressed the virtues of intermediate secondary schools which provided a practical education, and cited the success of London central schools.[96] He pointed out that continuation schools would be very costly and argued that intermediate secondary schools would give better value for money. Later the Education Committee explained their rejection of continuation schools in terms of the shortage of teachers, the high cost of school building and the difficulties involved in arranging day-release for young people employed in the West Riding's staple industries of agriculture, textiles and coal mining.[97] At first Labour members of the Council were sceptical of Jackson's proposals. They argued that the Fisher Act should be given a trial and that new legislation would be required for Jackson's scheme.[98] On being assured by Jackson that new legislation was not necessary, they withdrew their objections.[99] Jackson's scheme was then submitted to the Board of Education, but before the issue was fully resolved it was overtaken by the change in the economic climate. As a result of the onset of slump in the winter of 1920–1, the Board restricted expenditure on education and, in consequence, over nearly all the country the schemes for continuation schools were dropped.

Some progress, meanwhile, was being made with the provision of higher and more advanced classes in elementary schools. At first it was stressed that the existing work of elementary schools should be extended and deepened rather than new subjects introduced.[100] The energies of head teachers and the local inspectorate were channelled into this particular part of elementary education in the early 1920s.[101] Owing to the high cost of labour and materials immediately after the war, the Committee would not embark on projects with permanent buildings but preferred to use army huts as temporary accommodation.[102] The new handicraft and domestic science centres provided between 1919 and 1921 were housed in converted classrooms or army huts,[103] but the Committee put considerable effort into making separate provisions for the instruction of older boys and girls. Practical subjects, such as woodwork for boys and cookery and needlework for girls, were given prominence in the early 1920s. From the outset it was acknowledged that the development of more advanced work within the elementary schools and the proliferation of practical subject centres were to be only temporary measures.[104] In the long term the Authority wanted to concentrate older pupils into separate schools which were specially staffed and equipped for more advanced work with elementary school children. During 1919 and 1920 the special sub-committee concerned with the implementation of the 1918 Act did preparatory work in this area. Jackson and other members of the sub-committee accompanied J. W. Horne, the Senior Inspector for Elementary Schools, on visits to London central schools, and advice was sought there.[105] By the winter of 1920 the sub-committee was making progress with experimental schemes to set up central schools in Queensbury and Wombwell and local discussions had been held.[106] At this point, however, the onset of the slump prompted the Board of Education to issue Circulars 1185 and 1190, which instructed LEAs to take strict economy measures and to suspend new projects. Thus further progress was halted, at least temporarily.

Apart from retarding new developments, the economies of 1921 made surprisingly little impact on elementary education. By the time that the Economy Sub-Committee had completed its work and reported and the Education Committee had considered its recommendations, the immediate crisis had passed.[107] The Economy Sub-Committee proposed that small elementary schools should be closed because they were uneconomic, and also suggested that the age of compulsory attendance at school should be raised from five to six years and that children under five years should not be admitted to school at all.[108] The Education Committee willingly accepted the former recommendation, but commented that under the existing state of the law little progress could be made.[109] Closure of small non-provided schools could only be effected with the consent of the managers and this was hardly ever easy to obtain.[110] Later the Committee reported that villagers would almost always be strongly opposed to the closure of their own school, even if it had less than thirty pupils and could be clearly shown to be an uneconomic unit.[111] Consequently, progress in this direction proved to be a very difficult matter. With regard to the questions of the raising of the age of compulsory school attendance from five to six years and the exclusion of children under five altogether, there was disagreement. The Economy Sub-Committee pointed out that fifty-four out of 116 district sub-committees supported the former proposal and ninety-two the latter.[112] It was estimated that as a result of raising the school leaving age from thirteen to fourteen there were over 10,000 extra children in West Riding elementary schools, but it was pointed out that if children under five were excluded, approximately 10,000 school places would be freed.[113] The Elementary Education Sub-Committee, however, rejected this suggestion completely,[114] and it is interesting to note that when a similar proposal had been made in 1905–6, largely on grounds of economy, the Education Committee and the County Council had then reacted in the same way.[115] By 1922 the immediate crisis had passed and the Economy Sub-Committee's view was supported by only two members at the Education Committee's meeting. Although one of these was Sir James Hinchliffe, chairman of the County Council, the proposal to exclude children under five was dropped.[116]

Although restrictions on educational developments were still in force in 1923, the Board of Education agreed to receive a deputation from the West Riding to discuss arrangements for the most advanced children in elementary schools.[117] An interesting but unsigned memorandum (it seems likely that it was produced by the local inspectors for elementary education) was prepared for this meeting.[118] This document maintained that new provisions for the age range twelve–fourteen years were now urgently required, and it urged that, where possible, these developments should take place in schools separated from the ordinary elementary provision. It was stressed that West Riding parents had as much right to facilities for advanced instruction for their children as did parents in adjacent county boroughs.[119] The advice of the Board of Education was sought on central schools and their position in the general educational system.[120] As a result of this meeting the Authority embarked on a policy of providing what were known as 'middle schools'[121] in the West Riding, for the age range eleven–fourteen years. The term 'middle school' was not widely used outside the West Riding and was roughly equivalent to the term 'non-selective central school' which was used by many authorities. There were basically three ways of providing middle-school facilities:

(1)   the erection of new schools;

(2)   the reorganisation of existing buildings so that all pupils in the age range eleven–fourteen years in an area could be concentrated into one school which took no children under eleven;

(3)   the reorganisation of existing buildings so that all pupils in the age range eleven–fourteen years in an area could be concentrated into one school which also continued to take some children under eleven.

In the next few years the West Riding experimented with all three of these possibilities. Despite the restrictions on building, early in 1923 the Board of Education sanctioned the construction of middle schools at Wombwell and Rothwell.[122] Both of these projects took a long time to materialise, however, as there were troubles over sites and plans at Wombwell, and eventually, at the request of Rothwell and Stanley Urban District Councils, it was decided to give priority to the building of a new secondary school in that area.[123] Meanwhile, the Board of Education approved of the reorganisation of elementary schools in the South Elmsall district, which made it possible to open the first West Riding middle school at South Kirkby Moorthorpe in September 1925. By the beginning of 1926 this school accommodated 370 pupils between eleven and fourteen years of age, and by this date special middle-school classes, which provided for 360 pupils, had also been organised in connection with four other elementary schools.[124] Little more progress was made with reorganisation before the report of the Hadow Committee was published. Late in 1924 the Education Committee submitted a plan of future needs to the Board, in which it was stated that in the next seven or eight years seventy-one new elementary schools and twenty-two enlargements to existing schools would be necessary.[125] It was pointed out that only 8,000 out of 30,000 girls over eleven in elementary schools received instruction in domestic subjects and that the provisions for handicraft were even more seriously in arrears.[126] It was stressed that much new building was necessary: first, to keep up with the housing developments in the still rapidly growing coalfield in the south-east of the county and, secondly, to make the reorganisation of elementary education a viable proposition.

There was little opposition within the County Council to this reorganisation of elementary education, although Clough claimed that there was no demand for central schools[127] and on another occasion characterised middle schools as 'moonshine and mockery'.[128] In general, however, the three main political groupings on the Council all favoured reorganisation, although several Labour members showed some initial scepticism. Alderman D. Hardaker regarded middle schools as an inferior substitute for secondary education.[129] He was assured by Hinchliffe that middle schools were not intended as rivals to secondary schools. Hinchliffe pointed out that there were thousands of children in the top standards of elementary schools who would not receive the benefits of any form of higher education if it was not provided in middle schools. He concluded that the Board was anxious to experiment with these middle schools, and the fears of Hardaker and his friends were largely dispelled. The reasons for the relatively slow rate of advance before 1927 must be sought largely outside Yorkshire. The First World War brought an end to the building of new schools, and during 1919–20 the Authority refused to sanction projects because of the high costs. In January 1921 the Board of Education severely restricted building in Circular 1190, which was not finally withdrawn until 3 April 1924. The remainder of 1924 and the early months of 1925 proved to be a brief interlude of optimism. In June 1924 Jackson told the AEC that he trusted that 'the spirit of the Geddes Report has gone for ever from the world of education'.[130] He expressed the hope that by 1927 the school leaving age would be raised to fifteen, and that soon afterwards many children between the ages of eleven and fifteen would be educated in newly built or organised 'middle schools or junior technical schools or junior secondary schools or whatever name you like to call them'.[131] By November 1925, however, the state of the national economy induced the Board to issue Circular 1371, which stated that the cost of new and developing services must be largely met by economies on existing services.[132] In these circumstances the West Riding had to curb many of its new projects, at least in the immediate future.

The publication of the Hadow report in the last weeks of 1926 made a considerable impact on the West Riding, which was not surprising as Hadow was an 'added' member of the Education Committee and Jackson had also served on the Consultative Committee during the preparation of this report. In 1927 it was announced that in future West Riding elementary schools would be organised thus:[133]

1. Primary education
   (a) infants
   (b) juniors
2. Post-primary education
   (a) senior classes or departments
   (b) middle (central) schools or classes

It was acknowledged that reorganisation in an area as large as the West Riding would take a considerable time, perhaps as long as ten years. It was proposed to deal with the county district by district. Draft schemes for the various districts were prepared by administrators at Wakefield and then local conferences were held with district sub-committees and the managers of any non-provided schools involved.[134] Twenty-two such conferences were held between November 1928 and the end of March 1929, and they were normally attended by a representative of His Majesty's Inspectorate and the Committee's Education Officer or one of his Chief Assistants for Elementary Education.[135]

TABLE 3.2

*Reorganisation of elementary schools, 1930–1* [136]

|  | 31/3/30 | 31/3/31 |
|---|---|---|
| 1. Brought into effect | 4 | 17 |
| 2. Approved by Board of Education | 22 | 29 |
| 3. Approved by district sub-committees but awaiting approval of Education Committee, managers of non-provided schools or Board of Education | 19 | 32 |
| 4. Joint conferences held and approval of district sub-committees awaited | 21 | 16 |
| 5. Joint conferences pending | 35 | 2 |
| 6. In course of preparation or awaiting amendment | 4 | 10 |
| 7. Under consideration by managers of non-provided schools where non-provided schools only involved | 2 | 1 |

The slow progress made before 1929 is clearly shown in Table 3.3. In that year only 1,471 out of a total of 53,145 elementary pupils over eleven were in

TABLE 3.3

*Reorganised schools and their pupils, 1926–31* [137]

|  | March 1926 | | March 1929 | | March 1931 | |
|---|---|---|---|---|---|---|
|  | *Schools* | *Senior pupils* | *Schools* | *Senior pupils* | *Schools* | *Senior pupils* |
| Elementary schools limited to children over eleven | 1 | 370 | 3 | 863 | 28 | 9,056 |
| Elementary schools which in addition to providing specially organised courses of instruction for pupils over eleven also provide the usual elementary course | 4 | 360 | 5 | 608 | 10 | 1,400 |
| Total | 5 | 730 | 8 | 1,471 | 38 | 10,456 |

reorganised senior schools. Between 1929 and 1931 conditions were much more favourable and the planning of earlier years began to bear fruit. Under the minority Labour Government of 1929 the Board of Education issued Circular 1404, which increased the Board's capital grants for elementary schools from 20 per cent to 50 per cent in the period 1 September 1929 to 31 August 1932, as long as the expenditure represented an effective contribution to an approved reorganisation scheme. It was also announced that the Government intended to raise the school leaving age to fifteen in the future. The West Riding made provision for this in its Programme for Educational Development, 1930–3, which was approved by the Board in April 1930.[138] Although national economic fortunes worsened and the school leaving age was not raised, this brief period of relative expansion in education at least enabled the West Riding to provide places in reorganised schools for almost one-fifth of its senior pupils by 1931. Another factor which was important in this development was the agreement reached between the Authority and the Church of England over religious instruction in reorganised schools.

The religious problem was not allowed to dominate West Riding education in the inter-war years as it had done before 1914. Much of the credit for this must be given to the chairman of the Education Committee, Percy Jackson, who took a strong interest in finding a solution to the religious problem, not only at local but also at national level, through his work for the AEC and the CCA.[139]

Soon after being elected chairman, Jackson took the lead and proposed that there should be changes in religious instruction in the West Riding.[140] He wrote, 'I am of the opinion that in the general hope of reapproachment amongst the Churches the time is ripe for a reconsideration of the whole question of religious teaching.'[141] He wanted more time and attention devoted to the study of scripture and suggested that the West Riding Consultative Committee should look at the subject. Eventually it was decided to ask an outside committee of academics, teacher trainers and representatives of various Churches to prepare a new syllabus. This work was completed by the summer of 1922 and the new syllabus was well received both inside and outside the Riding. Indeed, by the end of the 1920s the West Riding Religious Instruction Syllabus was used by several other LEAs in England and had achieved a considerable international reputation.[142]

Once the provision of central schools was considered, it was realised that the question of religious instruction in reorganised schools had to be faced. From the outset it was clear that there could not be separate council, Church of England and Roman Catholic central schools in each area; yet the Churches did not wish to see their former pupils pass on to council central schools and the Council was equally determined that pupils educated in its schools should not be moved to denominational schools after the age of eleven. These matters were discussed in a preliminary way in 1919, and a deputation from the Church Schools Association for the Diocese of Wakefield gave their views on one occasion.[143] Soon afterwards the Bishop of Wakefield suggested that ex-Church school children attending council central schools should receive denominational instruction there.[144] The Committee pointed out that this was contrary to the Cowper-Temple clause and illegal, but proposed that ex-Church school pupils, whose parents desired it, could return to their old schools for about one hour's religious instruction per week.[145] The Board of Education was consulted about such an arrangement and raised no objections.[146] This did not prove of immediate importance, however, as central and middle schools were slow to emerge.

It was not until 1922 that the religious question arose in a form which was almost as acute as it had been in the years immediately after 1902. A proposal to reorganise the elementary schools in the Queensbury district and to create a central school led to problems, as one of the main schools involved belonged to the Church of England. Hinchliffe and Jackson were appointed to negotiate with the managers, and eventually it was agreed to transfer the premises to the County Council on certain conditions,[147] of which the most important were: (1) repairs were to be carried out by the Authority at its own expense, and (2) religious instruction in the Queensbury Church of England School and the Chapel Lane Council School was to be in accordance with the

West Riding syllabus, except that on one morning per week denominational instruction was to be available for children whose parents desired it. There can be little doubt that condition (1) contravened the 1904 Concordat which was still in force, but this particular provision had been ignored on previous occasions.[148] Condition (2), as far as the Church of England School was concerned, was in line with the 1904 Concordat, but there were doubts about whether the Chapel Lane Council School fell into the same category. Chapel Lane School had been transferred to the County Council much earlier and by the 1920s was clearly a provided school. Several Liberal and Labour councillors, led by W. Clough, questioned whether 'right of entry' into a council school should be given to a denominational clergyman. On the other hand, Jackson argued that there were to be transfers of scholars in connection with both schools, and maintained that the proposed compromise was in accordance with the spirit of the Concordat.[149] When the County Council considered this issue in January 1922, Clough mustered sufficient support in a close vote for the matter to be referred back.[150] In April, however, the Queensbury Urban District Council protested about the delay in providing a central school, and this prompted the Education Committee to return the matter to County Council without amendment.[151] The opposition was still led by Clough, who suggested that his fellow Methodist, Liberal Alderman Jackson, 'had "kow-towed" to Mr Fisher, Bishops, the County Councils Association and other "big guns" so much of late that he could not recognise a principle now when he saw one. The right of entry into council schools was not for sale'.[152] This time, however, an equally close vote went against Clough, and reorganisation at Queensbury proceeded. Nonetheless, the Queensbury episode made it amply clear to Jackson that if he took a compromise line on the religious issue, he still could not count on the automatic allegiance of those who normally supported him.

During 1925 and 1926 there were attempts at the national level to find solutions to the problems faced by the voluntary schools. Their buildings were often old and ill-equipped (particularly for older scholars), and at the same time their managers normally could not raise the funds required for modernisation. These problems were highlighted in the 1920s, first by the requirements in the 1918 Act that special provisions should be made for all of the more advanced pupils and, secondly, by the issuing of the Board's first 'black list' of unsatisfactory elementary school premises in 1925. The President of the Board, Lord Eustace Percy, negotiated privately with the Archbishop of Canterbury over these matters,[153] and soon Sir Percy Jackson and Sir Mark Collett, chairman of Kent Education Committee, were brought in as spokesmen for the local authorities. Eventually they agreed that it would be best if individual local authorities tried to find solutions in their own areas, with the possibility that legislation would follow later.[154]

Jackson took up this matter in the West Riding and hoped to make progress by revising the Concordat of 1904. In May 1925 it was shown that 107 transfers of schools from voluntary bodies to the County Council had taken place since 1904, and that seventy-one of these schools were still in existence.[155] On the other hand, it was pointed out that the original terms of the 1904 Concordat had been ignored in practice in the vast majority of transfers.[156] The right to give denominational instruction in a transferred school was exercised in only one case, and the original financial clauses had been applied in only a handful of instances. In 1904 the Committee had insisted that the trustees should put the premises into good repair before they were transferred. One of the main reasons why trustees wanted to transfer their schools, however, was that they could not afford necessary repairs, and in practice this condition was normally waived as long as the trustees agreed to forgo their right to rent. In 1925 Jackson proposed that the 1904 Concordat should be amended and the *de facto* practice of the Authority regularised. Jackson expected this regularisation to induce voluntary bodies to offer relatively large numbers of schools for transfer.[157] He stressed that the Churches did not even have the funds to put right the premises actually singled out for criticism by the Board.[158] He quoted the Archbishop of York as saying that 'it was the best offer they had had, and if schools had to be transferred he recommended Church authorities to accept it'.[159] Jackson assured his non-conformist friends that the Archbishops of York and Canterbury had told him that they were concerned not so much with dogmatic teaching in the schools as that Christian teaching should be given in them.[160] The militant non-conformists rejected Jackson's pleas for good will, and several Labour members, for various reasons, also voted against the changes in County Council.[161] Nonetheless, the amended Concordat was ratified by a majority of nine votes. The effects of the 1926 Concordat must have been disappointing to Jackson, for there was certainly no rush on the part of the voluntary bodies to transfer schools. The Roman Catholics were consistently opposed to transfers and the Church of England remained uninterested. The 1926 Concordat was ineffective; to come to grips with the problem of the comprehensive reorganisation of elementary education in the West Riding, Jackson had to open negotiations with the Church of England to try to find an agreement which would have much wider application than this innocuous but largely redundant Concordat.

By the beginning of 1929 many draft schemes of reorganisation were ready for submission to the Board of Education, but the Authority was reluctant to send them up before the managers of the non-provided schools involved had given their approval. Jackson commented that the Authority 'could not move an inch towards [reorganisation] until they had arrived at an agreement with the religious bodies'.[162] Church of England school managers were normally guided in such matters by the advice of their Diocesan Educational Associations, and in late 1928 and early 1929 Jackson and Brigg took part, on behalf of the Authority, in preliminary discussions with representatives from these Associations.[163] By June 1929 it was agreed in principle that there should be co-operation between the two sides and that this should take the form of a new Concordat. In essence the new Concordat was to incorporate the whole of the 1926 Concordat, with important additional clauses concerning religious instruction in reorganised schools.

With regard to all non-provided schools, which under reorganisation had to be attended by children who previously went to council schools, agreement was reached fairly easily. The West Riding Syllabus of Religious Instruction was to be taught throughout the schools, and the parents of all children admitted had to state on the admission forms whether on the two days per week when denominational teaching was given they wanted their children to receive that instruction or teaching under the West Riding Syllabus. This represented a concession on the part of the Church authorities.

With regard to reorganised council schools to which both council and non-provided primary schools were to send pupils, the negotiations proved more difficult. Both sides agreed that the West Riding Syllabus should be used in the schools and that on two days per week denominational instruction could be provided for children whose parents desired it. The Diocesan Associations agreed with the Authority that this denominational instruction should not normally take place on school premises, but suggested that when there were no other suitable buildings nearby it should be allowed to do so.[164] It was said that the Board had allowed such arrangements in Dorset.[165] The Board, however, was adamant that the Dorset circumstances were exceptional and completely ruled out this possibility in the West Riding.[166] The Education Officer also advised the Committee to refuse the Associations' request that headteachers should accept responsibility for the discipline of the children attending denominational classes away from the school premises.[167] The Diocesan Associations were informed that they could not be accommodated on either of these points.

The Inter-diocesan Committee[168] reconsidered these matters and probably realised that these points were ones which could not be conceded by the Authority, particularly in view of the Board's rejection of the Dorset precedent. In March 1930 the chairman of the Inter-diocesan Committee eventually informed the Authority that the terms of the proposed Concordat could be accepted by the Church. It is interesting that opposition on the Council to this new Concordat was very limited, for only Clough voted against it in the Education Committee and it passed through full Council unopposed. The much less important 1926 Concordat aroused considerable hostility but by 1930 public opinion inside and outside Yorkshire now favoured conciliation, so that reorganisation could proceed.[169] This certainly helped in the West Riding, for by the end of 1932, despite severe economic difficulties, the Authority had implemented twenty-four area reorganisation schemes. Four schemes involved only council schools, one scheme only Church schools and in two schemes the voluntary school managers still refused to participate; in the remaining seventeen cases, however, there was full co-operation on the lines of the 1930 Concordat. Children from forty Church of England schools had been transferred to council schools, and in four instances ex-council school children attended Church of England schools. According to the Education Officer, the 1930 Concordat was 'invaluable' in the reorganisation of West Riding elementary education.[170]

Progress with reorganisation was temporarily retarded by the financial crisis of 1931. In September the Board issued Circular 1413, which withdrew the special 50 per cent capital grants for new developments in connection with reorganisation. It was also intimated that capital expenditure was to be limited to: (1) the provision of accommodation necessitated by local increases in population, (2) urgent repairs, and (3) treatment of the worst schools on the Board's 'black list'. Some projects had to be abandoned, and all reorganisation schemes approved but not in operation had to be reviewed. It did not prove easy to modify schemes so that they could be accommodated in existing buildings, and in at least three areas further delay was caused by the raising of the religious question.[171]

During the crisis years, 1931–3, the Authority experimented with cheaper forms of school construction. Building with timber rather than brick was preferred for a short period, but by 1934 the difference in cost between brick and timber had so diminished that the county reverted to brick construction.[172] It was also about this time that demographic factors began to relieve the situation.

Children born in 1919 and 1920, years with high birth rates, were leaving school and being replaced by smaller numbers. This eased pressure on accommodation in some parts of the Riding, and the Committee even began to consider the question of raising the school leaving age to fifteen.[173] Such a change was favoured by the Liberals and by the Socialists, who had fared well in the 1934 local elections. It was argued that raising the school leaving age would alleviate juvenile unemployment. Hallam pointed out that it would be easier to find extra school accommodation in the north of the Riding than the south, where unemployment was more acute.[174] The Authority proceeded to organise a conference of all LEAs in the area to discuss this issue, and the proposal of a longer period of schooling was widely supported. The President of the Board of Education, however, soon made it clear that he did not favour raising the school leaving age at this juncture,[175] and the issue was then dropped at the local level.

Jackson, meanwhile, urged the Government to relax the restrictions imposed on capital developments in 1931.[176] He maintained that this was essential if education were to advance in the spirit of Hadow. During July 1935 the restrictions were finally removed[177] and 50 per cent central government grants for capital developments reintroduced.[178] As the Board prepared to implement the 1936 Act, the LEAs enjoyed a period of relative expansion for their service. In the West Riding reorganisation on Hadow lines gained pace again. Table 3.4 shows the progress made in the 1930s. In 1937 there

TABLE 3.4

*Proportion of children over eleven in reorganised schools and classes in the West Riding*[181]

| | % |
|------|-----|
| 1931 | 20 |
| 1932 | 20 |
| 1933 | 24 |
| 1934 | 28 |
| 1935 | 33 |
| 1936 | 39 |
| 1937 | 45 |
| 1938 | 49 |

was some criticism in County Council that plans for new senior schools involved buildings which were too lavish and that the building programme itself was too rushed.[179] These charges were denied by Alderman W. H. Hyman, the first Labour chairman of the Committee, who succeeded Jackson in January 1937. Hyman retorted to his critics, 'In the West Riding you have dozens of schools which are practically slum schools.'[180] The opposition to the building programme was easily outvoted.

It is not easy to make fair comparisons between LEAs with regard to progress with reorganisation. By 1938 55 per cent of the children over eleven in England and Wales were educated in senior schools or divisions.[182] This was a larger proportion than that achieved by the West Riding, but it must be stressed that progress in rural areas in the country as a whole was much less pronounced than in urban areas and that the West Riding administrative county (excluding county boroughs and Part III authorities) contained large rural areas. It is interesting to compare the West Riding's performance with neighbouring LEAs, as long as it is recognised that the problems encountered varied considerably from one authority to another.

TABLE 3.5

*Proportion of children over eleven in senior schools and divisions, March 1938*[183]

|  | % |
| --- | --- |
| England and Wales | 55 |
| West Riding County Council | 53 |
| West Riding Part III authorities | 71 |
| Lancashire County Council | 37 |
| East Riding County Council | 23 |
| North Riding County Council | 46 |
| Leeds County Borough | 29 |
| Sheffield County Borough | 43 |
| Halifax County Borough | 58 |
| Doncaster County Borough | 79 |
| Wakefield County Borough | 83 |

In 1939 the Committee decided that senior schools in the West Riding should be known as modern schools. Hyman and Brigg felt that this change would raise the prestige of the schools, and Hyman maintained that modern schools 'should approximate as near as they could make them to existing secondary and grammar schools'.[184] The concept of elementary education had developed a long way since the Authority had reluctantly taken over responsibility for it in 1904.

Although much had changed in elementary education, the religious question still persisted in the West Riding. The proportions of children on the registers of provided and non-provided schools in the West Riding changed significantly during this period. This trend is illustrated in Table 3.6.

The increase in the proportion of pupils in provided schools was greater in the West Riding than in England and Wales as a whole. In 1906 53 per cent of the elementary school children in England and Wales were on the registers of council schools and 47 per cent on the registers of voluntary schools,

TABLE 3.6

*Average number of pupils on registers in the West Riding*

|  | Provided schools | | Non-provided schools | |
| Date | Number | % of total | Number | % of total |
| --- | --- | --- | --- | --- |
| 1906 | 101,238 | 51 | 97,657 | 49 |
| 1909 | 119,661 | 59 | 84,155 | 41 |
| 1914 | 136,692 | 67 | 68,629 | 33 |
| 1919 | not available | | not available | |
| 1924 | 132,616 | 70 | 57,966 | 30 |
| 1929 | 144,567 | 73 | 54,041 | 27 |
| 1934 | 147,957 | 75 | 50,429 | 25 |
| 1939 | 120,518 | 76 | 38,345 | 24 |

but by 1938 the proportions were 70 per cent and 30 per cent respectively.

The 1936 Act gave permissive powers to local authorities to make grants (between 50 per cent and 75 per cent) towards the building or extension of non-provided schools for senior children over eleven years of age. The Authority, led by Hyman, negotiated with the Anglicans and Roman Catholics about this, and eventually it was agreed in principle that such grants could be paid. There was predictable opposition to this from Clough,[185] but in July 1937 the County Council agreed without a division, as Clough had died the previous May. When more specific proposals were put before the Authority in 1938, however, trouble arose. In June the Education Committee agreed to pay 75 per cent capital grants towards the provision or enlargement of four Roman Catholic and five Church of England senior schools. In presenting this to Committee Hyman praised the Roman Catholics for their generosity of spirit and fairness in negotiations and concluded that 'they had shown an anxiety to see that every Roman Catholic child could benefit by reorganisation and obtain the same type of education as other children in the Riding'.[186] Hyman described this as 'the most far-reaching and happiest piece of work they had accomplished in their programme of reorganisation'.[187] Hyman's joy was short-lived, however, for less than a month later the County Council rejected these proposals by thirty-nine votes to thirty-five. This division split both the Labour and Liberal groups on the County Council. Alderman A. Flavell (Labour) and Alderman W. J. Johns (Liberal) led the opposition, maintaining that preferential treatment was to be given to one section of the population.[188] Flavell harked back to 1902, claiming, 'Rome is calling the tune, but the West Riding ratepayers are called upon to pay the bill.' Hyman's final appeal to members was 'to end the religious controversy once and for all, and to have pride in the fact that having

TABLE 3.7

*Teaching staff of West Riding elementary schools, 1903–39*

|  | Head teachers | Cert. asst. | Cert. supply | Uncert. asst. | Supplement. teachers | Provis. asst. | Total |
|---|---|---|---|---|---|---|---|
| Appointed day | 1265 | 704 | – | 1925 | 665 | 35 | 4594 |
| 31-3-05 | 1265 | 832 | – | 1658 | 676 | – | 4431 |
| 31-3-06 | 1262 | 939 | 6 | 1795 | 875 | 63 | 4940 |
| 31-3-07 | 1274 | 1149 | 13 | 1630 | 911 | 48 | 5025 |
| 31-3-08 | 1278 | 1199 | 18 | 1919 | 885 | 95 | 5394 |
| 31-3-09 | 1283 | 1469 | 19 | 1933 | 788 | – | 5492 |
| 31-3-10 | 1284 | 1480 | 19 | 2130 | 708 | – | 5621 |
| 31-3-11 | 1264 | 1654 | 20 | 2108 | 601 | – | 5647 |
| 31-3-12 | 1276 | 1759 | 29 | 2094 | 568 | – | 5726 |
| 31-3-13 | 1284* | 1914 | 32 | 1947 | 532 | – | 5709 |
| 31-3-14 | 1297 | 2074 | 36 | 1814 | 531 | – | 5752 |
| 31-3-15 | 1292 | 2146 | 32 | 1693 | 517 | – | 5680 |
| 31-3-16 | 1255 | 2169 | 32 | 1509 | 503 | – | 5468 |
| 31-3-17 |  |  | not available |  |  |  |  |
| 31-3-18 | 1249 | 2201 | 46 | 1495 | 505 | – | 5496 |
| 31-3-19 | 1253 | 2200 | 51 | 1451 | 518 | – | 5473 |
| 31-3-20 | 1248 | 2163 | 50 | 1417 | 510 | – | 5388 |
| 31-3-21 | 1261 | 2197 | 50 | 1424 | 485 | – | 5417 |
| 31-3-22 | 1332 | 2111 | 50 | 1386 | 458 | – | 5337 |
| 31-3-23 | 1224 | 2057 | 40 | 1307 | 408 | – | 5036 |
| 31-3-24 | 1215 | 2180 | 35 | 1323 | 393 | – | 5146 |
| 31-3-25 | 1212 | 2249 | 40 | 1363 | 345 | – | 5209 |
| 31-3-26 | 1210 | 2360 | 46 | 1406 | 290 | – | 5312 |
| 31-3-27 | 1213 | 2460 | 51 | 1432 | 267 | – | 5423 |
| 31-3-28 | 1209 | 2528 | 51 | 1417 | 245 | – | 5450 |
| 31-3-29 | 1209 | 2583 | 50 | 1396 | 222 | – | 5460 |
| 31-3-30 | 1216 | 2639 | 51 | 1374 | 210 | – | 5490 |
| 31-3-31 | 1216 | 2678 | 51 | 1360 | 195 | – | 5500 |
| 31-3-32 | 1213 | 2705 | 47 | 1331 | 182 | – | 5478 |
| 31-3-33 | 1201 | 2731 | 51 | 1298 | 165 | – | 5446 |
| 31-3-34 | 1184 | 2798 | 51 | 1260 | 154 | – | 5447 |
| 31-3-35 | 1173 | 2837 | 49 | 1216 | 146 | – | 5421 |
| 31-3-36 | 1163 | 2877 | 48 | 1180 | 140 | – | 5408 |
| 31-3-37 | 1155 | 2898 | 53 | 1137 | 134 | – | 5377 |
| 31-3-38 | 1092 | 2855 | 58 | 1018 | 112 | – | 5135† |
| 31-3-39 | 1064 | 2831 | 56 | 948 | 105 | – | 5004† |

*In order to compare the position existing on this date with that on the Appointed Day, the following particulars of transfers to other education authorities should be taken into account.

| Education authority | Teachers transferred | | | | Date of transfer |
|---|---|---|---|---|---|
|  | HT | CA | UA | ST |  |
| Wakefield | 5 | 19 | 9 | 3 | 9 November 1909 |
| Dewsbury and Batley | 27 | 27 | 52 | 11 | 1 April 1910 |
| Sheffield | 3 | 11 | 6 | 1 | 1 April 1912 |
| Halifax | 2 | 4 | 8 | – | 9 November |
| Leeds | 6 | 1 | 13 | 3 | 9 November 1912 |

† Decrease mainly attributable to review of county districts.

once approved this, the rest of England will follow us',[189] but all was to no avail. Subsequently, the Council agreed to pay grants towards the enlargement of two Church of England senior schools,[190] but no progress was made with the other outstanding cases before the outbreak of war. Although the religious question did not dominate the educational affairs of the West Riding in the 1930s as it had done in earlier years, it was not until the post-war era, with its new legislative framework, that religious differences were reduced to a minor role in the educational politics of the West Riding Education Authority.

# CHAPTER IV

# *Higher Education 1890–1939*

### I    SECONDARY SCHOOLS

The West Riding Technical Instruction Committee took up the question of providing aid for secondary schools as early as 1891.[1] This aid was given directly by means of payments to schools and indirectly through county minor scholarships which enabled larger numbers of children to receive secondary education. By 1901–2 fifty-one schools (thirty-seven in the administrative county) were receiving direct grants from the Authority[2] and a slightly larger number were recognised as eligible to educate scholarship holders. The number of county minor scholarships awarded by the Technical Instruction Committee in selected years is shown in Table 4.1.

TABLE 4.1
*County minor scholarships*

| Year | Number |
|------|--------|
| 1891–2 | 186 |
| 1896–7 | 402 |
| 1901–2 | 398 |

These scholarships covered the costs of fees, books and travel. Travel grants were a particularly important element in rural parts of the county but, despite these allowances, county minors were less keenly taken up in districts such as Settle, Ripon, Skipton, Wetherby, Selby and Penistone than in more urban areas.[3] Maintenance grants were not paid on initial awards in the early years, but were given in certain circumstances when scholarships were renewed. From the Technical Instruction Committee's accounts it is not possible to calculate precisely how much money was devoted to secondary education, but it is estimated that in the early years of this century between

77

£6,500 and £7,500 per annum (roughly one-sixth of total expenditure) was allocated to it.

For the first time the public sector of education began to regard the grammar schools as part of its sphere of influence. Secondary schools were inspected by the Authority before they qualified for grants or scholarships, and on occasions special conditions were imposed before aid was given. The Authority was represented on the governing bodies of all aided secondary schools and exercised some measure of control over the level of fees and the curriculum. It was felt that in certain schools too much prominence was given to scientific and technical subjects; at the turn of the century this part of the secondary school curriculum could qualify for central government grants, whilst other important subjects remained relatively neglected.[4] The Technical Instruction Committee organised its own scheme of aid in a way which was specifically designed to avoid this tendency. Between 1893 and 1902 the West Riding campaigned nationally for county councils to be recognised as the local education authorities for secondary schooling, and in 1902 it appointed a full-time local inspector of secondary schools.[5] During the preparation for the Education Bill (1902) the West Riding impressed upon the Government that the organisation and supply of secondary education was 'the most important educational problem before the country at the present time',[6] and continued to urge that legislation should be passed to give the County Council full control over the development of post-elementary education.

During 1901 the Technical Instruction Committee obtained the services of A. H. D. Acland, who was widely regarded in Liberal educational circles as an expert on secondary schools. He had experience of setting up such schools in Wales under the Intermediate Education Act and felt strongly that priority should be given to this sector of English education. In 1892, in collaboration with a close colleague, he wrote:

> We do not assent to the vulgar view that the liberal education of the middle class is a matter outside the purview of the state. But, undoubtedly, the most urgent need of our time is to provide facilities for the secondary education of workmen's children, and, in the interests of all classes, it is highly desirable that this education should be given as far as possible in the same schools as those attended by the middle class.[7]

Acland, who was related by marriage to Milnes-Gaskell, chairman of the County Council, joined the Committee as an 'added' member at a time when it was under some pressure from secondary schools to increase their grants. From the outset Acland took a strong interest in the activities of the

Committee and was soon appointed to a two-member sub-committee which was to survey and report on the provisions for secondary education throughout the West Riding.[8] For more than two years Acland played a central role in this investigation, but before the findings were published a new and discordant dimension was added to the secondary education question.

The denominational issue affected secondary schools for the first time. In 1903 a new and increased scale of grants was introduced, but the militant non-conformists rejected the advice of successive Liberal chairmen of the Committee, Arthur Anderton and Henry Dunn, and insisted that schools which imposed religious tests on teachers, or which imparted denominational religious instruction, should remain on the old and less generous scale. This action predicatably aroused considerable anger amongst the Moderates on the Council, the Anglican and Roman Catholic communities and in the local Press. Although only a relatively small group of secondary schools was involved, led by the governors of the Dewsbury Endowed Schools Foundation they soon formed a pressure group to fight this policy.[9] Eventually the Board of Education informed the Authority that the policy seemed 'to be a violation of the Education Act 1902',[10] but the Committee stood its ground and held that the Board had no right to interfere. It is interesting to note, moreover, that when the Liberals were returned to power at Westminster, the central government copied the West Riding's practice and operated differential rates of grant along these lines for a short period.[11] In the West Riding several of the schools affected (for example, the Dewsbury Wheelwright schools) took steps to have their schemes amended to enable them to qualify for the higher grants.[12] Eventually in 1911, when the scales were further revised, much of the heat had gone out of this issue and differentiation was quietly dropped.

In February 1904 the Acland report on West Riding secondary education was published.[13] It was a long and meticulous survey, and showed that in 1901-2 3,100 pupils were attending secondary schools in the administrative county and a further 1,200 in the neighbouring county boroughs. Approximately 68 per cent of these pupils had received their previous education in public elementary schools[14] and about 26 per cent held scholarships of some sort.[15] An attempt was made to compare the proportion of the population receiving secondary education in the West Riding with the proportions in other parts of the country and even in several foreign states. The West Riding finished near the middle of the resulting league table, but it would be unwise to try to draw firm conclusions from such an exercise. The survey did show clearly, however, that attendance proportionate to population did vary greatly within the area and was lowest, to a marked degree, in the southern part of the county. Deficiencies in the supply of secondary schools for girls were also clearly illustrated. Of the 4,300 pupils in attendance only 1,500 were girls[16] and there were no provisions for girls south of Wakefield. The Technical Instruction Committee had identified this particular problem as early as 1892[17] but was unable to improve the situation because it had only very limited powers to aid the building of secondary schools.

In his report Acland recommended that secondary school accommodation for at least 2,500 pupils should be built.[18] He suggested that the majority of this should be for girls and proposed that ten new girls' secondary schools should be constructed in appropriate locations. He aimed at raising total attendance to 8,000, including 1,000 places for pupils (mainly girls) preparing for careers as elementary school teachers.[19] During the early years of this century both the Board of Education and the LEAs tried to ensure that as many students as possible who were training for teaching received some of their education in secondary schools. Consequently, the growth in secondary school provision became inextricably bound up with the expansion of teacher training; for example, in the West Riding some of the first secondary schools set up by the Authority were known for a few years as 'Secondary (Pupil-Teacher) Schools'. Acland advocated a policy of increasing considerably the number of county minor scholarships and of introducing awards for intending pupil-teachers, bursars and student and pupil-teachers, (see Chapter V) which were all to be tenable at least in part in secondary schools. Thus in order to attract and educate an adequate supply of elementary school teachers it was necessary to develop and expand a local system of secondary schooling. From the outset Acland realised that this would be a costly business and suggested that central government grants for this purpose would have to be considerably augmented.[20] Between 1904 and 1914 the West Riding sent so many memorials to the Board of Education and representatives attended so many meetings there, urging successive Conservative and Liberal governments to increase the central government support for secondary education and teacher training, that it would be tedious to list them all. These consistent efforts, however, produced few, if any, results, and Acland's initial and perhaps unjustified optimism regarding this issue was eventually dashed.

Under Acland's leadership the Higher Education Sub-Committee quickly launched its expansion programme. In 1903–4 recurrent grants to secondary schools were considerably augmented and building grants, normally at a rate of 33⅓ per cent, were introduced. Between 1903 and 1905 the number of county minor scholarships held increased from 373 to 764 and over 600 intending pupil-teacherships were created. These latter awards were soon phased out, but minor scholarships were consequently even further increased and the number held.in 1912–13 topped 1,500. After the publication of the Acland report, conferences were held with representatives from local areas to discuss the requirements for secondary schooling in their respective districts. Between June and October 1904 no less than twenty-seven of these conferences took place. Acland normally took the chair at these meetings and, as he was often one of the best informed persons present, he frequently took the lead in the discussion and usually put forward specific proposals. These conferences were designed to ascertain the wishes of the local people, but the Authority was not reluctant to take the initiative and stated that these occasions provided opportunities 'to afford information and guidance . . . and, where necessary, to arouse local interest in the subject generally'.[21] By the time that Acland resigned his position as an alderman in the autumn of 1907 to become the chairman of the Consultative Committee of the Board of Education, much had been achieved. The number of secondary schools in the administrative county had risen from thirty to fifty and the total number of pupils receiving secondary education had increased from 4,300 to about 8,000. There had been a particularly large increase in the provision for girls; in 1903–4 there had been twice as many boys as girls in attendance, but by 1907–8 the figures were roughly equal. Acland's contribution to these developments was of primary importance but the scheme was not implemented without opposition, which commenced during Acland's period of office and lasted for several years after his departure from Yorkshire.

One of the first problems which generated controversy concerned payments for West Riding pupils who attended secondary schools in the county boroughs. At first the county offered to pay full fees for scholarship holders but refused to make capitation grants for fee payers.[22] This did not satisfy the county boroughs, particularly Leeds and Bradford, and payments were demanded for all pupils from the county. If such payments were not agreed, the county boroughs threatened to close the doors of their schools to West Riding children after 31 July 1906. The West Riding, led by Acland, immediately countered this ultimatum by offering to pay grants on pupils who attended in the county boroughs because no county schools were accessible for them but was adamant that it would not pay on children who came from areas where West Riding schools were available. Acland maintained that 'it would be a suicidal policy to send children past the doors of our own schools'.[23] A few days later the county boroughs accepted this principle and the crisis was averted.[24]

At about the same time there was opposition to the Authority's policy of establishing new schools in certain districts. In December 1905 the Headmasters' Association approached the Board of Education unofficially about the situation in the Halifax area and complained that the proposed West Riding schools there would be detrimental to Heath Grammar School.[25] Soon afterwards Halifax made an official complaint to the Board about alleged competition with the borough's secondary schools, contrary to Section 2(2) of the 1902 Act.[26] The Board convened a conference, chaired by the Chief Inspector for Secondary Education, to consider this matter. There was a full attendance of local representatives and both sides of the case were argued very forcefully. Eventually the Board found largely in the West Riding's favour. However, the West Riding District Councils' Association, which often served as a focal point for opposition to the Authority's schemes in this period, persistently maintained that this problem was not unique to the Halifax area and cited examples from several other districts.[27] It was also often asserted that the small West Riding schools were inferior to those in the county boroughs, and that the multiplication of small schools was both educationally unsound and uneconomic.[28] On one occasion it was alleged that the West Riding schools did not employ specialist teachers. This was categorically denied by the Authority. On the other hand, Acland acknowledged that the smallest schools in the most rural areas had as few as eighty pupils, but stressed that the vast majority of new schools had between 150 and 400.[29]

It was also argued by opponents that the middle classes, who could well afford the full costs of their children's secondary education, benefited most from the Authority's scheme. This point was made both inside and outside the Council Chamber and emanated from both the right and the left.[30] It was made most commonly in connection with the preparatory departments operated by secondary schools.[31] In reply Acland contended that something needed to be done for the middle class as well as for the working class, but he denied extravagance.[32] Arguing on rather different lines, some commentators claimed that the new secondary schools depended too heavily on the rates and took 'a mere handful of fee-paying pupils'.[33] The Authority replied to this by producing statistics which showed that in 1907 43 per cent of the pupils in the new schools were fee payers and 57 per cent scholarship holders.[34]

Spokesmen for the rural areas of the county[35] often stressed that their districts were not interested in secondary schools and consequently did not receive commensurate benefits for the rates they paid.[36] In 1907 Alderman J. C. Horsfall, chairman of the Finance Committee, conceded that there was some substance in the rural interests' grievance,[37] although a special sub-committee on secondary education in rural districts had been set up as early as 1905. In March 1908 a petition was received from the Knaresborough district asking that the old grammar school there should be reconstituted as an experimental secondary school with a rural bias to its curriculum.[38] Eventually the Authority agreed to this and the new school opened in October 1908. Although the experiment cannot be described as an unqualified success, it was well regarded by the Board of Education. Some years later the Knaresborough Rural Secondary School received national recognition when the Board published an official pamphlet about its work.[39]

At the root of much of the opposition to the West Riding scheme was the question of cost. The District Councils' Association, which represented the vast majority of minor local authorities in the area, normally led the attack on this front, and in 1907 and 1911 it opposed the Authority's applications to the Local Government Board to increase its rating powers for higher education. On both occasions the Association stressed that it was not critical of expenditure on technical education but attacked the cost of the Authority's secondary scheme. In addition to highlighting minor 'extravagances', the Association maintained that (1) the Authority's building programme had resulted in an expensive over-provision of secondary schools in West Yorkshire, and (2) the Authority insisted, in a paternalistic way, on providing a standard of service which was in advance of the needs and desires of the vast majority of the rate payers. Nonetheless, the Local Government Board eventually allowed increases in rating powers on both occasions.

The West Riding blamed the financial plight of the Authority firmly on central government. It consistently argued that Board of Education grants for secondary schools should be increased and maintained that the costs of teacher training should be transferred entirely to the elementary education account. It insisted that it applied for increased rating powers most reluctantly and, in 1911, only after it had made stringent economies. Like other authorities, the West Riding was having to manage with shrinking 'whisky money' grants[40] (until they were stabilised in 1911)[41] during a period of inflation. In 1901 the West Riding met 92 per cent of its expenditure on higher education from central government grants and only 8 per cent from the rates, but by 1906 the proportions had changed dramatically to 47 per cent from grants and 53 per cent from rates.[42] Over the next few years the proportion paid from rates increased a little more,[43] and it is clear that, despite the efforts of all parties in the West Riding to put pressure on successive governments, the higher education services which expanded so rapidly after the passing of the 1902 Act were paid for, to a completely unprecedented degree, out of the rates.

Despite financial difficulties much was achieved in the period before the First World War. By 1914 the West Riding was educating a slightly larger proportion of the population in secondary schools than the national average.[44] The proportions of fee payers and scholarship holders are shown in Table 4.2.

In 1913 Percy Jackson, the vice-chairman of the Committee commented that Liberals believed the mixing of scholarship holders and fee-paying pupils 'to be of the greatest good for the future of the country. The scholarship holders are the pick of the boys and girls in our elementary schools, and they quicken the pace in the secondary school. It also seems of the highest importance that the children of all classes should in this way mix on terms of equality during their schooldays.'[45]

TABLE 4.2

*Pupils in secondary schools, 1907–14*

| Date | West Riding | | England and Wales | |
| | % fee payers | % scholarship holders | % fee payers | % free |
| --- | --- | --- | --- | --- |
| 1907–8 | 50 | 50 | n.a. | n.a. |
| 1908–9 | 52 | 48 | 67* | 33* |
| 1909–10 | 50 | 50 | 66* | 34* |
| 1910–11 | 52 | 48 | 65* | 35* |
| 1911–12 | 54 | 46 | 64 | 36 |
| 1912–13 | 55 | 45 | 64 | 36 |
| 1913–14 | 55 | 45 | 64 | 36 |

* Excludes Wales.
West Riding 'scholarship holders' is a slightly broader category than Board of Education 'free places'. Strictly comparable statistics are not available.

It must be stressed that the Authority owed a great deal to the pioneering work of Acland in this period. Although he lived outside the administrative county (at Scarborough) throughout his six years on the Committee and he never served as an elected member, he was given a relatively free hand to put his ideas on secondary education into practice.

Largely as a result of an increase in real incomes, the period of the First World War and its immediate aftermath witnessed a considerable growth in the numbers of secondary school pupils. Between 1913–14 and 1919–20 these grew by 64 per cent in England and Wales generally[46] and by 66 per cent in the West Riding.[47] Many of these new pupils were fee payers, for in the West Riding this category of scholars increased from 55 per cent to 61 per cent of the total during these years. The Committee, however, was determined that the number of scholarship holders should also grow. In 1919 it introduced senior continuation scholarships for the 16–18 age range, and announced that it would no longer restrict county minors to a fixed number but would make awards to all entrants who passed the qualifying examination.[48] This resulted in a rapid increase in new awards from 385 in 1917–18 to 799 in 1919–20 and to 1,158 in 1921–2.[49] More generous maintenance allowances for poorer pupils were also offered from 1919.

One of the more important factors which enabled the West Riding to take these measures was the passing of the Education Act of 1918. This removed the limitation on rating for higher education which the Riding had consistently opposed since 1902. From 1918 central government also undertook to meet 50 per cent of the cost of approved expenditure on higher education. In the light of these reforms the county felt able in 1920 to abolish its system of 'special' rating for secondary schools. Before 1920 any deficit accumulated by a school was covered by the levy of an additional 'special' rate upon the districts served by the school. After consulting the schools,[50] it was decided that both the capital and recurrent costs of secondary schools would be met from the general county rates as long as expenditure was kept within the limits of approved estimates.

The expansion in numbers strained the accommodation of some schools between 1918 and 1921.[51] This led the Committee to consider whether it should continue to allow the admission of pupils under ten to secondary schools. The issue of preparatory departments always generated political controversy, perhaps out of proportion to their importance. When the Authority had been searching for economies in 1910–11 it had been suggested that grants should no longer be paid in respect of children under ten but, after much disagreement, this proposal was not implemented.[52] By 1921, however, capitation grants had been abolished and the calculation of the cost of educating children under ten, as distinct from those over ten, became more difficult.[53] Cost, moreover, was only one aspect of the question, for it was pointed out that in crowded schools the admission of under-tens could keep out properly qualified pupils who were over ten. The Authority denied that this had happened, but predicted that unless appropriate action was taken, it could occur from September 1921.[54] The Labour and more radical Liberal members favoured the complete abolition of preparatory departments, whereas the more conservative, while acknowledging that preference should be given to older pupils where there were shortages of places, thought that they served useful functions. These two groups were evenly balanced on the Education Committee, a circumstance which led to forceful exchanges and close voting,[55] and the matter even went to a division in full County Council.[56] Jackson, who tended to favour the more radical line, was insistent that admissions of under-tens should be checked in both aided and maintained schools.[57] Eventually it was agreed that in schools with insufficient accommodation preference for places should be given to the over-tens.[58] This ruling prevented the admission of under-tens to nine schools during 1921–2,[59] and the proportion of under-tens in the schools fell from 10 per cent in 1920–1 to 4 per cent in 1927–8.[60] For most of the 1920s and 1930s the Committee adopted a neutral attitude to the relatively rare attempts to form new preparatory departments, although it was always stressed that no additional cost must fall on the Authority. Perhaps the most interesting example concerned Selby Girls' High, a maintained school, in 1933. The governors' plans were approved by the Committee, but the Board of Education refused to sanction the development, pointing out that it was now general practice to veto the creation of new preparatory departments.[61] Later (in 1939) after a dispute in Committee the Authority also decided, as a general principle, to oppose the setting up of further preparatory departments.[62]

In the early 1920s there was only one other issue in the secondary field which generated as much controversy as the admission of under-tens. This was the question of fees. In 1912 a minimum fee of six guineas (£6.30) per annum was fixed for all West Riding secondary schools.[63] When this matter was reviewed in 1921, it was decided, despite inflation, to make no alteration.[64] Soon afterwards, however, the County Council, as part of its 'Geddes economies' reduced the higher education estimates for 1922–3 by £25,000. At the next Education Committee meeting Jackson suggested that £18,000 of this could be saved if the fees for secondary schools were increased to nine guineas (£9.45). This proposal was criticised by several members, but eventually the reduced estimates were agreed.[65] To justify the increase the Authority pointed out that between 1913–14 and 1922–3 the average maintenance costs of secondary schools had grown by 74 per cent[66] and that many other LEAs had increased fees by between 50 and 100 per cent since 1914. It was also stressed that the generous provision of scholarships in the West Riding would prevent cases of hardship. Nevertheless, when this increase was considered by the County Council, the Labour group led determined opposition. T. H. Foulstone (Labour) complained that it was unreasonable to increase fees when wages were falling, and added that it would lead to serious problems in south Yorkshire.[67] On the other side, Miss H. Unwin maintained that the exigencies of the time made some such action absolutely necessary.[68] In a division the opposition was defeated by the close margin of five votes.[69] Although most of the schools accepted the increase, there were strong protests from several governing bodies,[70] and it was only after considerable pressure had been applied that the governors of Mexborough Secondary School agreed to implement the rise.[71] Between 1922 and 1924 there was a slight fall in the total number of secondary school pupils which must be attributed mainly to the increase in fees. In this period there were an additional 758 scholarship holders, but this was more than offset by a decrease of 920 in the number of fee payers.[72] The numbers of fee payers continued to diminish, although at a lower rate than for the years 1922 to 1924, for the remainder of the 1920s. Attempts by the governors of several schools to persuade the Committee to reduce fees, however, proved of no avail.

According to Jackson, after the 'Geddes axe' the Board of Education discouraged the Committee from awarding more scholarships, but this advice was disregarded.[73] The Board, however, influenced one important decision in this field. In September 1921 the Higher Education Sub-Committee agreed that children who were not from public elementary schools should become eligible to compete for county minor scholarships,[74] but the sub-committee did not agree that when such awards were made the parents should be subjected to a means test.[75] When this came to the Board's notice, it insisted on the application of a means test on grounds of economy.[76] The chairman of the sub-committee attacked this 'interference' and maintained that annoyance had been caused by the fact that 'the Committee's great scholarship scheme' had been 'checked somewhat'.[77] In 1924 the Board was approached again about this decision and it agreed to amend its policy. The Authority immediately abolished the means test.[78]

There can be little doubt that the development of the county minor scholarship scheme was given a high priority throughout the 1920s. Jackson was particularly proud of achievements in this field and told the Royal Commission on Local Government: 'We have the finest scholarship scheme in England.'[79] In 1919 the Committee had agreed to make awards to all candidates who passed a qualifying examination. Evidence suggests that the Board of Education was never entirely satisfied with this arrangement. In the early twenties the Board applied 'Geddes restrictions', and, although these were removed in 1924, the Authority was informed in 1925 that it should not, without the previous sanction of the Board, increase the percentage of free-place awards in secondary schools beyond 58.5 per cent (the proportion given in 1924–5).[80] In 1927 the number of children who passed the qualifying examination was greater than that previously approved by the Board. The Authority then asked that it should be allowed to make awards to all the successful examinees. The Board conceded that this could be done in 1927, but stressed that it wished to discuss the county's future policy.[81] After lengthy talks involving Jackson and Lord Eustace Percy, President of the Board, it was eventually agreed that the West Riding would not be pressed to modify its existing arrangements.[82] Table 4.3 illustrates the development of

TABLE 4.3

*Pupils in secondary schools, 1920–31*

| Date | West Riding | | England and Wales | |
|------|------------|---------------------|------------------|--------|
|      | % fee payers | % scholarship holders | % fee payers | % free |
| 1920–1 | 61 | 39 | 65 | 35 |
| 1921–2 | 59 | 41 | 62 | 38 |
| 1922–3 | 54 | 46 | 61 | 39 |
| 1923–4 | 51 | 49 | 62 | 38 |
| 1924–5 | 48 | 52 | 61 | 39 |
| 1925–6 | 43 | 57 | 60 | 40 |
| 1926–7 | 40 | 60 | 59 | 41 |
| 1927–8 | 37 | 63 | 58 | 42 |
| 1928–9 | 35 | 65 | 56 | 44 |
| 1929–30 | 33 | 67 | 55 | 45 |
| 1930–1 | 31 | 69 | 53 | 47 |

the scholarship scheme in the 1920s; the West Riding provisions were certainly amongst the more generous in the country.

One way in which the Authority deliberately attempted to broaden opportunities in this field was to institute a preliminary test in all elementary schools to discover as many suitable candidates for the county minor scholarship examination as possible. Thus, from 1922 all elementary school-children of the appropriate age were reviewed, and the immediate result was a sharp increase in the number of candidates taking the examination. From 1925 an intelligence test, set by Godfrey Thomson of Durham University, was also incorporated into the assessment procedure.[83] Despite these changes, however, there was still a significant number of children who, although recommended to sit for the examination, failed to obtain their parents' consent to do so.[84] Nonetheless, between 1922 and 1926 the ratio of scholar-ship winners to the total ten–twelve age group was improved from one in forty-eight to one in twenty-four.[85]

Progress in the secondary field was checked abruptly by the national financial crisis of 1931 and the consequent economies in public expenditure. Early in 1932 the County Council resolved to reduce the rates by one shilling (5p) in the pound and, according to Jackson, education had to be prepared to bear its share of the burden.[86] The Higher Education Sub-Committee was soon forced to adopt measures which it had consistently resisted in the 1920s. First, it was agreed that a fixed number of new county minor scholarships should be awarded in 1932–3; moreover, the allocation specified was about six hundred awards fewer than the number given in 1931–2.[87] Secondly, a means test was to be applied to the parents of minor scholarship winners.[88] Although such tests were commonly used by some other authorities, the possibility of introducing one in the West Riding had been ruled out as recently as 1927.[89] Thirdly, minor scholars' dinner and maintenance allowances, which had greatly increased in number between 1927 and 1931 and which cost the Authority over £20,000 during 1930–1, were put on to a new and less generous scale.[90] Fourthly, the fees for under-tens in preparatory departments were raised from nine guineas (£9.45) to £15 per annum, although the fees for older pupils remained at the former figure. With the exception of the last item, these economies were roundly condemned by Labour members. Hyman considered them 'an abomination', and predicted that 'thousands and thousands of the best brains of the Riding would find themselves unable to remain at their secondary schools'.[91] Jackson, who clearly disliked the measures, stressed, 'It is as hard for me as anyone to face up to the position, and meet myself coming back.'[92]

In making these economies the West Riding had acted in anticipation of Board of Education Circular 1421. When this document was issued it was severly criticised nationally, especially, but not exclusively, by left-wing organisations.[93] This pattern was mirrored exactly in the West Riding, with Hyman, Lady Mabel Smith and the veteran Alderman Hardaker leading the attack in Committee. Jackson adopted a rather more ambivalent attitude, and most of the Liberals and Conservatives tended to take the line that it was a necessary evil at a time of national difficulty.[94] The provision in the Circular which aroused the most hostility amongst the majority of the Committee was the stringency of the means test for minor scholarships. The Board's proposals were less generous than the measures adopted by the Authority earlier in the year. Eventually it was agreed that the Committee should suggest to the Board a scale which, although less generous than their own, was more liberal than the Board's. Pointing out that no county area had been more generously treated in this respect than the West Riding, the Board remained adamant and refused to budge from its original figures.[95]

By the end of 1933 the Authority found that it was saving more from the imposition of the means test than it had anticipated.[96] When the financial forecasts for 1934–5 were prepared, it became clear that £4,400 could be saved under the heading of scholarships without reducing the number of awards below the level of 1933–4.[97] In these circumstances, the Higher Education Sub-Committee decided to keep spending at the same level but to award more scholarships.[98] In this respect the Authority returned to a position which was broadly comparable with the situation prior to the imposition of the economies. In 1935 the Committee also felt able to improve the maintenance allowances for county minor scholars.[99] Early in 1936 the Board relaxed some of the restrictions of Circular 1421 and removed the maximum limit on the number of minor scholarships which could be awarded by local authorities.[100] At this juncture, the Education Officer, Hallam, presented a largely noncommittal, but perhaps slightly discouraging, memorandum to the Higher Education Sub-Committee about the consequences and costs of making all places in secondary schools dependent on success in the scholarship examinations.[101] If implemented, this would have resulted in the eventual exclusion from the schools of all pupils falling into the category of 'fee payers' in Table 4.4 (below). The sub-committee, however, decided to take no action on this matter.

During the inter-war years capital developments in the field of secondary education were relatively modest. Between 1919 and 1939 the Authority built eight new secondary schools (including Adwick-le-Street Grammar School which was completed after the outbreak of war) and provided completely new buildings for five existing schools. As a consequence of the extensive building programme before 1914, the West Riding found itself able to cope with the large expansion in pupil numbers between 1916 and 1920 rather better than many other education authorities. The one part of the county which was a notable exception to this was the mining area in the south and south-east of Yorkshire. In this district, where the population was still growing rapidly, there was low attendance in proportion to the population and an undisputed shortage of places. The Authority was well aware of this problem from the early 1920s, and seven of the eight schools built during the period were situated in mining areas. Nonetheless, as Binns told the Board in 1939, a succession of economic crises had considerably retarded the Authority's building programmes.[102] During 1938–9 the Board imposed further restrictions and indicated that new projects would only be sanctioned if it was established that they were necessary on health grounds. The Committee put seven such cases to the Board in 1939, and, after complicated negotiations, it was agreed that the Authority could go forward with the five most urgent projects.[103] At this juncture, to Binns' annoyance, these schemes had to be postponed as Air Raid Precaution work took priority.[104]

In general the 1930s were a period of consolidation for secondary education. Table 4.4 shows that the balance of fee payers and scholarship holders was held fairly constant during this period.

The reasons for this steady rather than spectacular progress in the 1930s were undoubtedly connected with the economies, but other factors, particularly with regard to the later 1930s, must not be overlooked. The successive chairmen of the Committee, Jackson and Hyman, attached considerable importance to the reorganisation of elementary education, and there can be little doubt that priority was given to the setting up of senior schools during this period.[105] Hyman, moreover, made no secret of the fact that he was sceptical of the value of expanding secondary education of the grammar school type.[106] On the other hand, it must be remembered that only one county (London) had more pupils in secondary schools in the mid-1930s than the West Riding, and only one county (Durham) had more pupils in

TABLE 4.4
*Pupils in secondary schools, 1930–8*

| Date | West Riding | | England and Wales | |
|------|---------|-----------|---------|-----------|
| | % fee payers | % scholarship holders | % fee payers | % free |
| 1930–1 | 31 | 69 | 53 | 47 |
| 1931–2 | 29 | 71 | 52 | 48 |
| 1932–3 | 30 | 70 | n.a. | n.a. |

| | % fee payers | % scholarship holders | % holders of special places paying partial or full fees | % full fee payers | % partial fees | % free |
|------|---------|-----------|-----------|-----------|-----------|-----------|
| 1932–3 | n.a. | n.a. | n.a. | 49 | 2 | 49 |
| 1933–4 | 32 | 67 | 1 | 48 | 4 | 48 |
| 1934–5 | 32 | 66 | 2 | 48 | 5 | 47 |
| 1935–6 | 31 | 65 | 4 | 48 | 6 | 46 |
| 1936–7 | 31 | 64 | 5 | 47 | 7 | 46 |
| 1937–8 | 30 | 64 | 6 | 46 | 8 | 46 |

Strictly comparable statistics for the West Riding and England and Wales are not available.

proportion to population.[107] It is generally true, however, that the 1930s tended to be overshadowed in the development of secondary education by three earlier periods. These three critical stages were, first, the 1890s, when the Technical Instruction Committee took the crucial decisions to involve the Authority in this work in the first instance; second, the five years after the passing of the 1902 Act, when Acland built up a sound basis for a permanent system; and, finally, the 1920s, when under Jackson's leadership the Committee, despite difficulties, made important efforts towards broadening educational opportunities throughout the community. Table 4.5 illustrates the progress made before 1939.

TABLE 4.5

*Secondary school pupils per 1,000 population, 1901–38*

| Date | West Riding | England and Wales |
|------|-------------|-------------------|
| 1901–02 | 3.1 | n.a. |
| 1913–14 | 5.5 | 5.2 |
| 1919–20 | 9.1 | 8.5 |
| 1929–30 | 12.6 | 10.4 |
| 1937–8 | 13.2 | 11.4 |

## 2   FURTHER EDUCATION

Throughout the period 1889 to 1939 further education in the West Riding aroused far less controversy than did the schools. The pioneering work of the 1890s, when the Technical Instruction Committee normally left voluntary bodies to manage evening classes, was considered in Chapter I. The 1902 Act, however, transferred the management of sixty-nine evening classes from school boards to minor authorities or district sub-committees.[108] During the next few years, and especially after 1907, the Committee encouraged public authorities to take over the management of evening classes, and the number of schools controlled by public and quasi-public authorities increased from 131 in 1904 to 377 in 1914, whereas those under voluntary and quasi-voluntary bodies fell from 134 to 68.[109] By 1925 only 4 per cent of the schools were still under voluntary control.[110] The Committee maintained that co-ordination and rationalisation were more easily achieved when schools were managed by public bodies.

During the Edwardian period there was considerable national concern about the provisions for the further education of school leavers. This subject was examined by the Consultative Committee of the Board of Education during 1907 and 1908, and at the same time the new chairman of the Higher Education Sub-Committee, E. Talbot, persuaded the Authority to launch a campaign to expand and to improve the co-ordination of provisions in this field. An organising master and mistress were appointed to stimulate developments in rural districts, where it had been clearly shown that there was comparatively little interest in evening classes.[111] Head teachers of elementary schools were encouraged to impress upon their older pupils the opportunities provided by evening classes and open letters were addressed to the parents of all school leavers stressing the value of attendance at night school. Talbot and his vice-chairman, Percy Jackson, made personal contributions to this campaign, addressing meetings at the thirty chief local centres for evening school work in the Riding in 1908–9.[112]

Although the Committee claimed that it was satisfied with the response to this campaign, in terms of student enrolment the results must have been disappointing, for during this period the numbers attending evening classes grew steadily rather than dramatically, as is shown in Table 4.6.

TABLE 4.6
*Numbers of students enrolled in West
Riding evening and technical classes
1892–1914*

| Date | Students |
|------|----------|
| 1892–3 | 12,289 |
| 1900–1 | 21,680 |
| 1903–4 | 24,376 |
| 1906–7 | 30,310 |
| 1909–10 | 36,278 |
| 1913–14 | 34,639 |

In many ways the inter-war years witnessed unprecedented progress for the further education scheme, but the early 1920s were not typical in this respect. During the session 1920–1 there was a strike of members of the West Yorkshire Association of the National Union of Teachers over a new scale of remuneration for evening instruction.[113] As a result 157 evening schools and four technical schools remained closed,[114] and only about 17,500 students enrolled for classes, compared with about 31,000 in 1919–20.[115] Comparatively soon after this the 'Geddes economies' took their toll. The rates of pay for part-time teachers were reduced, the teaching duties of head teachers were increased, the fee regulations were amended and the closure of some schools was enforced.[116] No longer were teenagers who enrolled shortly after leaving day schools to be admitted free, and the remission of fees to students who achieved a high standard of attendance, a measure which had been practised by some managers since 1904, was ended.[117] The Committee also suggested that thirty-six selected schools should be closed at least temporarily, but local managers, greatly influenced by the economy drive, proceeded to shut down no fewer than 110 schools.[118] This overreaction quickly prompted the Committee to ask the managers to reverse these policies before permanent damage was done to further education.[119] During 1924 most of the restrictions were removed and by the mid-1920s student numbers had largely recovered from their nadir of 1922–3. In 1925 the Authority was again trying to encourage the attendance of teenagers at evening schools. Head teachers of elementary schools were required to issue free admission tickets to all school leavers, and publicity literature was circulated throughout the area. By 1926–7 the number of students enrolled topped 40,000 for the first time, even exceeding the figures for the pre-1914 period, when Barnsley, Dewsbury and Wakefield had formed part of the administrative county. The following year the West Riding's performance in further education was compared with other parts of the country. It was shown that in the West Riding 25.4 students per 1,000 population attended evening classes compared with 12.8 in English counties generally.[120] Only Cumberland registered a higher proportion amongst county authorities, and the figures of 29.2, which was the average for the West Yorkshire county boroughs, was only marginally greater than that achieved by the much more rural West Riding.[121]

During the late 1920s and 1930s student enrolments grew steadily (see Table 4.7), and by 1937–8 the West Riding students taking further education courses represented a proportion of 45.4 per 1,000 population.[122]

TABLE 4.7
*Numbers of students enrolled in*
*evening, technical and art Schools, 1926–38*

| Date | Students in West Riding institutions | West Riding Students in institutions under neighbouring authorities |
|---|---|---|
| 1926–7 | 40,854 | 6,602 |
| 1929–30 | 44,567 | 7,479 |
| 1932–3 | 46,948 | 9,207 |
| 1935–6 | 53,044 | 11,441 |
| 1937–8 | 57,218 | 12,907 |

Progress was not greatly affected by a protracted, and sometimes acrimonious, dispute between the Authority and the Board over the application of Circular 1421 to further education.[123] The Board pointed out that the West Riding received a lower proportion of income from fees in further education than any other English county, and maintained that this proportion should be increased.[124] It proposed, first, that recent day school leavers should be charged a small registration fee for attending evening classes; secondly, that the full remission of fees for good attendance should cease; and, thirdly, that a graduated scale of fees for the various years of senior and advanced courses should be introduced. The Higher Education Sub-Committee, with the support of the majority of the local managers, resisted these demands. After lengthy correspondence and visits to London by Jackson, Hyman and Hallam a tentative and uneasy compromise was reached. The Board dropped its first demand and it was agreed that partial remission of fees (80 per cent) could be given for certain specified courses only. The third request, however, proved particularly intractable. The Authority wished to keep to its practice of prescribing a minimum fee for all technical courses and leaving considerable discretion to local managers. Matters were soon further complicated by the West Riding's suspicion that Lancashire was receiving more lenient treatment from the Board over this issue. The Board was adamant that all authorities were being required to introduce graduated scales and insisted that the West Riding could not be an exception. Eventually the Authority submitted a graduated scale which was lower than the one proposed by the Board for county authorities. At this juncture, almost two years after negotiations had commenced, the Board agreed to accept this scale, to the Education Officer's surprise.[125]

Probably the most important single achievement of the inter-war years in this field was the creation of the Yorkshire Council for Further Education in 1928. The catalyst for this development was an HMIs general report on further education throughout Yorkshire, issued in 1927. Although largely favourable, the report suggested that there was a need for greater co-operation and co-ordination between the different LEAs in the county. A special sub-committee, chaired by Percy Jackson, considered this report and proposed that the West Riding should convene a conference of all the Yorkshire LEAs to discuss future co-operation and the possible creation of a joint board.[126] Contemporaries acknowledged that Jackson was the prime mover of this project[127] and it is clear that Jackson had discussed his ideas with Lord Eustace Percy, President of the Board, who strongly supported the scheme.[128] The conference was duly held at York on 30 April 1928, with Jackson in the chair. At the meeting Jackson stressed the advantages of co-operation between the large towns which were the natural centres for higher technical education and the surrounding county areas which could supply an important number of students. He felt that co-ordination was essential to maximise opportunities for students and to prevent the wastage of scarce resources through the duplication of facilities. There was no real opposition and it was unanimously agreed to set up the Yorkshire Council for Further Education, on which would be represented employers, trade unions, technical and art teachers and all the Yorkshire LEAs. Later Jackson was elected the first chairman. The Council operated through a series of interlocking committees for the various industries and local areas of the region. From the outset it was made clear that the Council should act in an investigatory and advisory capacity, and it was not given executive powers which might interfere with the autonomy of individual LEAs. Within a short time the Council played an essential role in the rational planning and development of the facilities for technical and further education throughout the county. During the 1930s the Yorkshire Council was often cited by the Board of Education as an example of the success that could be achieved through the co-operative efforts of neighbouring LEAs, and other regions were urged to emulate Yorkshire's pioneering scheme.[129]

During this period the Committee was deeply concerned with the provision of specialist technical education facilities for two of the three staple industries of the county. Although instruction in connection with the textile trades was largely concentrated in the county boroughs (with the exception of important facilities in Keighley), the administrative county took major responsibility for agricultural and mining education.

## 3  AGRICULTURAL EDUCATION

From the outset the Technical Instruction Committee was eager to promote agricultural education, but was pleased to delegate the provision of the instruction to the newly created Department of Agriculture at the Yorkshire College (later Leeds University). This Department received grants not only for relatively advanced in-college courses, but also for the organisation of much elementary work in the localities. The East and North Ridings also made similar arrangements with the college with regard to their agricultural work. In 1898, in conjunction with the East Riding, the Technical Instruction Committee took the lease of a farm at Garforth which acted as a centre for practical instruction for both authorities. Three years later the North Riding agreed to join the scheme, and the Yorkshire Council for Agricultural Education was created. This body, on which the Councils of the three Ridings were equally represented, was destined to control the development of agricultural education in the region for the next forty years and an intimate connection with the Agriculture Department at Leeds University was retained throughout this period.

In 1918 the Yorkshire Council made it clear that it did not regard the farm centre at Garforth as adequate for long-term requirements and proposed that another site should be purchased.[130] It was soon agreed that a new residential agricultural institute should be set up on the site.[131] In 1925, after complex negotiations with the Ministry of Agriculture, the Yorkshire Council purchased suitable land at Askham Bryan.[132] Although the land was soon used for practical work, the scheme to build the institute was much delayed by disagreements and by economy cuts. Eventually the foundation stone was laid in November 1936, and the buildings were largely completed by the outbreak of war in 1939.

About this time a bitter dispute came to a head, which ended with the West Riding's withdrawal from the Yorkshire Council. The fundamental difference concerned the staffing of the new institute. Leeds University proposed that its Professor of Agriculture should become the Principal of Askham Bryan and hold both appointments jointly.[133] This view was supported by the East and North Ridings. The West Riding Committee was firmly opposed to this policy. Walter Hyman, who was completely dissatisfied with the university's sub-degree work in agriculture, argued that a resident Principal should be appointed.[134] Hyman claimed that agricultural education had been neglected because of the association with the university, and maintained that 'nothing worthwhile could be done for the agricultural education of school children and farm labourers until the Council did it for themselves ... nothing has been done [by the university] apart from producing a few BScs who have got fat jobs'.[135] The Committee wished, in many ways, to bring agricultural education into line with other branches of technical education and to administer it directly from Wakefield. Further negotiations proved fruitless and the West Riding gave notice that it intended to withdraw from the Yorkshire Council in March 1941. The Ministry of Agriculture tried unsuccessfully to dissuade the Authority from this course of action, and intimated that it had been particularly satisfied with the close association between the Yorkshire Council and the university. It pointed out that it did not intend to establish new grant relations with a local authority during wartime.[136] This incensed Hyman even further,[137] and in this extremely acrimonious atmosphere the West Riding proceeded to sever its connections with the Yorkshire Council and to set about creating its own scheme for agricultural education.

## 4  MINING EDUCATION

When the Technical Instruction Committee commenced its work, it found education for the mining industry neglected. Schemes for remedying this situation, however, were soon put forward by the Mining Departments of the

Yorkshire College and Firth College, Sheffield. Both colleges had some experience of such work, and the Committee was pleased to use their services. It was soon agreed that the colleges would look after the needs of their respective parts of the coalfield and would also participate jointly in the setting up of a new centre for mining education at Barnsley. After initial difficulties, the Barnsley Mining School developed successfully in the years before the First World War, and throughout this period the universities steadily decreased the amount of direct teaching which they undertook in the pit villages, concentrating more and more on the organisation and inspection of the local classes.

During the First World War mining education experienced a period of decline. Overtime at the collieries took up most of the miners' time and apparatus and teachers were in short supply. Staff shortages in the Mining Departments of the universities exacerbated matters further, and the newly created county borough council in Barnsley changed the emphasis in the former West Riding mining school, which developed into a much more general technical college. When the Board of Education reviewed the facilities for mining education in the county in 1918, it was clear that all was not well and the Committee was advised to appoint an organiser for mining education. In view of the continued development of the coalfield and the importance of the industry to the county, the Committee acted upon this recommendation.[138] The new organiser soon proposed that the provisions should be restructured.[139] Elementary instruction continued in the local evening schools but advanced work was concentrated into six (later seven) centres. County mining scholarships were instituted to enable a small number of miners to take full-time degree or diploma courses at the universities, but the latter largely lost their direct connections with part-time instruction. During the 1920s and 1930s, with the help of large grants from the Miners' Welfare Fund, the Committee concentrated on building up the seven advanced centres. Completely new mining and technical institutes were constructed at Dinnington, Mexborough and Whitwood and the facilities at the other main centres were considerably improved.

## 5   AID TO UNIVERSITIES

The financial aid given to Leeds and Sheffield Universities by the County Council was by no means restricted to agriculture and mining. In the early 1890s the Committee stressed that it would only pay grants for work done at its request and that its aid was not intended as a source of profit to the colleges.[140] This policy was amended by the mid-1890s, however, and general grants were given to the Yorkshire College from 1896–7 and to Firth College, Sheffield, from 1897–8. In many ways the aid provided by local authorities in the 1890s enabled the colleges to branch out into new fields and was crucial to their growth and development.[141] During this period local authority grants to the colleges were more than twice as large as those from central government.[142]

When the universities were granted their charters in the early years of the twentieth century, the Privy Council attached considerable importance to their obtaining substantial grants from the West Riding.[143] The Authority eventually agreed to share a general grant of £6,000 between Leeds and Sheffield and to continue several smaller payments for earmarked purposes. Apart from cuts between 1911 and 1913, when the Authority was forced to restrict its expenditure on higher education generally,[144] these grants remained largely unchanged until 1924. During the early 1920s Michael Sadler, the Vice-Chancellor of Leeds, encouraged by the University Grants Committee, launched a vigorous campaign to obtain larger grants from local authorities for his institution. Sadler, who served as an 'added' member of the Committee, knew Percy Jackson well, and the negotiations for increased grants were conducted in a friendly spirit.[145] It was decided that the Yorkshire universities would share the proceeds of a penny rate. This was an extremely generous increase, as the annual sum involved approached £39,000. Partly in consequence of this decision, during the mid-1920s the Yorkshire universities received well over a quarter of their recurrent income from local authorities, whereas the average for all English universities was only just over one-tenth.[146] On the other hand, the Yorkshire universities fared badly in the economies of 1931–2, when, despite protests, the grant from the West Riding was reduced by 17½ per cent,[147] which was a larger cut than that experienced by most parts of the educational service. Later, in 1936, when there were some signs of economic recovery, the Committee invited the universities to discuss their grants with a view to restoring them to their former level. At this juncture, Sir Ernest Bain, chairman of the Leeds University Finance Committee, made a strategic error which lost the universities several thousands of pounds.[148] Bain told Jackson and Hyman that Leeds University was now prosperous and did not require an increase in the West Riding grant. Largely as a result of this encounter, deputations seeking increases for both Leeds and Sheffield in 1937 and 1938 were unsuccessful.

Throughout the period the West Riding also helped the universities and their students by awarding county major scholarships. In 1892–3 the

Authority awarded twelve county majors and six free studentships at the Yorkshire College. Although the studentships were phased out, the number of county majors increased considerably during the inter-war years and, despite some retrenchment in the early 1930s, the Authority was making about seventy awards per annum in the years immediately prior to the Second World War.[149] Even before 1914, however, the West Riding scholarship scheme had a high reputation, and was highly praised by the Senate of Leeds University in 1912.[150] In that year it was shown that there were considerably larger proportions of students receiving local authority grants at Leeds and Sheffield than at other universities in the country, and these students, to an important extent, came from the administrative county of the West Riding.[151]

Relations between the Authority and the universities were normally most cordial, but the one major exception to this was the dispute with Leeds over agricultural education.[152] When the West Riding withdrew from the Yorkshire Council for Agricultural Education, and the Ministry refused to consider the Authority's new scheme for grant purposes, Hyman blamed Leeds and proposed that the university's general grant should be reduced by £7,000 for 1942–3. Members of the County Finanance Committee were concerned about the rather spiteful nature of this proposal and reduced the cut to £1,500, and when the matter was discussed in Council several members clearly opposed the policy altogether.[153] This reduction could have had serious consequences for the university during wartime, but it was only applied for one year. During 1943 Binns approached the Vice-Chancellor at Leeds, on behalf of Hyman, and asked him whether the university would make a friendly gesture to the West Riding with regard to agricultural education; it was understood that if this was done the cut would be restored.[154] The university complied and this untypical episode came to an end, for over the whole period the West Riding consistently gave much greater support to its local universities than was usual in other parts of the country.

# CHAPTER V

# The Education
## and Training of Teachers

Throughout the whole of its existence the West Riding Authority was characterised by its active and lively interest in the quality of the teaching which went on in its schools. From the earliest meetings of the Education Committee members exhibited an acute awareness of the need for an adequate supply of well-trained teachers. To help the county's teachers maintain and improve the quality of their work, programmes of in-service courses were arranged each year and the staff of county advisers and inspectors played a key role in this work.

In 1903 the future elementary school teacher was still generally recruited from among the more promising pupils in the elementary schools themselves, and became an intending pupil-teacher for two years, usually from fourteen to sixteen, and then a pupil-teacher until the age of eighteen, when he might take the King's Scholarship examination for an award which would help to pay for a two-year training college course. Those who took college courses became trained certificated teachers. Other pupil-teachers went directly into the schools at eighteen as uncertificated teachers; while serving in the schools they could take an examination and become certificated teachers. After the Education Act of 1902 the policy of the Board of Education was directed increasingly towards ending this system and drawing recruits to the training colleges from secondary schools. The change to this from the pupil-teacher system took a quarter of a century or so to achieve fully and its attainment required a much wider provision of secondary schools than existed in the nineteenth century.

When the Board issued its report recommending that the normal education of a future teacher should involve attendance at a secondary school at least until the age of sixteen and no commitment to teaching as a career until sixteen or seventeen,[1] the West Riding was comparatively well placed to respond to this initiative through the work of its Technical Instruction

Committee in fostering secondary schools in the 1890s. In 1904 the West Riding instituted a scheme providing for the appointment of 465 intending pupil-teachers and 430 pupil-teachers annually. In 1907 the Authority decided to end the intending pupil-teacher scheme and to make a substantial increase in the number of county minor scholarships to secondary schools available for boys and girls between the ages of ten and sixteen or seventeen. Reliance was placed on the desire of a considerable proportion of those scholars to become teachers at a suitable age, without having been previously pledged as intending pupil-teachers. Bursaries were introduced in 1907 for those who wished to stay at secondary schools from sixteen to seventeen in order to qualify for entry to a training college. At seventeen awards were offered to enable students to proceed directly to college for two years or to spend one year as a student teacher before going on to college.[2]

This extensive provision of various awards and grants for those intending to become teachers in the early years of the century was the product of the belief that the supply of trained teachers was inadequate. The financial difficulties that the county experienced over its expenditure on higher education, which is referred to elsewhere (pp. 15, 83), made it necessary to reduce the number of minor scholarships originally planned in 1909. In subsequent years the Education Committee continued to indicate its concern lest an insufficient number of persons should come forward to train as teachers. In 1911 it resolved that the Government should be urged 'to adopt some scheme whereby the preliminary education and training of a sufficient number of boys and girls in the area of every education authority as teachers in elementary schools shall be provided for, and that adequate funds for such purpose shall be granted by Parliament'.[3] The need for more recruits to teacher training became a theme running through the minutes and memoranda of the Education Committee in the years immediately before the First World War. In 1913 the Education Department estimated that 520 bursars or pupil-teachers were needed annually, yet the number was declining markedly – from over 600 in 1907 to 223 in 1912 – as is clear from Table 5.1. The running down of the pupil-teacher system did itself seem to be causing some of the difficulty. If most of the recruits were to be drawn from the secondary schools, the numbers staying until the age of sixteen needed to be greatly increased. Against the estimate that 520 bursars should be recruited at the age of sixteen, there were only 391 pupils aged sixteen attending West Riding secondary schools in 1912. Early leaving from the secondary schools was seen as the main problem; 30 per cent of those at school at fourteen left before they reached the age of fifteen, while 50 per cent of the fifteen-year-olds left before they were sixteen.

TABLE 5.1

*Number of pupil-teachers and bursars*
*appointed for the first time during the school years*
*1905–6 to 1920–1*

|  | Pupil-teacher | Bursars |
|---|---|---|
| 1905–6 | 398 Pupil-teachers | — |
|  | 672 intending PTs |  |
| 1906–7 | 623 Pupil-teachers | — |
|  | 613 intending PTs |  |
| 1907–8 | 393 Pupil-teachers | 246 |
| 1908–9 | 305 Pupil-teachers | 232 |
| 1909–10 | 184 Pupil-teachers | 245 |
| 1910–11 | 120 Pupil-teachers | 219 |
| 1911–12 | 68 Pupil-teachers | 206 |
| 1912–13 | 21 Pupil-teachers | 202 |
| 1913–14 | 17 Pupil-teachers | 223 |
| 1914–15 | 51 Pupil-teachers | 257 |
| 1915–16 | 37 Pupil-teachers | 244 |
| 1916–17 | 48 Pupil-teachers | 269 |
| 1917–18 | 21 Pupil-teachers | 340 |
| 1918–19 | 4 Pupil-teachers | 320 |
| 1919–20 | – Pupil-teachers | 307 |
| 1920–1 | – Pupil-teachers | 287 |

*Source: Annual Reports*

The problem had not been resolved when the war began and brought with it an intensification of the shortage of qualified teachers. The Authority offered full-time posts as teachers to student teachers, without further training, after three months of practice in a school. The demands of the armed forces and of the booming wartime economy served to diminish further the supply of teachers. Moreover, accommodation difficulties became so acute during and immediately after the war that the Education Committee decided to provide hostels for teachers at Grimethorpe, Bolton-on-Dearne, Hemsworth and South Elmsall.[5] But the supply of entrants to teaching in the West Riding, as in the country generally, was much affected by the general inflation of wages and prices during the war and in the months which followed it, and by the failure of teachers' salaries to adjust to this situation. Salary scales were still local at this time, each authority having its own (the West Riding's certainly did not lag behind those of many other areas). What was really a national problem needed to be handled on a national basis and the establishment of the Burnham Committees to settle teachers' salaries nationally from 1919 removed this question from the area of local decision-making.

The West Riding sought to stimulate recruitment in 1921 by circulating to the parents of all pupils between fourteen and sixteen at secondary schools a letter about the improved prospects of teachers and about help with the cost of training. The Committee pointed out that teachers had 'the following privileges (1) assistance towards the cost of training, (2) a steady and healthy employment with good holidays, (3) improved prospects as regards salary, and (4) pension and lump-sum payment after service without contribution from the teacher'. In order to encourage boys and girls to stay at school until sixteen and to take up bursarships, the Committee now offered 'intending teacher grants' at the rate of six shillings (30p) a week for boys of fourteen and eight shillings (40p) for those of fifteen, the grant for girls being a shilling (5p) less in each case. Bursars received free tuition at secondary schools, travelling expenses and maintenance allowances of £25 per annum for boys, £20 for girls.[6] The drive to attract more entrants to teaching, of which this letter formed a part, was to mark the end of two decades of fears of a shortage of teachers. Fears of a surplus and measures to reduce the numbers being trained were more typical of the 1920s and 1930s, both nationally and in the West Riding. Reductions were eventually achieved by limiting further the number of students training colleges might admit, but as early as 1923 the county was obliged to introduce parental means tests in respect of all grants or bursaries which it offered. The policy of the Government from that year was to refuse to pay grant on expenditure connected with any sort of maintenance allowances or scholarships, unless authorities undertook previous inquiry into parents' means and reduced the value of any award in accordance with income scales.[7]

The only other major change in the arrangements for the education of future teachers up to the age of eighteen before the major reforms of the Second World War period was the abolition of the student teacher system. The Departmental Committee of the Board of Education, whose task was to consider the training of teachers, recommended that this should be abolished in its report in 1925. The Board indicated to LEAs that it proposed to follow this recommendation and expected the system to be ended in 1927 unless there were some very strong reasons for keeping it. A year of service in an elementary school between leaving a secondary school and entering a training college at eighteen had for some while seemed to be of little value to those in a position to assess its worth. In 1921 the Principal of Bingley Training College reported to the authority that she believed it to be 'of no great value and in some respects positively harmful'. She added that the almost unanimous opinion of training college authorities was that students would do better to remain as full-time pupils in secondary schools for the additional year.[8] In spite of opposition from some of the Part III authorities, the West Riding abolished the system and used the money thus released both to assist bursars to stay at school for an additional year and to make the scale of grant aid more generous for students at college.[9]

While the Education Committee sought to make adequate provision for intending teachers up to the age of eighteen through intending teacher grants, scholarships and bursaries, from the earliest days of its existence it was becoming clear to the Authority that it would need to make provision to train future teachers after the age of eighteen. In 1904 there were four institutions which trained teachers situated geographically in the West Riding: Leeds University, University College, Sheffield and Ripon and York Diocesan Colleges. They trained a total of 368 students, of whom 104 were from the administrative county area. On the assumptions which the Authority made about the number of West Riding teachers training outside the area and the number who would be needed, there appeared to be a shortfall of 650 training college places for women and 150 for men.[10] After making deductions in respect of government grants and student fees, the net annual cost to the rates of providing and maintaining the necessary additional training college accommodation was said to be £13,800. A conference of other northern authorities was held in Bradford in December 1904, as a result of which a deputation was sent to the President of the Board of Education on 21 February 1905 to urge that more state assistance should be given to the training of teachers.

In view of the urgency of the situation, it was suggested that a training college for 200 women students should be established at once and that the premises of Knaresborough Grammar School – which was closing – might be considered for this purpose. Before a decision had been taken on this, the Board amended its training college regulations to provide for a building grant of up to 25 per cent of the total cost of buildings and sites for new colleges. Even with this grant, the burden which would fall upon the county's higher education rate if a college were built would have been such that implementation of the scheme seemed impractical. In a paper which he wrote for the Higher Education Sub-Committee in March 1905, Acland, the chairman, spelt out the problems. Representatives of the rate payers would naturally wish to see a reasonable return in their district for expenditure undertaken and this would take the form of a supply of trained teachers. There was a need for some scheme to prevent authorities which spent little or nothing from taking advantage of authorities which did provide training college places. He suggested a national pooling arrangement, whereby every authority would contribute on the basis of the number of pupils in its schools – rather like that which has operated since the Second World War. In the absence of any such scheme, the only way in which the Riding could make sure of a reasonable return for money spent out of the rates on training teachers would be to bind the teachers it trained to serve for a number of years in its own schools. Acland admitted that this was not educationally a desirable practice, but believed that unless the West Riding was willing to run the risk of having its teachers tempted away without any return for expenditure on training either in service or in money, there was no other course open.[11]

The need to provide training college places was continually before the Education Committee in 1905 and subsequent years. In 1906 the Government increased the grant in aid of sites and buildings for training colleges from 25 to 75 per cent. The West Riding was also encouraged by a further change in the regulations introduced by the Liberal Government in 1907, when grant aid was withheld from any new college which imposed denominational membership requirements on members of its staff or governing body. The regulations also sought to forbid any religious teaching distinctive of a denomination in such an establishment. The Authority had already indicated that it would not be interested in giving assistance to proposals from the diocesan colleges at York and Ripon to build undenominational hostels, and on 22 October 1907 the Education Committee formally resolved 'that a residential training college be erected in the West Riding to provide accommodation for 200 women students'. The Committee was anxious to avoid placing the new college in a Part III authority's area, since it wanted the schools to be used for practice to be under its own control.[12] The County Architect suggested a number of sites. He thought the most suitable were those at Nab Wood in Shipley, Newall Estate in Otley, and Lady House Estate in Bingley. The latter site was said to be most healthy, 'with pure air and beautiful surroundings, and its isolation from a scholastic point of view is in its favour'. The Bingley site was purchased and the college built at a total cost of £60,000, of which the Board of Education provided £45,000 by way of grant. Runciman, President of the Board and MP for a West Riding constituency, laid the foundation stone for the administrative block on 24 May 1909. One of the five halls of residence was named after Acland to mark the part he had played in bringing the college into existence.[13]

Bingley Training College opened in September 1911. The first Principal was Miss Helen Wodehouse, who came from the post of lecturer in philosophy at Birmingham University. The appointing committee had interviewed eight applicants and then sent a deputation to visit the schools and colleges at which the five strongest candidates worked before a decision was finally taken. The Higher Education Sub-Committee delegated power to manage the institution to a special standing sub-committee which became, in effect, the governing body. 102 students were admitted when the college opened on 2 October 1911. The formal opening ceremony was performed by the chairman of the Council, Sir John Horsfall, on 21 October and the address was given by the Vice-Chancellor of Leeds University, Michael Sadler. Various members of the university's staff lectured at the college during its first year and the Education Committee formally minuted its thanks to the university for the help then given.[14]

The Authority made training college provision for men through an agreement with Leeds City Council to take fifty places – twenty-five entrants annually – at the new college which was being built on Beckett's Park Estate in Far Headingley. The buildings were completed in time for the September 1912 entry and the County Council undertook to pay the fees for fifty West Riding students for a period of ten years, whether the places were taken up or not. For its part Leeds gave the West Riding representation on the managing body and guaranteed provision of this number of places. The agreement was not extended beyond the initial period, for experience showed that the number of male students from the West Riding was falling far short of twenty-five (during the First World War the number did not exceed six in any year). When the position was reviewed in 1921, it appeared that only two out of fifty-five boy bursars appointed in 1919 had entered training college. Fourteen were awarded senior scholarships to proceed to universities and a number had withdrawn.[15]

The number of applications from women for admission to Bingley did not show similar signs of falling off in the post-war years. In 1924 the number of new students admitted was reduced from 102 in the previous year to ninety-seven in response to an instruction from the Board of Education which imposed a general reduction of 5 per cent on admissions to all training colleges because of the danger of unemployment among teachers in elementary schools.[16] The number of students increased to take up the full capacity of the college again in the later 1920s, reaching a peak in 1929 when there were 208 in residence. The fall in the birth rate led the Board to require reductions in the entry again from 1932 and by 1934 the student body had been reduced to 162. The contraction in teacher training in the 1930s saw the actual closure of certain colleges in other parts of the country. The good reputation which Bingley had come to enjoy was affirmed by the report which followed a full inspection by a group of HMIs in 1924. The drawing power of the college among potential students was emphasised in the report. Half the places were reserved for West Riding students, while the rest were filled mainly by students from other parts of the North and Midlands. It had long since ceased to be a 'local' college in the narrow sense. The Authority was commended for consistently taking a great interest in the college and for its 'ready and generous' response to suggestions for improvement made by the staff and by the Board's inspectors. Self-government by the student body and teaching, both effective and enlightened, by a well-qualified staff were said to characterise the college.[17] The investment by the county of effort and finance in the foundation and maintenance of the college was clearly fully justified.

Generous treatment of the college by the Authority in the years following the war was the more welcome since the Board had ended the special training college grant to local authorities, which had amounted to about three-quarters of the annual operating deficit, and now included colleges in the general higher education deficiency grant, at 50 per cent of recognised expenditure, as part of arrangements to simplify the very complicated pre-war system of numerous special grants for different activities in this field. For 1919–20 the net cost to the county of current expenditure at Bingley rose from £4,900 to £7,295.[18] Voluntary colleges continued to receive much more generous grant aid and the sixteen LEAs which had training colleges by this time made vigorous representations to the Board. Four years later the representations resulted in additional grant being made available on a temporary basis. This additional grant eventually became a permanent feature of arrangements, when the Treasury brought in a measure which enabled it to collect the cost of its additional grant from those authorities which did not provide colleges. Even so, these provisions still resulted in LEA provided colleges being treated less generously than voluntary colleges and the matter was aired repeatedly in the Higher Education Sub-Committee.[19]

Alongside these arrangements for the initial training of teachers on a full-time basis, the Authority built up and fostered a system of part-time sessional and vacation courses designed to maintain and enrich the quality of teaching available in its schools. The sessional courses were divided into special courses dealing with particular subjects and intended for secondary, technical and certificated elementary school teachers, and general courses in a group of subjects designed to meet the 'more pressing requirements' of uncertificated and supplementary teachers. The latter usually occupied two evenings a week as well as Saturday mornings and were given at centres for uncertificated and supplementary teachers. With the passage of time and the wider acceptance of fuller initial training it became possible to reduce the number of centres; the centres at Barnsley, Pontefract and Harrogate were closed in 1908 and those at Skipton and Doncaster the following year. The fee charged for courses for uncertificated teachers was usually £2 per year, that for classes for supplementary teachers £1. Those attending were eligible for grants to help them with the fees and sometimes with travelling expenses.

Special courses ranged over a wide variety of subjects. In 1908 they included modern languages, various sciences, commercial subjects, drawing, history, geography, mathematics, needlework and physical instruction. The courses which were provided in French and German at Leeds University were described as being of BA standard. Candidates were required to attend for two years and to take examinations at the end of each, a diploma being awarded to those who were successful. By contrast, the course in general history consisted of ten lectures, beginning with the remains and achievements of prehistoric man and ending with 'Progress in the 19th Century, its Meaning and Signs of Realization'. Grants were available to those who were actually teaching the subject they studied or could show that they were likely to do so.[20]

Quite apart from the general and special courses, vacation courses were held each year from 1905. In the early years a course in the general theory of education was held at Scarborough and in 1908 it was attended by 146 teachers, of whom 135 were grant-aided by the West Riding. The main lecture course on the general theory itself was given by J. W. Adamson, Professor of Education at King's College, London. The additional courses in different subject areas were given by other well-known experts. Arthur Smithells, Professor of Chemistry at Leeds University, gave the course in teaching elementary experimental science, and the report on the course which went to the Higher Education Sub-Committee later commented that 'the number of superstitions and absolutely unscientific ideas which were exposed is hardly credible'. In the same year a geography course was held at Oxford and teachers were given assistance to attend vacation courses at Cambridge and London. A group of twenty-two teachers was sent to take a vacation course at Boulogne, twenty-four were given grants to attend a course in physical education at Silkeborg in Denmark, while a further seven teachers received grants to enable them to stay with French families. It may be of interest to note that some members of the Education Committee and one or more of the County Council's inspectors visited each of these vacation courses, both at home and overseas, and that detailed observations on the courses themselves and in many cases on the progress, assiduity and achievement of individual teachers were circulated to the Higher Education Sub-Committee.[21]

The construction of Bingley Training College meant that the county now possessed excellent premises in which to house its residential vacation courses, and in 1912 an exploratory course was held there. Its success led the Higher Education Sub-Committee to hold a full vacation course at the college in August 1913. This included a general course lasting a fortnight, four special courses lasting three weeks and two courses in physical instruction lasting for two weeks. A total of 227 attended, 160 of them with the aid of grants from the West Riding. After a break of two years during the First World War the Bingley vacation course was resumed in 1919 and became an important feature in the county's educational calendar. By the 1930s half of the accommodation was reserved for teachers from outside the Riding and the gathering of teachers took on a national character. The list of persons who lectured at Bingley included such well-known national names as Lord Eustace Percy, Professor Cyril Burt, Sir Michael Sadler, Mrs Sidney Webb, Sir Henry Hadow, Professor Ernest Barker and Sir William Rothenstein. The Education Committee regarded the Bingley course as an opportunity for teachers to meet some of those recognised as leaders in the work of education as well as giving participants the opportunity to compare experiences and discuss difficulties. The annual vacation course was always very much under the immediate control of the county Education Officer, and in a report to the Board of Education in which he spoke of its achievements, HMI Maxwell-Lyte commented that the smooth operation of the course was largely due to the personal superintendence of J. H. Hallam and his wife.[22]

The outbreak of war in 1939 led to a rapid reduction in the supply of teachers. The surplus of the 1930s, with the enforced cuts in admissions to the training colleges, gave way to shortage, as men teachers in considerable numbers and some women went to various forms of war service. By 1941 the output of newly qualified teachers from the colleges had been greatly reduced. The number of men students in the colleges had been cut by 59 per cent when compared with 1938, while the number of women students had fallen by 15 per cent – even though the state encouraged young women to take up teaching as a form of war service. It was clear that it would be essential to train a large number of additional entrants to the teaching profession as quickly as possible and on an emergency basis as soon as the war ended. In 1943 an office committee was set up in the Board of Education to work out a plan. The committee considered at some length a scheme submitted by Binns by which trainees would be based on selected schools and would gradually take on increased teaching loads. Lecture courses were to be provided for groups of trainees at nearby technical colleges. But the committee preferred a scheme suggested by one of its own officials, under which about fifty emergency training colleges would be set up, each with about 200 students who would undertake a course lasting for one year, two-thirds of the time being spent in training and one-third in school practice. The colleges would be run by LEAs as agents for the Board, with all finance coming from the Exchequer.[23]

As early as January 1944 efforts were being made to find buildings in the county which would be usable as emergency colleges without expensive adaptation, but towards the end of the war such buildings were extremely difficult to find. Eventually one emergency college was established in Oatlands School and the Beechwood Hotel at Harrogate and another in a former miners' hostel at Stanley, Wakefield. Both colleges were designed to provide for 150 students. It was expected that both would open in the spring of 1947, but delays in the preparations at Harrogate meant that it could not open before August. The Harrogate college was residential and at first took only men students. It was to have closed in November 1949, but the Ministry extended this deadline to accommodate another intake of students and it remained open until 1951, thus producing a total of 443 qualified teachers. The college at Stanley only operated for one year, after which the building had to be handed back to serve its original purpose. This was a day college and took both men and women students. Although it was also only open for one year, 147 qualified teachers were trained there.[24]

The operation of the emergency training scheme depended on the goodwill of both local authorities and teachers' unions. The Ministry made it clear that it wanted authorities to be willing to second teachers for service as temporary lecturers in the colleges, and the West Riding agreed to this in principle in 1945.[25] In May 1946 the Committee changed its attitude and refused to second for more than a year – in spite of the opposition of the Education Officer, who felt that there was some inconsistency in the public and vigilant determination of the chairman of the Education Committee to raise the school leaving age when he was not, apparently, prepared to support the steps essential to secure the necessary teachers. The Committee, however, fearing that the schools that lost permanent staff and had only temporary replacements would suffer, instructed the Education Officer to convey their change of policy to the Ministry. The Minister wrote back in forceful terms, urging the Authority to stand by its earlier willingness to second for the full length of the emergency college scheme. The sort of difficulty which would arise if any limitation were imposed on secondment was already clear from a letter from Binns, now Chief Education Officer for Lancashire, whose authority wanted to appoint a West Riding teacher as a lecturer in one of the emergency colleges it was going to run: 'We in Lancashire are going to run six of these emergency colleges for the benefit of the country as a whole and unless we get the support of other authorities we cannot do it.' With these representations from the Ministry and from Lancashire before it, the Staffing and Salaries Sub-Committee rescinded the resolution it had taken in May and agreed to secondment for the full term of the emergency training college scheme.[26]

The scheme required that trainees were to follow further part-time courses of study and reading during their two-year period of probation. It was not always practicable to arrange programmes of courses specifically for emergency-trained teachers, but the West Riding took a very active interest in their further training. County Council inspectors became responsible for all probationers in their areas. Each member of the Authority's professional staff was appointed as supervisor to a small group of probationers with whom he maintained personal contact, advising and guiding them on their programmes of further study. Full use was made of existing courses being run in technical colleges and schools of art in both the county and the county boroughs. The emergency training scheme certainly recruited a large number of valuable entrants to the teaching service: in 1962 it was reported that of the 630 teachers trained under the scheme then serving in the West Riding, 105 were head teachers in primary and secondary schools, seventy were deputy heads and 206 held posts of special responsibility.[27]

Quite apart from the immediate shortage of teachers caused by the war itself, the national teacher training system had met with increasingly severe criticism in the years before the war. Both the Permanent Secretary and the Principal Assistant Secretary in charge of teacher training at the Board of Education were convinced of the need for a thorough inquiry and far-reaching reforms. In the summer of 1939, therefore, the Board approached the Treasury to sanction the expenditure involved in setting up a committee of inquiry. The outbreak of war in September delayed matters but the inquiry was held during the war by a committee with Sir Arnold McNair as chairman. This committee's particular recommendations were indeed far-reaching, but in some ways its contribution to the creation of a generally receptive attitude to new ideas was more important. It was especially significant in the West Riding with its strong traditions of concern with the quality of teacher training. The new Education Officer, Alec Clegg, attached the greatest importance to the improvement and extension of facilities both for the initial and the continued training of teachers, and the creation of a group of new permanent colleges in the post-war years was largely due to his initiative in seizing the opportunities presented by the Ministry of Education's currently expansive and reforming attitude. In institutional terms, the principal fruits of this period were Bretton Hall, Lady Mabel and Ilkley Colleges of Education, along with Woolley Hall, which became a permanent centre for the continuing education of teachers.

Soon after taking over from Binns, Clegg received a visit from Cyril Winn, Staff Inspector for Music, and one of his colleagues. Winn pointed out that nowhere in the country was there a college for the training of music teachers. The West Riding, with its reputation for good music teaching, would be an admirable place to set up a specialist college. The Ministry did not intend to establish such a college itself but was concerned to find an authority which would do so and to give it full support. Newell, the HMI accompanying Winn, suggested that if a college were established it might include also art and drama. This approach was very much in line with Clegg's own view of the importance of considering education, particularly education in the arts, as a whole. The establishment of such a college in the county would obviously enhance the work already being done in the schools.[28] The ideas which came from this discussion were elaborated more fully in a paper which was prepared for the Post-War Education Sub-Committee the following February. Music and art tended to be taught as isolated subjects and training in them was often narrow, yet they had the common purpose of stimulating and training the sensibilities of children. Thus any training college for students specialising in music should also include intending teachers of art and possibly drama. The aim would be for each student who left the college to have a broad understanding of the arts generally and of their effect on the education of children. The ultimate aim for the specialist college was to be a lofty one, doing for music, art and drama 'what the Carnegie College does for Physical Training'. The new system of pooling training college expenditure which was to come into effect from April 1946 had been announced by the Ministry, and this enabled the Education Officer to point out that the proposed college would cost the West Riding exactly the same for maintenance whether it was established in the county or by some other authority. The 'spin-off' from its presence would thus be a cost-free gain.[29]

In the late 1940s building controls, the rationing of building materials and the issue of costs all pointed to the need to seek large existing buildings – perhaps mansions or hotels – and converting them for college use, rather than buying sites and constructing purpose-built colleges on them as had been the case with Bingley in the less restrictive atmosphere at the beginning of the century. The positive aspect of this constraint was that the new colleges were likely to be situated in attractive surroundings. Bretton Hall (which had been the residence of Lord Allendale) lay in an unspoiled estate between Wakefield and Barnsley. The particulars prepared when the post of Principal was advertised stated that this was 'one of the most beautiful estates in South Yorkshire'. The low figure put on it by the District Valuer caused the Education Officer some perturbation, for 'the Miners' Welfare Committee are, I know, ready to outbid us'.[30] But in the end the County Council managed to purchase the Hall and over two hundred acres of grounds early in 1947, at a price of £35,000. Over £100,000 was agreed to meet the cost of adaptations and alterations.[31] The college took its first students in 1949.

Although in the nature of things it was not a matter which received public notice, the three years or so of negotiation and adaptation of the buildings were a time when the Education Officer and the advisory staff for music and the other arts devoted a good deal of time and energy to planning the first local authority specialist college to provide teachers with a training in the arts. In this they worked closely with HM staff inspectors for art and music, Dickey and Winn. Moreover, there can be no doubt that G. N. Flemming, responsible for teacher training at the Ministry in these years, was not merely sympathetic to the establishment of Bretton Hall and the other new colleges in the West Riding, but also gave a quite remarkable amount of help.

The establishment of Lady Mabel College for physical education teachers also owed much to close co-operation between the Education Officer, specialist advisers and the HMI most directly concerned. In the course of seeking premises for use as emergency teacher training colleges, Earl Fitzwilliam's enormous mansion, Wentworth Woodhouse, near Rotherham, had been considered but was not thought to be suitable without more expenditure on alterations than could have been justified for temporary use.[32] It came to mind when the senior woman physical training inspector for the north-eastern area, Miss Ruth Foster, visited Clegg on 24 October 1946. She had been asked by the Ministry to advise on the establishment of new physical training colleges for women and had been impressed both by the newly appointed team of physical training organisers in the Riding and by the approach to the subject which was being adopted. She wondered whether the Authority would be prepared to establish a specialist college. The Education Officer set about trying to secure a lease on the greater part of Wentworth Woodhouse with a view to establishing the proposed college there.[33] Six days after Miss Foster's visit, Flemming wrote from the Ministry giving the Education Officer further encouragement: 'In case you have any doubts on the point, this is just to assure you that we are very anxious to expand the facilities for training teachers of physical training.' He went on to inquire whether there was anything which 'you would like us to put officially to the Authority, either in relation to Wentworth Woodhouse generally or in relation to the PT College suggestion in particular?'.[34]

There was at the time an acute shortage of places for women who wished to train as physical training specialists. It was decided to plan for an entry of sixty students a year, with a total of about 170 places for the three-year course and a further thirty places for trained teachers who wished to take a one-year course in physical training. By January 1947 fairly detailed plans had been drawn up in both the academic and the architectural areas. The Policy Sub-Committee considered the matter on 21 January and approved the proposals in principle. Subject to formal approval by the Ministry, further negotiations with Earl Fitzwilliam were to be undertaken. These were successfully concluded in time for the premises to be leased for fifty years from 1 November 1947, at an annual rent of £800.[35] Although every effort was made to get the buildings ready on time, when the college opened in 1949 the initial intake of fifty students spent their first term in emergency accommodation in Harrogate and only moved into Wentworth Woodhouse in January 1950. The college was named after Lady Mabel Smith, County Councillor for many years, member of the Education Committee and sister of the seventh Earl Fitzwilliam, who involved herself very actively in the affairs of the new college until her death in September 1951.

The foundation of Ilkley Training College, which was to specialise in the training of teachers of housecraft, had its origins in the severe shortage of teachers of domestic science. Since the Ministry would not authorise new buildings but would support proposals for adaptations of existing buildings, for a proposal from the West Riding to set up such a college to be successful it would have to be linked with the acquisition of suitable existing premises. Both Hyman, then chairman of the Education Committee, and Clegg were keen to find a suitable building and early in 1949 thought they had found one in Nostell Priory, Wakefield. The Education Officer put the proposal to Flemming and discussed the plan with HMI Miss Briant. Flemming welcomed the proposal warmly and offered to do all he could to forward it. In his reply he suggested, 'In putting the matter to your Committee you can say that you have verified from us that there is a serious need for more training places for housecraft teachers.'[36]

The twists and turns which led to the abandonment of the proposal to house the college at Nostell Priory, and which eventually led to its being housed at Ilkley, form a complicated web of events, not now of great significance in their detail. One factor was the enthusiasm which Hyman showed to have the college housed at Harlow Manor Hotel in Harrogate – at that time a requisitioned building which the Leeds Regional Hospital Board also had its eye on. Two weeks after hearing from Flemming of the Ministry's likely sanction of the Nostell Priory project, Clegg was writing to HMI Miss Briant inviting her to meet his chairman and to look over Harlow Manor. Many of the Education Committee also favoured the Harrogate building and it was clear that Nostell Priory was far from ideal for the required purpose. Two requisitioned hotels in Ilkley, which had been thought of as possibilities for emergency training or adult education colleges two or three years earlier, were now brought into the picture – Ben Rhydding Hotel and Wells House Hotel. In May 1949 the Committee decided to consider these and the deputation that had looked over Nostell Priory and Harlow Manor was authorised 'to visit and inspect both of these'.[37] In the course of the summer the Ministry came to favour Wells House, Ilkley, and this would have been the personal preference of the Education Officer, but the Education Committee eventually showed that it preferred Harlow Manor, Harrogate, concluding that the additional time and money needed to convert the latter would be far outweighed by the cultural advantages of Harrogate over Ilkley. The Ministry now took a very firm line in a formal, official letter to the Authority. Any attempt to acquire Harlow Manor might lead to a dispute between the Ministries of Health and Education and would have to be referred to an impartial body for decision. In any case, Wells House would be cheaper, easier to adapt and available for students much sooner. The current shortage of housecraft teachers meant that any delay in opening the college should be avoided. The West Riding Education Authority was, therefore, asked to reconsider the decision it had taken. The matter was reconsidered and on 29 September the Education Officer was able to report that negotiations were now starting for the acquisition of Wells House Hotel, Ilkley.[38]

It was another year before the negotiations were completed and the County Council itself formally agreed to the purchase, adaptation and furnishing at a total cost of £238,000. The opposition of Hyman – who, though obviously influential, was no longer chairman of the Education Committee – continued to the last. He spoke against the motion at the Council meeting on 18 October 1950, on the grounds that to put the college in Ilkley was educationally unsound: 'There are no drama, music or literary and debating societies there. There is nothing.' In reply Alderman Mrs Ryder Runton outlined the case for adapting Wells House Hotel, denied that Ilkley was culturally deficient and said she believed the opposition policy could be summed up in a three-word headline: 'Hyman wants Harrogate'.[39]

As with the other specialist colleges, Bretton and Lady Mabel, the aim of the Authority was that Ilkley should not only be involved with specialised work in housewifery, laundry and cooking but should also be concerned with the contribution which its own specialism could make to the personal development of each child. It was hoped that a well-developed art course would encourage students to study the design and quality of domestic furnishing and equipment. Other subjects, too, were seen as contribution to this. History, for instance, might well be concerned with the development of home-making in all its aspects in the past.[40]

The taking over of mansions and hotels for use by the education service did lead to a certain amount of criticism on the grounds that it seemed to be an unduly lavish way of providing facilities – even though it was in fact more economical at the time than new buildings would have been. There was one such outburst of public criticism in 1952 which centred on Wentworth Woodhouse. The *Sunday Express*, under the headline 'Keep-fit girls live in £250,000 temple', explained that tennis courts that had served the Earls Fitzwilliam and their famous house parties were deemed inadequate. New courts were laid out and for this purpose a hillside was levelled. Villagers at Wentworth were reported as saying that 'the past glories of the mansion have been eclipsed by what is now going on'. The matter was aired in the Council Chamber three days later, when County Councillor Sutcliffe, an Independent from Hebden Bridge, also raised the question of expenditure on facilities at Bretton Hall, 'What the Education Committee are visualising I don't know. Perhaps they are going to stage "Lohengrin" on the lake. I am sure the chairman would look nice in a gondola. Then the Socialist members could probably stage the "Volga Boatmen" with Alderman Hyman as coxswain. . . .' Fuller Smith, the Conservative chairman of the Education Committee, replied to the criticisms before the Council, and a long and detailed letter justifying the expenditure on the new colleges appeared over his name in the *Yorkshire Post* three days later.[41] It should perhaps be said that the immediate result of the establishment of the three colleges was an additional annual supply of 290 teachers in subjects in which there were great shortages. While the cost fell on all LEAs in proportion to their school populations, the county which housed them undoubtedly received greater educational, cultural and economic benefit from the colleges than any other. From the West Riding's viewpoint, they certainly represented a good bargain.

The subsequent expansion of these three colleges and of Bingley, and the establishment of a day training college at Swinton, were largely consequences of shortages in the supply of teachers, national, local or both. The raising of the school leaving age to fifteen and the immediate post-war shortages had persuaded the Ministry of Education of the need for more teachers in the later 1940s, but by the mid-1950s the Ministry was beginning to fear that too many teachers might be being produced. For over a century the Education Department at Whitehall, the Board of Education, the Ministry and now the Department of Education and Science (DES) have always had difficulty in estimating accurately future requirements for teachers and throughout this time there have been centrally inspired periods of expansion and contraction in the colleges. When in 1953 the West Riding proposed that Bingley and Bretton should be increased in size to help to meet the needs arising from the high birth rate of the post-war years, the Ministry rejected the proposals. By 1955 the Education Officer had reason to believe that the Ministry intended to close Bretton. Centrally it was thought that problems of teacher supply would have been overcome by 1958 and that some contraction in the number of college places was needed. For various reasons, Bretton seemed to be a suitable candidate for closure. By 1958 the central government had changed its view. The 1957 bulge in the birth rate had not been expected. Thus there were comparatively fewer births in 1954, 1955 and 1956 and many more than were expected in 1957 and 1958. 'Crowding up' of the colleges became Ministry policy and this national expansion of student numbers was reflected in West Riding colleges.

But parts of the county and some of the heavily industrialised county boroughs suffered from an acute shortage of teachers even when the national supply position appeared to be in balance. The Yorkshire AEC, as well as the West Riding and other individual authorities, devoted much time and energy to pressing on the Ministry the need to take action to help unattractive areas. The Education Officer feared that even after the introduction of the three- (instead of two-) year training course for the teacher's certificate from 1961, the position in these areas would remain unchanged. He feared that children in drab areas with little in their backgrounds to help them educationally would be taught by teachers whom nobody else wanted.[42]

One of the areas of the Riding where the shortage was worst was in the south. By 1960 the Ministry doubted whether the colleges would be able to admit any more students than they had in 1958 and 1959 and was inclined to turn to the more economical expedient of setting up non-residential colleges in populous areas for mature students. One had already been established on an experimental basis in Leeds and the Ministry considered that the success with which it was meeting justified investigating the possibility of establishing further temporary day colleges on the same pattern. The Ministry had thought of setting up such a college in Sheffield but was advised that school practice difficulties ruled that out, so L. G. Cook of Teachers Branch at the Ministry suggested orally and informally to the West Riding's officers the possibility of the county's setting one up. The requirements were accommodation (perhaps school premises) which could be used without extensive alterations and proximity to a large concentration of population (somewhere near Rotherham in the southern mining and industrial area was suggested) and a start should be made by September 1960 or 1961. The Education Officer was keenly interested in the idea and a hunt began for suitable premises. Mature students attending college daily from their homes were quite likely to seek posts after training within daily travelling distance of their present homes, hence a day training college in an unattractive area which suffered from a severe shortage of teachers could make a worthwhile contribution to meeting an authority's staffing problems. Within a week Clegg wrote to the Ministry suggesting the new building nearing completion intended to house the secondary technical school which existed in Mexborough Technical College premises.[43]

The proposal to use the new technical school building provoked a great deal of opposition in the Mexborough and Swinton area and at one time it looked as though the Ministry would not give its approval. While Teachers Branch favoured the scheme, Schools Branch and Further Education Branch were hostile, since it involved losing school or further education accommodation. These conflicting interests became clear at a meeting the Education Officer attended at the Ministry on 24 February. Eventually the Ministry agreed to the colleges being established in the secondary modern school buildings at Swinton and arrangements were made to open in January 1961. Although the college was regarded as providing accommodation for 200 students, the Ministry agreed that it might take up to 250. There were about 500 applications for admission in the first year and of these about half seemed to be suitable for training; many either lacked the minimum academic qualifications or were too young to take the two-year course, and the college did take rather more three-year students than the Authority had hoped it would need to do. In the event only about 30 per cent of the 185 students admitted were suitable for the two-year course;[44] fifty-seven more students came in January 1962. Both the national situation and the success of the college in recruiting students led the Ministry to suggest in 1962 that if a suitable site could be found, the college might be made permanent. In due course the college got its own purpose-built premises at Scawsby. The success of the college at Swinton and at Scawsby stimulated the establishment of an outpost in the Castleford area for the training of mature students as a way of helping to overcome the shortage of teachers in that district. This operated as an annexe of Lady Mabel College.[45]

The expansionary path which the Ministry was now following in teacher training may perhaps be said to have entered its final and most impressive phase of growth from 1965, when a drive was launched to increase the number of practising school teachers from 290,000 to nearly half a million. Ironically enough, it was launched in the very year when the birth rate began a steady decline. A very great expansion of the number of places for students in the colleges was then planned and pushed through in the late 1960s. A campaign was also launched to bring back married women teachers to the schools.[46] In the West Riding colleges numbers had increased from 1,026 to 1,536 between 1960–1 and 1964–5; by 1972–3 the total had reached 2,708 students and further expansion was still envisaged. Ilkley, for instance, was planning to increase its student body to 750, whereas ten years earlier it had numbered barely 200. Yet although a falling birth rate was to lead to the closure of some colleges and a very severe reduction in the numbers being trained in the mid-1970s, the Authority was still facing a very real struggle to staff its schools in some divisions in the last decade before it ceased to exist.

The divisions which could recruit full-time teachers were usually the same as those which had a generous supply of trained married women willing to return to the classroom. Divisions near the large northern county boroughs and those which included or were near suburban areas or residential commuting villages could recruit without difficulty. Difficulties over the recruitment of married women to help on a full- or part-time basis arose in such areas as Hemsworth, Don Valley, Staincross, Mexborough, Rother Valley and Goole. Attractive residential districts in the northern part of the county such as Ripon, Harrogate and Skipton had an abundant supply of full-time staff and really had no need to call upon part-time teachers.[47] In this respect, as in so many others, the striking social and economic contrasts between different areas of the Riding meant that within the one authority the national situation was mirrored – a dearth of teachers in less attractive areas coupled with an ample number in more pleasant places.

The maintenance of the quality of teaching received much attention during the last thirty years of the Authority's existence and the single most important development here was the establishment of a college devoted entirely to the further education of teachers. If there could be said to be one place where the Ark of the Covenant of West Riding Education was kept during the Authority's last two decades, that place was Woolley Hall. In a paper which the Post-War Education Sub-Committee considered in October 1945 the Education Officer argued that the first concern of an education authority was to appoint good teachers and then to maintain their enthusiasm and technical proficiency. In due course it was to be the function of Woolley Hall to meet the need for 'the continued training of new recruits and the refreshing and enlivening of older teachers'. The Education Committee agreed with the paper and the hunt began for a suitable large house which would provide hostel accommodation for up to sixty students, along with ancillary rooms for practical subjects, a hall, a small stage and a few acres of grounds. Apart from cleaning staff, there would only be a warden. The teaching staff would be provided separately for each course.[48]

A number of premises were considered before Woolley Hall was acquired for this purpose, including Kirklees Hall near Brighouse, Eshton Hall in Gargrave and Ingleborough Hall in Clapham. By May 1946 the Ministry's approval in principle was sought for the acquisition of Woolley Hall, a large house five miles from Wakefield, in order that the District Valuer might be asked to undertake his valuation. Since this was the first case of the acquisition of a building for quite this purpose, the Ministry felt it would need to get the Treasury's agreement before it could give general approval, and to avoid delay advantage was taken of the approval already given by the Ministry for the valuation of large houses with a view to accommodating two schools for handicapped children to get the District Valuer to report on Woolley Hall. This house offered just the sort of accommodation that was needed but a good deal of renovation and adaptation would be required.[49] The uniqueness of a further education college for teachers meant that administratively it did not fit neatly into the Ministry's established pattern. While it served the schools and the teachers, it could not be the responsibility of either Schools or Teachers Branches; instead it came within the orbit of Further Education Branch whose main concern was technical education. The repair and development of the building had to be financed from minor building funds a little at a time, for no place could be found for this as a major further education project. Eventually the Authority felt that it could not go on using Minor Works money when so many schools were in urgent need of repair and the Ministry then suggested (in 1960) that an additional allocation might be sought from the national Minor Works pool specifically for Woolley Hall, and this the Education Committee did.[50] Woolley Hall had been opened in 1952 by Sir John Maud, then Permanent Secretary, Ministry of Education. Miss Diane Jordan, who as a member of the advisory staff had played an important part in formulating the ideas behind the project, became the first Warden. The popularity of Woolley Hall courses and conferences among teachers testified to the value they placed on it and the success of the project: in 1972–3 more than 6,000 teachers applied for day or residential courses there. Its characteristic appeal was said to be that it was not so much a place where instruction was given as one where views were exchanged, problems considered and solutions generated by colleagues facing similar issues. The demand on Woolley Hall by school teachers became so great that the institution was no longer able also to meet the needs of the further education and youth service staffs, and Bramley Grange was opened as a second centre to accommodate their requirements in 1968. It may not be too much to say that the concept which governed the establishment of Woolley Hall and its implementation has been the most significant single development in the post-war county education service.

Many courses for teachers continued to flourish outside the new institution. The Bingley vacation course, which had been temporarily broken off during the Second World War, was resumed after the ending of hostilities. To some extent the themes of the county's vacation courses have reflected quite closely the contemporary concerns of the educational world, such as the modern school in the early 1950s or education and social handicap in 1969. During the post-war years there was an enormous explosion in the number of sessional courses of varying lengths and on all sorts of topics which the Authority provided and which teachers attended. There were thirty of these courses in 1953; by 1972 there were ten times as many. The total number of teachers from the Authority's service attending courses in that year was about 1,800. This development might be seen as an index of the mutual desire of Authority and teachers to maintain and improve the quality of the service offered by the schools.

The Plowden Committee found that in 1965 only fifty out of 164 LEAs employed their own inspectors.[51] The West Riding had always regarded them as having an essential part to play in sustaining the quality of education in the county. The first inspector had been appointed as early as 1891, when the Technical Instruction Committee was anxious to ensure that the institutions and classes which it aided were giving value for money. An assistant inspector, a woman inspector of domestic subjects and a number of occasional inspectors of special subjects were all appointed before 1900. As has been shown already, until the years between the wars the Authority relied heavily on inspectors of elementary and secondary schools to carry some of the duties which might elsewhere have fallen upon administrators, while leading members of the Authority itself became sufficiently closely involved in day-to-day affairs to formulate policy suggestions and even to handle fairly routine matters which administrative officers were dealing with in other LEAs.

After Hallam was made Education Officer, he – and later his two successors, Binns and Clegg – attached considerable importance to the contribution which inspectors made. In the early 1950s there were seven inspectors, each responsible for rather more than 150 schools, as well as a senior inspector, an inspector of special schools and an inspector of technical colleges and institutes. Their duties were very varied. They were expected to stimulate and encourage good work, to share in the conduct of teachers' courses, to carry out inspections of schools and to follow up suggestions made in reports by HMIs. The Authority relied almost entirely on their advice in deciding the number of teachers to be employed in each school and they undertook duties connected with the assessment of candidates for county major awards. Finding out the answers to questions from the Education Committee and the Education Department seems to have become a major task in itself, for in 1953 it was found that up to 100 inquiries per month were being submitted to the inspectors. Advisory staff differed from inspectors in a number of important respects, the most fundamental being that they were concerned with one subject only. There were advisers in art, music, handicraft and physical education. All of these were taught widely in the schools, yet they tended to be subjects in which the general training college courses gave rather less grounding than in the teaching of English, geography, history or mathematics. The earliest appointment of advisory staff in domestic science, art, handwork and physical training dated from the early years of this century. In 1906 the Authority believed that the only way of finding the sort of physical education adviser it needed was by looking abroad and it came to an arrangement with the Danish Government to hire the services of one of their specialists for six months each year. The rather special needs of physical education led to more advisers being appointed in this subject than any other. Every pupil's timetable included physical education, despite the fact that it was possible that none of the teachers in many of the smaller schools had studied it and consequently a good deal of advice and support would be needed from outside the school.[52]

In the mid-1960s there was some pressure for the appointment of specialist inspectors or advisers in mathematics and science. The Education Officer resisted this, partly because he felt that it ran counter to the lessening of the importance of subject divisions in the work of the primary and modern schools. The fundamental reason for avoiding the singling out of any of the general subjects of the curriculum for such specialist attention was the danger that the person responsible for it might become 'liable to the occupational disease of the specialist which is that the subject becomes more important than the child'.[53] This movement away from the specialist was one reason why the reorganisation of the inspecting and advisory staff took the form it did during 1969 and 1970. The main reason why the reorganisation was undertaken was to adapt this essential element in the county's education service to the changing circumstances and changing ideas in the schools and colleges. The growth of larger schools meant that by 1968 eighty-seven heads of schools received salaries larger than those paid to inspectors. The latter had also lost ground by comparison with training college staffs. There were schools that were under-visited and neglected, partly because of long-standing vacancies. Thus any reorganisation would need to strengthen the structure of the advisory staff by creating an increased number of senior posts. Above all, 'a much more integrated attack is required upon the total education of the whole person and it is therefore increasingly inappropriate that the advisory force maintained by the Authority should itself represent disintegration into spheres of interest rather than a team of people who, after consultation, bring a co-ordinated influence to bear on current problems.'[54]

The main features of the reorganisation were that the advisory service should form four area teams, each under the general direction of an area adviser. The title of inspector was to be discontinued and the advisory hierarchy was to consist of a chief county adviser (the former senior county inspector), area advisers, area advisers in further education, senior advisers and advisers. The salary adjustments that were a condition of the introduction of the new arrangements had to be cleared by the Prices and Incomes Board. Thus during the last four years of the Authority's existence the function of each team of advisers was to give general support and encouragement to its schools, while each individual member of a team was responsible for a limited number of schools in the area. In most areas the team contained someone who could give advice on the teaching of a specific subject.[55] There can be no doubt but that the advisory staff was a principal and efficient agent of the Authority in influencing the quality of the education offered in its schools and colleges.

One further initiative designed to strengthen and support those schools which needed additional help was a novel scheme for the appointment of advisory teachers which received the approval of the Education Committee in 1968. There were a variety of reasons why schools might stand in need of temporary short-term help from a gifted teacher: domestic reasons might prevent members of staff from attending refresher courses and they might become set in their ways, or schools which had staffing difficulties might have to appoint an undue proportion of probationers. A small group of advisory teachers, not exceeding six in the first instance, were to be appointed for the purpose of giving such short-term help. They would be at the disposal of the Education Officer acting on the advice of the appropriate County Council inspector. Four of the six posts were in the Shipley, Castleford, Skipton and Hemsworth areas, another was appointed to develop nursery and play group work in the south of the Riding and the sixth was employed in assisting the horticultural advisory service. Two years later the Education Committee felt sufficiently confident of the success of this scheme to authorise the appointment of a further four advisory teachers. Apart from their work in schools, advisory teachers gave valuable help in teachers' centres (of which there were eighteen in the county) and with in-service training.[56] This particular development was really still in its infancy when overtaken by local government reorganisation, but some of the successor authorities have since taken the advisory teacher scheme further.

# CHAPTER VI

# Social and Welfare Provision
# 1902 – 74

## 1    MEALS AND MILK

Even before the introduction of compulsory education in the 1870s and 80s brought to notice poverty-stricken children whose semi-starved condition rendered their instruction impossible, voluntary organisations had experimented in providing school dinners and had established the positive contribution which sound feeding could make to the educational capacity of the children. It was reported in 1871 that 'the teachers agree in their opinion that those who are thus fed become more docile and teachable'.[1] The work of the voluntary organisations and the demand for some public provision became widespread towards the end of the nineteenth century, but it was against the background of the condition of many recruits for the army at the time of the South African War that the central government began to give more attention to this issue. The report in 1904 from an inter-departmental committee on physical deterioration[2] was directly responsible for the Provision of Meals Act in 1906.[3] This Act permitted LEAs to make available existing premises, equipment and staff for the provision of meals. They were bound to make a charge for meals unless satisfied that the parents were unable to pay. It was thought that the food itself for poor children would often be paid for by voluntary bodies. Where no such funds were available, LEAs could apply to the Board of Education for permission to raise a rate of up to ½d. to cover this cost.

The West Riding Education Committee had followed closely the progress of this measure and had appointed a special sub-committee to consider the Bill and to prepare evidence for the Commons Select Committee on it. The measure came into effect on 31 December 1906 and at its meeting in January the County Council delegated to the Education Committee the execution of the new legislation in the county area.[4] Its more dispersed population distribution meant that the need for this provision seemed less pressing in the county area than was the case in some of the larger Yorkshire cities such as Bradford, where 2,500 children were being fed by 1908. It was not until the summer of 1908 that the Education Committee finally decided that conditions in the West Riding required them to implement the provisions of the Act in certain districts. In the winter of 1908–9 the Board of Education agreed to make orders putting the Provision of Meals Act into effect in East and West Ardsley, Rothwell and the Worth Valley districts.[5] By 31 March 1909 just over 11,000 meals had been supplied, most of them without charge to the necessitous children.[6] The Act required LEAs to operate through canteen committees and in the Riding the district sub-committees of areas for which orders were obtained constituted themselves into canteen committees, co-opting for this purpose head teachers or other suitably qualified persons.[7]

The number of children receiving meals under the Act varied greatly from one year to another, depending on local conditions. In 1910 the divisional clerk in the Mexborough district reported that twenty children of casual labourers who were working short-time during exceptionally severe weather were attending school without sufficient food, and recommended that the Act should be invoked. The national coal strike of 1912 led to a large temporary increase in the number of meals provided. The Authority appointed a special sub-committee which visited the districts from which applications for meals had come and orders were made in respect of 128 parishes. During the last two weeks of March 81,350 meals were provided out of the rates, while in April no fewer than 222,564 were provided. Once the strike was over, barely more than 20,000 were supplied for the remaining eleven months of the financial year 1912–13.[8] In the early years the meal provided for necessitous children was usually breakfast rather than dinner and it seems to have consisted of tea or cocoa and bread (with butter or jam or dripping), buns or tea cakes.

The Education (Provision of Meals) Act of 1914 made three important changes in the existing law. It legalised the provision of meals during school holidays, repealed the limitation of expenditure to ½d. rate and abolished the need to apply to the Board of Education for an order sanctioning expenditure out of the rates on food.[9] Moreover, the Board made grant aid available for the first time to the extent of 50 per cent of the previous year's expenditure. The Government expected that the outbreak of war in August 1914 would produce an exceptional amount of distress among the industrial population and the Board issued a circular asking authorities to give early consideration to ways of dealing with a large and sudden increase in the provision of suitable meals for all elementary school children likely to require them.[10] The effect of the war was in fact to stimulate most of the industries of the West Riding and to usher in a period of prosperity. By the summer of 1915 the Education Committee reported that the provision of meals had been discontinued throughout the Riding.[11]

Industrial strife and depression in the years following the First World War again produced sharp fluctuations in the number of school meals provided. In the summer of 1919 the Education Committee agreed to put into effect the Provision of Meals Acts in a number of mining areas. During the miners' lockout of 1921 meals were provided on the most extensive scale to date and a supplementary estimate for £9,750 was agreed to meet the costs involved, even though these had been considerably reduced by gifts of food from voluntary relief funds, local subscriptions and voluntary service.[12] The total cost of meals provided at this time amounted to £10,642. By law the Authority was bound to recover the cost from the parents, unless it was satisfied that a parent was unable, by reason of circumstances other than his own default, to pay the amount. The difficulties involved in charging and collecting small sums from individual parents were considerable and four years later the chairman of the Education Committee reported that £6,773 had been collected and £3,476 excused, leaving a balance of £393 still outstanding.[13] Similar emergency arrangements continued to be made at the time of other disputes, most notably in the protracted miners' lockout of 1926.

The provision of meals in elementary schools on a more permanent basis in the Riding dates from 1929, when the district sub-committees for Hoyland, Featherstone and Wombwell asked for a medical survey of schoolchildren. This led to the establishment of a 'provision of meals centre' in each of these districts. From 1936 the County Medical Officer instituted regular investigations, which resulted in a considerable number of children being certified as in need of additional nourishment. Where there were not enough children to justify the setting up of a provision-of-meals centre, meals were provided on a contract basis by a café or by a housewife. One consequence of the Hadow reorganisation of elementary education by the setting up of senior schools for children over the age of eleven during the 1930s was that pupils attending these schools were sometimes drawn from quite large catchment areas and could not get home for a mid-day meal, and a number of school canteens were opened to provide meals on payment. Head teachers often ran these, with the Authority providing the necessary equipment and paying overhead costs. At the outbreak of the Second World War in 1939, 7,650 dinners were provided daily, 3,000 of these being provided on a contract basis.

Milk had been used from time to time as a valuable constituent in meals for necessitous children. The National Milk Publicity Council sponsored a scheme for the supply of milk to milk clubs in schools at a charge of a penny (0.4p) for a third of a pint, and from the end of the 1920s such clubs came to be set up in some of the county's schools, the Authority paying for the milk when the parents were too poor to be able to do so themselves. As part of the Government's proposals for the utilisation of surplus milk the Milk Marketing Board was given a subsidy, so that the price of a third of a pint of milk to schoolchildren could be reduced to a ½d. (0.2p). This new milk-in-schools scheme came into effect on 1 October 1934,[14] and was available to secondary as well as elementary pupils.

Quite apart from arrangements made in elementary schools under the Provision of Meals Acts, the need for providing a mid-day meal in secondary schools for pupils living some distance away from school had been accepted by the Authority since 1904. The steady growth in the numbers attending secondary schools necessitated the continuous development of this provision. School dinners were supplied on the basis that the pupils paid the full cost. In the case of scholarship holders, maintenance allowances for those eligible could take the form of a grant to cover the cost of school dinners, in whole or in part. In 1923–4, 341 scholarship holders received dinner grants to a total value of £2,374. In that year between 3,000 and 4,000 dinners were served daily and these were available in forty-five of the fifty-one maintained secondary schools. The price charged varied from 5d. (2p) in one school to 1s. (5p) in four schools; most schools charged 8d. or 9d. (3½p or 4p).[15]

It was the Second World War which made the school dinner a normal part of the life of every school. Outside the secondary schools it had been mainly the poor and undernourished children who were fed, and nationally school feeding 'had a bad reputation with parents, teachers and children alike . . . in many places, no "decent" child would attend'.[16] When the expected widespread destruction by bombing failed to materialise, the Board of Education began to urge local authorities to expand the school meals arrangements, particularly with the needs of evacuated children in mind, and if possible to make wider provision for local children as well. In the West Riding the Authority implemented the Circular as fully as it was able, relying on interesting more head teachers in school feeding with a view to gaining their co-operation and help in the buying of foodstuffs for canteens for which they themselves were to be largely responsible.[17]

Immediately after Clement Attlee became Lord Privy Seal, at the time when the war situation became very grave in June 1940, he urged on the Food Policy Committee of the Cabinet a massive expansion of school canteens to see that children got the right food within the limits imposed by wartime shortage and rationing. The Minister of Food, Lord Woolton, supported this call for expansion but the Board of Education felt such ideas were impractical and that the response from parents would be comparatively small. It argued that such communal feeding was 'outside the proper function of local education authorities'. The outcome of this clash of ministerial opinions was that the Board undertook a limited expansion forthwith and authorities were encouraged to follow this policy by being offered more generous grant aid.[18] This was the start of the major expansion of the school meals arrangements. As the food shortages became increasingly severe, the Board of Education was driven to ask authorities to expand the school dinner and school milk schemes over the next four years.[19]

These national developments were reflected in the West Riding. Overall there was an enormous expansion of facilities from 1940, each step in the expansion taking place as a consequence of a new initiative on the part of the Goverment or as a result of a particular local need becoming apparent in some part of the Riding. All kinds of accommodation – cloakrooms, domestic science rooms, church halls, etc. – were converted into emergency kitchens and canteens. The arrival of groups of evacuees at different stages in the war sometimes made necessary urgent local arrangements, as at Skipton where Christ Church Parochial Hall was hired in 1941 to provide dinners for evacuees from Brighton.[20] Successive waves of expansion served to throw additional burdens on teachers and in 1942 the Authority formally agreed with the West Riding Teachers' Association that there should be consultation in the initial stages of each new scheme for meals.[21]

The need to ensure that children received a balanced diet in spite of the food shortage also meant that the milk-in-schools scheme assumed a new importance. As in other parts of the country, dairies were showing an increasing reluctance to supply milk in third-pint bottles. The payment authorised by the Government did not make it worth their while to undertake the bottle washing and filling involved at a time when labour was in short supply and expensive. In the West Riding about 150,000 third-pint bottles were needed daily and about half of these were supplied under contract by co-operative societies and half by other suppliers. Between October 1941 and the following March the overall shortfall in supplies had amounted to about ten per cent of requirements and several co-operative societies had refused to renew their contracts to supply bottled milk, being willing only to supply the milk in bulk for schools to serve out as best they could. The Supplies Committee, therefore, sought to build a County Council dairy in Wakefield and if this venture were successful it planned to build three more. The Ministry of Food, however, made it clear through the Board of Education that it would not be appropriate for the West Riding to establish a milk bottling and distribution plant, since there were also severe shortages of machinery, labour and materials. An increase in the price which local authorities were permitted to pay to contractors overcame the problem and most dairies were again willing to supply the milk in bottled form.[22]

In coping with the rapid expansion of the meals service to protect children against the danger of malnutrition in wartime when labour and materials were in very short supply, the Authority often had to set up very large, extemporary, central kitchens in outbuildings to provide food for one or two thousand children daily, the food being transported to schools in containers and eaten on desks in classrooms. When it was considering the shape of education after the war in 1943, the Education Committee thought that priority should be given to the provision of kitchens and dining-halls at schools. The school dinner itself should be free and an integral part of the school day. The school dinner was valuable from the nutritional and from the social point of view, yet even in wartime some parents still refused to let their children have dinner at school out of a sense of independence – school feeding was still associated in many minds with being 'necessitous' in the Poor Law sense. The best way of overcoming this prejudice would be to make the meal free for all. The additional burden on teachers might be met by improving staffing ratios.[23] The question of making a charge for dinner was a national matter and the Government tended to regard this as part of the wider issue of family allowances. Eventually, in 1946, the Government postponed the introduction of free dinners for all 'until school canteen facilities are sufficient to meet the expected demand', which postponement has, in effect, proved to be of indefinite duration. School milk became free from August 1946.[24]

In the transition from war to peace, the Ministry overhauled arrangements for meals and their supervision. In conformity with Ministry suggestions, the West Riding authorised divisional officers to employ assistants to help teachers with dinner supervision in primary schools. It was also obliged to set about ending 'head teacher canteens', a scheme under which the heads ran the dinner service, financing it out of receipts from parents together with sums payable by the Authority, and for which the Authority also provided equipment. This arrangement was most often found in the smaller schools and the headmaster's wife was sometimes the cook. The Ministry required that this system should be replaced by central accounting of receipts and central payment of outgoings. Quite a number of heads regretted this change.[25]

Ministry control over school meals was tighter than that over any other aspect of the education service. After the war the local authorities were in some ways little more than agents running a system which was paid for by the

Treasury. The Ministry fixed to two decimal places the costs per meal (costed separately for food and overheads). Consequently an overspending of 1d. (0.4p) per meal in the West Riding represented an annual deficit of £10,000 chargeable to the local rates. A firm control over all aspects of the day-to-day running of the service was maintained by fierce scrutiny of every item of expenditure. The charge for meals and the minimum protein value per meal were fixed nationally; from 1964 parental income scales qualifying for the provision of free meals were also fixed by the Ministry. Equally close control was exercised by Whitehall over the school milk arrangements.

From 1954 the Ministry of Works no longer supplied the equipment for use in preparing school meals, and the Authority was able to specify its own requirements for new kitchen equipment. For much of the 1950s most dining still took place in classrooms or inadequately heated prefabricated buildings with much condensation. The increase in new school building and the upgrading of older premises meant that a decade later a widespread improvement had been achieved. The school dinner was also made more attractive in many schools by the replacement of linoleum-topped folding tables and backless benches by octagonal tables and wooden chairs. The increase in the number of pupils staying to school dinner which was so rapid in the war years continued at a more leisurely pace in the quarter of a century following 1945. In 1971 the Authority decided as a matter of policy to introduce a cafeteria and choice-of-menu service in secondary schools which was intended to replace the 'family service' pattern of meals at which the same food was served to all children. It was hoped that this would reduce the amount of food wasted.[26] In any case it was in line with the tendency to treat older children in a more adult manner at a time when the age of responsibility was being lowered from twenty-one to eighteen.

2    THE SCHOOL MEDICAL SERVICE

In contrast to the arangements for provisions of meals and milk, there was little tradition of voluntary effort associated with the medical requirements of schoolchildren. Before 1907 practically all the work which was carried out was initiated by LEAs, for although there was no statutory obligation for the authorities to conduct the medical inspection of pupils, they could do so by virtue of their powers concerning elementary education.[27] Although the West Riding Education Committee had made some headway in this respect before 1905, it had no system of inspection and the Authority clearly stood in the shadow of some neighbouring local education authorities, like those in Bradford, Leeds, Barnsley, Keighley, Wakefield and the East Riding, all of which by this time had appointed medical officers.[28] However, the position of the West Riding reflected the situation in most other LEAs, over two-thirds of which had also not made school medical inspection arrangements by the end of 1905.[29]

After negotiations with the Sanitary Committee a scheme was eventually formulated in November 1905, and the following year some of its proposals, including, for example, the notification and inspection of outbreaks of infectious diseases in schools, began to be implemented.[30] The Education (Administrative Provisions) Act of 1907 required LEAs to make arrangements for the medical inspection of schoolchildren, and in the West Riding a special sub-committee was established to set up the necessary machinery.[31] It was decided not to appoint a school medical officer but to expand the Health Department and utilise the staff of the County Medical Officer.[32] Similarly, at local level the existing local medical officers, many of whom were general practitioners, were made responsible for school work, although ten school medical inspectors were appointed by the Education Committee to work from various centres throughout the Riding.[33] The difficulties facing the embryonic school medical service were formidable, for there were approximately 200,000 children on the elementary school registers in an administrative area encompassing nearly 3,000 square miles, and index cards, measuring rods and other equipment had to be hastily provided.[34] These difficulties, in particular the enormous geographical area which had to be covered, help to explain why the West Riding lagged behind the county and non-county boroughs in the provision of medical inspection.

For administrative reasons medical inspections in the West Riding did not begin until September 1908.[35] The smooth running of the service depended on co-operation between the teachers and the school medical inspectors and the former quickly became involved in inspection by providing the inspectors with information relating to attendance, clothing, housing and home conditions, by notifying parents when their children were to be examined and by completing index cards.[36] From the outset it was clear that large numbers of children were in a poor physical condition. Between 1908 and 1916 on average less than half of the children examined each year (47.74 per cent) were free from defects. In 1909, for example, children in three age groups – five, seven and thirteen – were inspected and it was discovered that 21.49 per cent had verminous heads, 16.86 had defective vision (this figure excludes the five-year-old category), 15.78 had more than four carious teeth, whilst the incidence of skin diseases was an added cause for concern.[37] In addition, outbreaks of epidemic sickness created further difficulties for the medical service. In the year ending 31 March 1909, for example, no fewer than 258 schools were temporarily closed (in the previous year the figure had been 315) because of outbreaks of measles, scarlet fever, diphtheria and other infectious diseases.[38]

The logical corollary of the discovery of such a wide range of ailments was ameliorative action. Initially, however, school medical inspectors had extremely limited powers, for they could only dismiss children with infectious diseases from school and advise parents. Accordingly, it was decided that the scope of the service should be expanded, although the development of school clinics and the appointment of school nurses, which had taken place in some county boroughs, was not thought feasible for geographical reasons. Moreover, a feeling existed in the West Riding at this time that school nurses were of limited value. Consequently the Authority decided instead to promote the establishment of parochial Care of Children committees. The advantage of such committees was that they were to be based on the district sub-committee system and would therefore cover the whole of the administrative area of the Riding. In addition, because they were to be voluntary bodies consisting of selected members of the district sub-committees plus co-opted members, the Authority was not involved in any additional expenditure.

In 1909 J. R. Kaye, the County Medical Officer, indicated how the Care of Children committees were to be organised and what were to be their aims. They were to encourage the improvement of home conditions, to deal with 'exceptional' cases and to secure the assistance of such local agencies as 'the district nurse, Guilds of Help, charitable organisations, surgical aid societies and hospitals'.[39]

Between 1909 and the First World War the functions of the West Riding school medical service were considerably extended in other ways. Investigations were undertaken into the sanitary conditions of schools (cleansing and disinfecting premises, heating and ventilation) and the Authority's bacteriological laboratory was utilised in the control of infectious diseases.[40] In 1911 arrangements were made for the provision of spectacles at concessionary prices and the first eye clinics were formed to ensure that children with defective vision received appropriate treatment; this new departure led to the appointment of an eye specialist in 1914.[41] A major new development was the introduction of free dental treatment for schoolchildren in 1914. It was originally planned to appoint ten dentists but by the end of 1914 only three were in office.[42]

During the First World War the West Riding school medical service suffered the same inevitable dislocations as other sections of education and local government. Perhaps the most pronounced difficulty was the serious depletion of staff, which necessarily resulted in a reduction in the number of inspections so that only children known to be ailing were examined.[43] Nonetheless, although progress was retarded significant developments took place. The school nurses, for example, carried out their duties so successfully that many Care of Children committees considered their own activities to be superfluous. Large numbers of committees ceased to exist, although it had been intended that school nurses should merely be an adjunct to the committees.[44] Another advance concerned the extension of medical inspection to some eighteen secondary schools in 1914.[45] Thereafter the County school Medical Officer pressed for the adoption of inspection in all the Riding's secondary schools and this was finally achieved in 1920. There was a sharp rise in the incidence of tuberculosis during the war. Accordingly, the Education Committee, together with district tuberculosis officers, paid particular attention to the treatment of children suffering from the disease, and before the war had ended proposals had been ratified for the provision of a children's sanatorium and open-air schools.[46] The Committee had worked in close co-operation with the Public Health and Housing Committee on the tuberculosis issue and in July 1918 an important administrative development occurred when the two committees established a joint Child Welfare Sub-Committee to deal with the health of children from the pre-natal period to the end of their school lives.[47]

It was not until the passing of the Education Act in 1918 that education authorities were obliged both to diagnose and to treat certain medical defects in elementary schoolchildren and to provide for the medical inspection of pupils in secondary schools.[48] The West Riding, in common with many other LEAs, had therefore acted in advance of national legislation and the inter-war years saw both a steady expansion in existing medical facilities and the development of the service in new directions. The number of school clinics grew from twelve in 1919 to 117 in 1938, and the number of minor ailments which were treated increased from an annual average of 31,219 between 1921 and 1928 to an average of 49,975 per year in the period 1929–36. Several of the clinics (a total of seventy-two in 1938) were connected with the child welfare centres which grew up after the passing of the Maternity and Child Welfare Act in 1918, and an important relationship between the school medical service and the maternity and child welfare service was created in this period. There also emerged new types of clinics – ultra-violet light centres, aural clinics and institutions providing immunisation against diphtheria. This latter service began in 1931 and the West Riding was one of the first county authorities to offer immunisation, although some of the large county boroughs had pioneered this development.[49] The number of school nurses also grew and their duties became a vitally important element of the school medical service. Much of their work was carried out in the homes of children, particularly those who were socially disadvantaged, and the school nurses provided a valuable link between parents, the school and school clinics by acting as health visitors. The West Riding school dental service also saw large increases in its personnel, its workload and in the number of children treated.[50] Even so, the scope of the dental service in the West Riding was less extensive than in many urban and county authorities where the school population was less widely distributed. In 1938, for example, the number of children treated, expressed as a percentage of the total number of scholars, was 40 in the urban authorities, 38 in the county authorities but only 29 in the West Riding.[51]

From 1920 onwards a 'Health Week' was organised each year to improve health and hygiene, and in 1924 there emerged proposals for the hospital treatment of children suffering from squints, ear diseases and disorders affecting the adenoids and the tonsils.[52] Two years later, however, it was found that the scheme was inoperable because parents could not afford to pay the hospital fees.[53] Accordingly, on the advice of the Child Welfare Sub-Committee, the Education Committee agreed in July 1926 to make a grant to hospitals which treated children suffering from these complaints. It was also agreed that parents were not to be asked to refund any part of the cost of treatment.[54] The Board of Education acquiesced in this policy and between 1 April and 1 October 1927 1,899 children received treatment at voluntary hospitals in the East and West Ridings.[55] Thereafter hundreds of children each year were able to take advantage of the scheme. Efforts to combat tuberculosis continued unabated, particularly in the industrial south of the Riding where the incidence of the disease was particularly high. After a considerable amount of local pressure Sir George Newman, Chief Medical Officer of the Board of Education, finally opened the county's first open-air school at Wombwell on 2 June 1932.[56] The school, which accommodated sixty children, had a southern aspect and was equipped with windows 'so fitted that the rooms can be exposed to the fresh air when conditions permit'.[57] In providing for the health and welfare of its children the West Riding County Council was prepared to co-operate with neighbouring authorities. In 1937, for example, the County Council, in liaison with the county boroughs of Sheffield, Doncaster, Rotherham and Barnsley, established the foundations of the child guidance service by opening a clinic at Sheffield to provide 'skilled psychological advice on children who present problems of behaviour or of disordered personality or even those children who have peculiar difficulties in school work which are not due to mere dullness or mental defect'. The clinic was opened in August 1937 and by the end of that year had dealt with 94 cases, fifty-six of which were from the West Riding. The Board of Education was enthusiastic about the venture, for at this time such clinics were rare – two years later there were only twenty-four fully staffed and twenty-four partially staffed child guidance clinics in the country.[58]

During the Second World War the school medical service was put under severe pressure, although the West Riding County Council, in common with other local authorities, endeavoured to maintain the service to the best of its ability and to comply with the directives emanating from central government.[59] With the evacuation of children from the cities in case of air attacks came the serious danger that the incidence of some infectious diseases, especially diphtheria, would quickly reach epidemic proportions as urban carriers came into contact with the more susceptible rural population. Consequently, the Ministry of Health and the Board of Education asked authorities to arrange for the mass immunisation of children against diphtheria. An extensive campaign was launched in 1941–2 and the West Riding played its part in this national drive by securing the immunisation of children and by promoting local propaganda.[60] The campaign was extremely successful and the total number of diphtheria notifications in England, Wales and Scotland was reduced from 63,192 in 1941 to 24,275 in 1945.[61] The West Riding Authority also provided for the treatment of cases of infectious and other communicable diseases, including measles and whooping cough, which under normal circumstances did not require hospital attention.[62] The cost of this treatment was borne by the Ministry of Health. However, the limitations on the normal service, the dislocation caused by the evacuation of children, the large number of defects discovered in the evacuees, staffing shortages and the special problems caused by contagious diseases such as pediculosis, scabies and impetigo all contributed towards demands for the immediate extension of the service.

These demands were largely met by the provisions of the Education Act of 1944 which broke new ground by requiring all LEAs to provide medical and dental inspection and treatment in all types of maintained primary and secondary schools and by making medical inspection compulsory for the child.[63] The local authorities regarded this as an invitation to establish a full range of consultant clinics. However, the National Health Service Act of 1946, which came into force in 1948, enabled LEAs to make arrangements with the regional hospital boards for free specialist and hospital treatment of children and made the Boards responsible for appointing all specialists.[64]

This was regarded as a retrograde step by the West Riding County Medical Officer, who opposed the separation of responsibility for preventative and curative medicine. Nonetheless, an agreement was concluded between the school medical service and the Boards and in the post-war era there was a general transfer of many of the service's specialist clinics to the hospital authorities. The only clinics provided on a large scale by the West Riding school health service in the period 1948–74 were those concerned with child guidance, speech therapy and minor ailments. An important exception, however, was the establishment of two audiology clinics by the West Riding in 1961, in response to the growing concern about hearing loss in children. The statistics relating to the history of West Riding school clinics in this period reveal two principal developments: a drastic reduction in the number of cases treated once the National Health Service offered free treatment, and a sharp increase in the importance of child guidance, indicating an increasing awareness of psychological maladies among children.

Medical inspection continued to be the mainstay of the school health service. There were several changes in the arrangements for inspection, one of the most important of which was the reduction in the number of routine examinations in the 1960s in favour of selective medicals. Routine inspections of children entering the primary schools continued because of their overwhelming medical and educational importance but the inspection of other age groups became largely selective. Regular visits of school nurses to conduct hygiene inspections and vision and hearing tests continued, however, leaving doctors free to deal with serious cases. These changes were accompanied by the availability of a wide range of specialist clinics, the eradication of epidemic diseases through immunisation and national developments such as the growth of the welfare state, the provision of free medical treatment and a tremendous improvement in living conditions. Not surprisingly, therefore, there was an enormous and inevitable improvement in the health of schoolchildren in the post-war era.

From the end of the Second World War until 1956 the school dental service was dogged by staff shortages, largely because the remuneration was considerably lower than in National Health Service practice. Thereafter, however, a more efficient use of manpower was arranged through the provision of permanent dental clinics, which meant that dentists were no longer peripatetic and did not have to arrange for the transportation of their equipment from school to school. The first dental clinic was established in 1937 and by 1972 fifty-eight clinics were in operation. The shortage of staff meant that the number of children inspected declined significantly (from 117,611 in 1948 to 71,978 in 1950) and although there was some improvement in the 1950s, the

1948 figure was not surpassed until 1958. For the years that followed there was a gradual improvement and by 1972 205,068 children were inspected.[65] The workload of the dental service therefore increased substantially but the dental health of children was a permanent source of anxiety. The proliferation of sugar-based foods and sweets, which were particularly attractive to children, prevented a substantial reduction in the percentage of children requiring treatment.[66] No survey of the work of the West Riding School dental service would be complete without reference to the orthodontic service. In 1953 a centre with laboratory apparatus was established at Wakefield and clinics were also set up at Brighouse, Castleford, Harrogate and Tadcaster which were equipped for minor orthodontic work. The orthodontic service made considerable progress after the early 1950s and became one of the leading services of its kind in the country.[67]

### 3   SPECIAL SCHOOLS:
#### MENTALLY AND PHYSICALLY HANDICAPPED CHILDREN

After 1870 there was a growing awareness not only of the existence of a large number of underfed and unhealthy children in schools but also of a considerable proportion of pupils who were epileptic or mentally and physically 'defective'. The state, however, did nothing to improve the plight of such children until 1899 when the Defective and Epileptic Children Act was passed, which permitted school boards to provide special education, although few did so.[68] In the West Riding no school board or urban and rural district council in the administrative county was providing special classes or schools for handicapped or epileptic children when the 1902 Act was implemented. Each authority had only a few 'defective' children and considered that the formation of classes or the financing of boarding-out accommodation was unjustifiable.[69]

Unfortunately the provision of special education for handicapped children remained inadequate in the Riding for the next four decades. Initially the Authority claimed that it was preoccupied with the enormous task of bringing the 1902 Act into operation and was not 'able to give the matter the proper attention'.[70] By 1906 the Education Committee was asserting that as a Royal Commission on the Care and Control of the Feeble-Minded had been established, it had 'stayed [its] hands' as it was 'desirous of ascertaining the views of the commissioners before taking any definite step'.[71] It was not until 1 January 1915 that the Elementary Education (Defective and Epileptic

Children) Act 1914 came into operation and local authorities were compelled to make suitable provision for the education of mentally handicapped children over seven years of age.[72] The West Riding now accepted that a residential school in the county would 'ultimately' be needed.[73] Three years later LEAs were obliged to provide educational facilities for physically handicapped children.[74]

The West Riding tackled the problem of handicapped children in these early years (1902-18) by relying exclusively on the facilities provided by other authorities throughout the country. The latter, however, did not possess enough places to cater for the number of children involved, even if the Riding had been prepared or able to undertake the necessary expenditure. Thus in 1906, when it was recognised that there were over 250 'strikingly defective' children in the Riding, only eight were in attendance at special schools.[75] Similarly, although there were approximately forty cases of severe epilepsy, only one child was provided for and in succeeding years the total number of handicapped children dealt with increased only slowly to sixty-five in 1913 and to 104 in 1916.[76] Before the 1914 Act was passed the Authority admitted that there was a general lack of accommodation but vindicated itself by claiming that 'having regard to the permissive character of the Act of 1899, Local Education Authorities hesitate to expend money on buildings'.[77] In any case the Authority could not compel parents to send their children to special classes or schools unless these were easily accessible. As a result, many parents in rural areas refused to send their children away from home.[78]

In the inter-war years the West Riding, along with other LEAs, continued its piecemeal approach to special education. The number of children in special schools by March 1921 was 103 and by March 1939 the figure was 239, although the total number of cases diagnosed rose each year, and in 1931, for example, there were 667 children who were mentally handicapped or epileptic.[79] In many ways developments in the Riding reflected the national situation, for there were 13,563 mentally handicapped children in special schools throughout the country in 1914 and by 1939 the number was 17,000, although as early as 1924 twice that number had been shown to be feeble-minded in returns by the LEAs.[80] During this period no special school for mentally 'defective' children was built by the West Riding and the same inactivity was evinced elsewhere.[81] Quite apart from parental resistance to a child's being sent to what came to be called 'the daft school', the setting up of the Wood Committee, which sat between 1924 and 1929 to examine the educational provision for mentally handicapped children, led to delay. Since its recommendations might affect the structure of special education, authorities were unwilling to take action until the Committee reported, and indeed the Board of Education Circular 1927 encouraged them not to make any expenditure in this direction. The Wood Committee made the important recommendation that within the ordinary school system various types of specialised provision should be made for one comprehensive group of backward children, but shortly afterwards the international economic depression deepened and building projects were again shelved.[82]

The Education Act of 1944 made special educational treatment part of the general duties of LEAs, which now had to provide education for all children in accordance with their ages, aptitudes and abilities. This development was to some extent inspired by the report of the Wood Committee and differed fundamentally from earlier educational legislation, which had segregated the handicapped from the rest of society and had dealt with their education quite separately. The West Riding Education Authority had become fully aware of the acute shortage of special education accommodation in the county, and after consultations with other Yorkshire authorities, it incorporated ambitious schemes for the building of several new schools in the Development Plan.[83] Proposals were advanced for seven day schools and a similar number of boarding schools for educationally sub-normal boys and girls, four boarding schools for delicate children, four for physically handicapped children, four for maladjusted children and three for epileptic, partially deaf, educationally sub-normal and deaf children. However, detailed problems involving the acquisition of suitable properties, finance and staffing arose; by 1954 no day special schools existed in the county and the Authority had only opened four boarding schools catering for the worst group of the mentally handicapped, comprising some 200 children.[84]

The next two decades saw an enormous expansion of the special educational provision. Arrangements were made for home tuition for a number of particularly delicate and ailing children and child guidance clinics assisted in special educational activities, including the establishment of remedial centres for children of normal ability who, for a variety of reasons, had become educationally retarded. Each year the school medical officers decided which children required special school placement and which could be educated in normal schools, and the progress of children attending special schools was constantly assessed.[85] Between 1954 and 1964 four new day schools for the educationally sub-normal were opened and by 1974 eight more had been built, but the increased provision is perhaps best illustrated by the rise in the number of children attending special schools – in 1949 the figure was 507, in 1958, 1,345 and in 1972, 3,605.[86] Notwithstanding this increase in facilities, in accordance with the principles of the 1944 Act, handicapped children were educated wherever possible in normal schools, support being provided for teachers and parents by the staff of the school health service.

Under the 1944 Act a procedure was prescribed for ascertaining which children were ineducable and were therefore the responsibility of the health or hospital authorities. Many parents found this arrangement distressing and the Education (Handicapped Children) Act of 1970 abolished this procedure and transferred responsibility for all handicapped children to the LEAs. In the West Riding this immediately doubled the work of the Special Schools Sub-Committee, for the Education Authority now assumed responsibility for an additional 1,100 children, some of whom were severely sub-normal.[87] Inevitably the Education Committee had to face difficult administrative problems, as a section of the Medical Department's staff had to be absorbed and additional classrooms and equipment had to be provided. The new duties of the Authority were indicative of the tremendous progress which had been made since the early years of the century when the West Riding had only provided education and training for a handful of handicapped children.

Both nationally and locally blind and deaf children fared rather better than those with other handicaps. As early as 1893 the Elementary Education (Blind and Deaf Children) Act made it compulsory for blind and deaf children to attend schools, and school boards were given the duty of providing education for them.[88] Most of the children were educated at voluntary schools and the boards and the state were made jointly responsible for reimbursing these institutions. Thus by the early years of this century the vast majority of blind and deaf children were being educated. Before the Appointed Day the school boards in the West Riding had arranged for the education of thirty-eight blind and fifty-nine deaf children, and before the end of the First World War the Education Committee was providing education for every blind and deaf child within its administrative area.[89] In addition, the Authority assisted a number of blind children over the age of sixteen by taking up its powers under Part II of the Act of 1902. These powers enabled the Higher Education Sub-Committee to award technical exhibitions to children for whom the Education Committee had previously undertaken responsibility.[90] After the 1914–18 war, however, the duties of the Committee with respect to the blind were greatly extended by the Blind Persons' Act of 1920, for the education service became responsible for the care and training of all blind persons in the county.[91] The Act was administered through the existing approved societies for the blind, and training, home teaching and visiting were provided. These duties were not relinquished until immediately after the Second World War, when they were transferred to the Health Service as part of the important national changes in the administration of health and education.

In the post-war era the education of blind and deaf children in the West Riding continued to be carried out largely in special schools run by neighbouring authorities. Nonetheless, there was one development which took place within the Riding itself. This concerned the establishment of a boarding school for children throughout the county suffering from the double handicap of deafness and educational sub-normality. Proposals for the school at Bridge House, near Harewood, were agreed in 1947 and by 1949 fifteen boys were being cared for.[92] At Bridge House boys were able to 'live in a school environment and be assessed in a way that [was] hardly possible anywhere else',[93] and the school therefore made a significant contribution to the county's special education facilities.

## 4   THE YOUTH EMPLOYMENT SERVICE

Following the passing of the Labour Exchanges Act in 1909,[94] LEAs were given the opportunity of providing an employment service themselves for those leaving elementary schools by the Education (Choice of Employment) Act 1910.[95] Within ten years the Ministry of Labour had appointed and was financing juvenile advisory committees in 130 areas. In 100 other areas LEAs had chosen to take up their powers under the Act of 1910 and had set up Choice of Employment Committees acting as sub-committees, with costs shared between the LEA itself and the Ministry of Labour. The conflict between the 'education' and the 'Ministry of Labour' interests led to an inquiry into the position by Viscount Chelmsford on behalf of the Prime Minister and he reported in 1921. Until his report[96] was published and a decision on it taken by the Government, applications for powers under the Act of 1910 were frozen by the Board of Education. Thus when in 1919 the West Riding decided to take up its powers under the 1910 Act, submitted a draft scheme and even appointed a Juvenile Employment Sub-Committee, the Board of Education postponed any approval of the scheme and consequently no grants could be claimed. The Education Committee was, therefore, 'reluctantly compelled to abandon the idea of carrying out any of the provisions of the above-mentioned Act'.[97]

In order to avoid conflicting and overlapping administration, Chelmsford recommended that any LEA exercising its powers under the Education Acts of 1910 and 1918 to enter this field should also undertake the administration of the Unemployment Insurance scheme for all persons up to the age of eighteen. All LEAs were to be given six months in which to make up their minds about whether to undertake this two-fold duty or leave it all with the

Ministry of Labour. The Board of Education terminated its approval of any existing schemes as from 30 June 1922.[98]

The prospect of having to undertake the administration of the Unemployment Insurance Act deterred the West Riding from pursuing this matter any further. Since any unemployed young person was required to report to the local office (whether under the Ministry of Labour or the Education Committee) daily in person to qualify for benefit, this would have involved the establishment of additional offices and clerical staff and, in effect, a duplication of the labour exchange machinery which the Ministry of Labour had already set up. The Committee felt that while these proposals might meet conditions in the large boroughs, they were quite unsuited to large counties in which circumstances varied as much as they did in the West Riding. When the Authority had put forward its scheme in 1919 it had also intended to provide part-time day continuation schools in the near future under the Education Act of 1918. This development would in any case have made frequent and close consultation with employers essential, in order to adjust arrangements for attendance so as to meet industrial conditions. But two years later the prospect of establishing and requiring attendance at day continuation schools had receded and this reason for consultation with employers had disappeared: 'The grounds remaining for such consultation would thus have relation mainly to juvenile employment and unemployment insurance; and there is not the same argument for linking this service with the education service proper.'[99] Two years later, when it appeared that some Part III authorities in the county themselves wished to exercise these powers, the county agreed to take the necessary formal action as a Part II authority to enable them to exercise on behalf of the County Council its powers in this matter within their own areas, on the understanding that any expenses incurred would not fall on county funds and that any repayments from the Ministry of Labour under the Unemployment Insurance Act should be made directly to the Part III authorities.[100]

Although not operating juvenile employment bureaux, the county did make some educational provision for unemployed boys and girls in the 1920s and 1930s. The Ministry of Labour offered LEAs a grant of 75 per cent of the total cost of centres and classes expressly for the unemployed. At times when the amount of juvenile unemployment increased markedly, the Ministry of Labour increased its grant to 100 per cent. Up to 1934 those between the ages of sixteen and eighteen years who were in receipt of unemployment benefit were required to attend as a condition of benefit, and those between fourteen and sixteen were encouraged to attend on a voluntary basis. No authority existed to require the attendance of the unemployed aged between fourteen and sixteen until the Unemployment Act of 1934 was passed which contained such powers. The Act also placed on LEAs a statutory duty to organise and conduct courses of instruction for unemployed juveniles. Before 1934 some classes that were started had had to be closed after a week or so because attendances could not be maintained on a voluntary basis. Even some of those over sixteen who stood to lose their benefit preferred to do so rather than attend classes.[101] During the later 1930s junior instruction centres became a semi-permanent feature in some parts of the Riding. At Mexborough an average of 400 boys were in attendance, while at the Pontefract centre the average stood at about 200 boys in 1935 and 1936.[102] The increased industrial activity and prosperity which the Second World War brought with it put an end to these activities.

The Education Act of 1944 revived the prospect of day continuation schooling for all to the age of eighteen and the Authority re-opened the question of its setting up an employment service for school leavers. The scheme which was adopted for the juvenile employment offices to be housed ultimately in the county colleges which, it was still hoped, were to be set up to bring into effect the legislation for day continuation schooling. The youth employment offices were thus regarded as discharging an essentially educational function and were therefore to 'be linked closely in this way with a main feature of the Further Education Development Plan'.[103] At committee level the issue began to receive attention in the autumn of 1947, when the Director of Education for Rotherham inquired whether the County Council was going to exercise its powers in this field or whether it was willing to allow Rotherham to administer the service in county areas adjacent to the borough. The Education Officer suggested to the Education Committee that it should itself organise a service to cover the whole of the administrative county and work began on drafting a scheme. Proposals were considered and approved by the Policy Sub-Committee at its meeting in January 1948. These provided for the service to be administered through the divisional executives and county divisional areas, with a trained juvenile employment officer on the staff of each divisional office. There were also to be area juvenile employment sub-committees. An administrative assistant was to be appointed to assist in the preparation and establishment of the service and he would subsequently become the Juvenile Employment Officer for the county.[104] The full model scheme was sent forward for approval by the County Council in May 1948, although the Employment and Training Act of 1948[105] required certain adjustments in the scheme. The new Act also established 12 January 1949 as the last day on which authorities not at present exercising youth employment powers might submit proposals for doing so.[106]

When the scheme came into being in 1949 it had twenty-three full-time offices, forty-one subsidiary offices and a total staff of seventy-two. This proved to be excessive and in 1951 the Committee decided to reduce the number of staff to sixty-one, with nineteen full-time and twenty-nine sub-sidiary offices. The constitution of youth employment committees was also revised in 1951. While education interests felt keenly that there was an essential unity about choice of employment, continued education and leisure-time provision for young people, any employment service would clearly fail in its purpose if it distanced itself from the world of employment. It seemed clear that the initial suggestions for membership of youth employment committees gave too little weight to this latter point and in December 1950 the Committee instructed the Education Officer to have discussions with the Ministry of Labour on ways of according more adequate representation to employers and employees. The consultations led to the production of a revised list of nominating bodies for employers' and employees' representatives. The local youth employment sub-committees were to be constituted in the following proportions:[107]

| Body | Representation |
|---|---|
| Authority | 4 |
| Employers | 4 |
| Employees | 4 |
| Teachers | 4 |
| Co-opted | 2 |
| | 18 |

During its early years the youth employment service's work was largely confined to those leaving the modern schools. It did not have staff suitably qualified to meet the more specialised needs of the grammar and technical schools. In 1949 the Ministry of Labour 'intimated the desirability of their specialised vocational guidance service for grammar and technical schools continuing to be administered by them . . .', and it was agreed that this should continue until such time as the Authority could extend its own service.[108] Both Hyman and Clegg wanted to expand the service to include this more specialised work, but while the existing staff were able to concentrate on the needs of local businesses and undertakings, they were not familiar with the sort of careers that sixth formers might expect to move to. The story of the development of the youth employment service in the 1950s was not one of 'roses all the way' and after one of the bouts of questioning that arose the county decided to make the two additional appointments thought necessary if it were to take over the vocational guidance of the older school leaver from the Ministry of Labour. It took over this service in 1956.

By 1964 the service was staffed centrally by a County Youth Employment Officer and two deputies, along with the two careers advisory officers concerned with guidance for older school leavers, a senior clerk and a clerk-typist. At the district level there were eleven area youth employment officers, thirty assistant youth employment officers and over sixty clerks and clerical assistants. Area youth employment officers exercised a good deal of independence in their day-to-day work and the County Youth Employment Officer's supervision really did no more than ensure that the broad lines of county policy were followed. Since many of the larger employers in the geographical county of the West Riding were situated in county boroughs which had their own youth employment services, it was essential for there to be close co-operation with the borough youth employment officers if careers advisory work with leavers was to achieve its logical aim of placing them in employment. Continuing close relations with the boroughs were the responsibility of the relevant area youth employment offices. Thus the Calder youth employment officer was concerned with maintaining contact with employers in Huddersfield and Halifax and the Don Valley area officer with those in Doncaster. This decentralised approach was really the only practical way of approaching youth employment and careers advisory work in such a large and varied authority as the West Riding, and in a report on the careers advisory service in 1964 inspectors from the Central Youth Employment Executive commented on the excellent relations which had been established by some area officers with employers. Virtually throughout this period, however, the provision of adequate careers advice for the older and better qualified school leaver was a matter of great difficulty and, perhaps, of some concern. The localised emphasis which best suited the needs of the majority of leavers did not lend itself to progress in work with older pupils. If the local officer (whose main work was – and was known by the schools to be – with pupils of lower academic attainment) were to undertake with older pupils blocks of work too small for the acquisition of useful expertise, this was not likely to produce a satisfactory service. At the same time, the small specialised staff at the central office was handicapped by its very smallness and by its geographical situation, which virtually excluded any extensive participation in follow-up interviews, the interviewing of casual callers, placement in employment and the review of progress of young employees. It was to meet this situation that the Education Committee authorised in 1967 an increase in the number of specialist careers officers from two to eight and decided that they would be located away from the county headquarters in groups of areas.[109]

During the last few years of its existence, the Authority transferred responsibility for this service from the Assistant Education Officer for Further Education to the equivalent officer for Secondary Education. This was a logical development, which recognised the increasing importance of advice before leaving school and of the involvement with the secondary schools of those concerned with employment. A closer and more continuous relationship was established with the schools, while an increasing number of teachers who are concerned with giving careers advice attended courses provided by the Authority.[110]

## 5  SPECIAL WORK IN SECTORS OF EDUCATIONAL DEPRIVATION SINCE 1944

Immediately after the war the Committee used its powers under the 1944 Act to supply needy children with shoes and clothing, to provide boarding accommodation and to set up a scheme of aid for pupils from families with low incomes. Under this scheme children from poor families qualified for free school dinners, grants for the purchase of school uniforms and maintenance allowances if they were older than the statutory school leaving age. The Children's Act of 1948 made the Home Office responsible for children in public care, and local authorities were required to set up Children's Committees with professional Children's Officers. In the West Riding the implementation of this Act was put in the hands of the Health Committee and a twenty-seven-man Children's Committee was created.[111] Experience soon showed that there were serious gaps in the legislative provisions of 1944 and 1948, and several categories of children in difficulties who urgently required help fell outside the scope of this basic national framework. The West Riding, led by the Education Officer, focused its attention on these problem sectors in the post-war period and sought to find means of helping these unhappy children.

From the 1960s Clegg put a series of important but depressing memoranda concerned with distressed, discarded and difficult children to the Committee.[112] These children usually came from inadequate homes and aften lived in deprived neighbourhoods. It was estimated that they constituted 10–12 per cent of the total school population and represented a tragic waste of human potential.[113] Some of these youngsters rebelled against society, and their aggressive and disruptive behaviour caused enormous problems for their teachers; others became completely withdrawn, which was equally worrying. Through articles, books, speeches and broadcasts the Education Officer tried to focus national attention on these neglected groups of children. He often illustrated the nature of the problem by quoting several appalling case studies drawn from experience in the West Riding.[114] He recognised that social and educational deprivation was more highly concentrated in some parts of the county than others, and he was determined that there should be special help for schools in these areas. Accordingly, in the 1960s and 1970s the West Riding became one of the country's leading exponents and practitioners of compensatory education.

The Education Officer was well aware that many of the national reports on education (Early Leaving, 1954; Crowther, 1959; Newsom, 1963; Robbins, 1963; Plowden, 1966) had shown that at every level of education there were those who were placed in a disadvantageous position through social inequality. Plowden, however, was the first report to recommend a plan of action which concentrated on districts of acute social deprivation, to be known as Educational Priority Areas (EPAs). Plowden advocated positive discrimination in favour of EPA schools and proposed that these schools should be given extra help with their buildings, staffing, books and equipment. In 1968 it was agreed to implement this recommendation in the West Riding, using local resources.[115] In future, schools designated by the Committee as 'in special need' were to qualify for extra help and attention. Provision was made for these schools to have additional teaching staff and more non-teaching assistance. Their capitation allowances were to be increased and priority was to be given to nursery education and play group schemes in the neighbourhoods of these schools. Schools in 'dirty' areas were to become eligible for more frequent redecoration, and funds were to be made available to install baths or showers where necessary.[116] At about the same time the DES launched its own scheme and EPA schools designated by the DES qualified for additional help from central government funds. The DES, however, adopted a much more stringent definition of an EPA school than the Authority, for by 1971 only thirteen primary schools in the West Riding were designated EPA schools by the DES but over 100 such schools were receiving extra help from Wakefield.[117]

During the 1960s and 1970s an extraordinarily diverse educational welfare programme was implemented. The Committee attempted to promote close collaboration between the education, medical and child care services, as well as repeatedly requesting information from the schools about children at risk and cases of violent indiscipline. Moreover, the importance of community involvement and the necessity for well-maintained and tidy schools was consistently emphasised. In addition to these general policies, more specific measures were taken. In 1970 an Assistant Education Officer was appointed with special responsibility for children in difficulty, and the following year a working party on compensatory education was set up.[118] This consisted of teachers and elected members in equal numbers and its recommendations were normally accepted by the Education Committee. In October 1971, for example, the working party suggested that social welfare should be organised on a school 'pyramid' basis (with contributory primary and middle schools as the base and a secondary school as the apex). This proposal was accepted and in some large schools, or pyramids of schools, consultative welfare committees were formed, consisting of teachers, welfare officers, medical officers, social workers and other representatives.[119] The consultative committees were able to consider the problems of individual children and to suggest appropriate treatment. The Authority allocated a considerable sum to compensatory education, and eventually £60,000 per annum was provided in an effort to overcome some of the difficulties which beset disadvantaged children.[120] This money was expended in several different ways. Liaison teachers were appointed at large schools, or pyramids of schools, and their role was to act as teacher–social workers and investigate those children whose education was being retarded by home circumstances.[121]

One of the interesting experiments conducted in the West Riding in this field of educational provision was the EPA 'action research' project set up at Denaby Main. Altogether five of these projects, which were financed by the Social Science Research Council and the DES, were established under the overall direction of A. H. Halsey.[122] Four were sited in the centres of large cities, but it was felt that Denaby Main in the heart of the Yorkshire coalfield exhibited most clearly the characteristics of an EPA as described in the Plowden Report. These included the existence of a large proportion of semi-skilled and unskilled manual workers, large families in receipt of state welfare benefits, overcrowding, poor school attendance and truancy, and a larger-than-average proportion of retarded, disturbed or handicapped pupils.

In January 1969 the West Riding project began with the arrival of the project director, Michael Harvey, although the research officer, G. A. N. Smith, and his wife had started a little earlier.[123] The project team were provided with a wide brief – to improve educational standards and teacher morale in the area, and to involve parents and the community more closely in the educational process.[124] However, because the project was only scheduled to run for three years, and because of limited financial resources, it was decided to conduct small-scale schemes and to concentrate resources on relatively few children.[125] Both the schools and the project organisers agreed that pre-school provision should be the major priority and, with the assistance of the West Riding Education Authority and the Government urban aid programme, they provided extensive facilities.[126] A policy of positive discrimination was employed and those schools which were regarded as being most in need received the major share of the resources.[127] Heavy emphasis was also placed on improving reading ability and a reading programme was implemented 'geared to the needs of the child who [had] failed to read by the end of the primary stage'.[128] About half of the project's resources were channelled into these two schemes. The other main development was the promotion of firmer links between educational institutions in the district, and between them and the community. The focal point of this aspect of the project was Red House, which 'increasingly became the project itself'.[129] Red House was opened as a special centre in January 1970, the cost of purchasing and adapting the building being met by a grant from the Joseph Rowntree Charitable Trust, and the salary of the Warden and his wife being paid by the Oxford University Chest. The scheme, which included the provision of residential accommodation for children, received the full support both of the Authority and of Sir Alec Clegg, who, in his book *Children in Distress* (1968), had advocated the establishment of residential hostels to provide short-term facilities for schoolchildren during periods of crisis at home. The Authority provided more than moral support, however, for it agreed to accept responsibility for the running and maintenance of the centre.[130]

The centre at Red House fulfilled a number of roles and the team and their helpers engaged in several different activities: they helped to co-ordinate the work of the Education, Medical and Social Services Departments; they provided a home visiting service; they offered assistance, including residential provision, for pupils of all ages who were not responding 'normally' at school and who were often under duress at home; they provided general assistance and support to primary schools (transport, help with under-achievers and workspace, for example); they established links with students at Scawsby College with the aim of promoting mutual assistance between college and schools in the EPA; and they also provided connections with the youth service in the area, encouraging home–school relationships and fostering general community development.[131] Although the project came to an end in December 1971, Red House continued to operate with the financial backing of the Authority, which in turn received grants under the Government's urban aid programme.[132]

The West Riding EPA project made a useful contribution to compensatory education and underlined the necessity of mobilising the community and of relating the school to the community, especially in deprived areas. The project organisers concluded that although most of their work had been on a small scale, there were indications that several schools were adopting some of the methods developed at Red House and that 'schools who in the past have perhaps accepted that they would be overlooked, have become militant in their demands for new resources'.[133] Although the project did not lead to a dramatic change in the levels of performance in the schools, it did create a new atmosphere in which schools were willing to experiment with new techniques and developments. The Authority believed the project to have been well worth while and to have brought about some noteworthy achievements. As a direct outcome of the activities at Red House, for example, the Committee appointed pre-school home visitors in other areas.

Another sector for which the Authority first made provision in this period was immigrant education. The West Riding received comparatively few immigrants in the years following 1963, when the first large-scale arrivals of non-English-speaking people in this country took place. In January 1967 there were approximately 131,000 immigrant children in Britain, but DES figures revealed that only 841 of these were in the West Riding (0.3 per cent of the county's school population).[134] Nonetheless, the problems which the Education Committee faced were considerable and were not revealed by the general statistics, for the rapid influx was largely confined to two areas, Batley and Keighley. The Authority was naturally concerned that the misleading picture presented by the overall figures should be corrected. This was particularly the case in 1968, when the Government allocated £3m in aid to areas of high immigration. When the West Riding was denied any assistance under the scheme Sir Alec Clegg felt constrained to write to Sir Herbert Andrew, Permanent Under-Secretary of State at the DES, informing him that the figure of 0.3 disguised the fact that in the spring of 1968 7.2 per cent of the children attending schools in Batley were immigrants.[135] Thus, although the West Riding was not regarded as an area of high immigration, the Education Committee's difficulties with Pakistani and Indian children in Batley and Keighley were similar to those experienced by such neighbouring local authorities as Bradford, Leeds and Huddersfield, which were renowned for the size of their ethnic minorities.

The assimilation of Pakistani and Indian children into West Riding schools did not really begin to constitute a serious problem until about 1965, when the number of children involved began to rise steeply. The difficulty was that particular schools were put under a considerable strain in attempting to cater for the needs of pupils who came from completely different social, cultural and religious backgrounds and who often spoke no English. In response to this situation the Batley Divisional Executive suggested in

January 1965 that a special immigrant centre should be formed.[136] The Authority accepted this proposal and a centre was established at a junior/infant school in the middle of the town. Extra staff and facilities were made available at the centre and opportunities for immigrants and local school children to integrate with the local community were provided. The centre continued to operate until 1972, by which time the number of non-English-speaking children of junior age arriving in the area had become small enough to be dealt with by the individual schools.[137]

By the summer of 1965 some schools in the excepted district of Keighley were also under pressure and it was decided to employ two welfare assistants in two local immigrant classes. The following year summer vacation classes for immigrant children in Keighley were instituted to ensure that language skills gained during the school terms were retained, and shortly afterwards similar classes were also organised in Batley.[138] A working party on the problem of educating immigrants reported in 1967 and thereafter several different lines of action were followed:[139] a double classroom unit was set up at Park Road Primary School, Batley, to reduce the waiting list for the centre; teachers trained to teach immigrants were recruited; and at secondary level special classes were formed within the schools to help pupils learn the English language.[140] The Authority organised sessional and weekend courses and conferences on the education of immigrant children for the benefit of teachers. In addition, special camping holidays were organised for immigrants, and in some cases immigrant nursery units were added to schools. These were undoubtedly beneficial to the children but they also allowed the staff to meet parents, many of whom spoke very little English.[141] There were also a number of supplementary staff appointments. Educational visitors were appointed at two schools with a large number of immigrants, an additional educational welfare officer with special responsibilities for immigrants was appointed, and some non-teaching assistants were employed in classes where there was a disproportionate percentage of immigrants.[142]

From the outset the Committee planned to integrate the new arrivals with the local community but had decided against the dispersal of immigrants by compulsory direction to other schools. The Authority considered its approach to have been most successful and commented in 1974, 'It is encouraging that after many years there are now clear indications that Asian parents are becoming more involved in the life of the school community and better able to understand the opportunities available from the English school system.'[143]

## 6 PRE-SCHOOL EDUCATION

Prior to 1914 a much larger number of under-5s attended elementary schools than did so in later years, but the rather more sophisticated concept of 'nursery education' as such developed later. The Education Act of 1918 permitted LEAs 'to provide or aid nursery schools for which grants might be made available by the Board of Education'.[144] The first nursery school to be administered by the West Riding was at Castleford, and this was opened in January 1937. At the outbreak of the Second World War only one other nursery school had been built by the Authority,[145] but by this time there were 102 recognised nursery classes in the Riding, with a total accommodation of 3,672 places. The number of children actually attending the schools was only 2,206; Binns attributed this to the scattered nature of the population and the long distances between the classes and children's homes. He concluded: 'For this reason, nursery classes generally will not fill up to the limit of the accommodation in a county area.'[146]

Nonetheless, the outbreak of hostilities in 1939 transformed the attitude of both the Government and the LEAs towards pre-school education. Mothers with children under fourteen were never mobilised but there were official and social pressures for them to engage in paid or voluntary civilian work, and approximately 12 per cent of mothers with very young children were so employed. Many other mothers participated in voluntary work.[147] Consequently, there was a powerful incentive to make nursery provision available as quickly as possible, so that women with children could be released to play their part in the war effort. This sense of urgency was certainly felt in the West Riding. In December 1941, for example, £2,500 was made available 'in order to avoid delay in the establishment of nursery classes in schools',[148] and during the war some 300 nursery classes were set up, mostly in prefabricated buildings. The classes were staffed by qualified teachers and by women who were swiftly trained as members of what was called the Child Care Reserve.[149] This enthusiasm for nursery education persisted in the Authority's Development Plan, which included proposals for building 241 nursery schools of forty places each, 129 of eighty places each and thirty-eight of 120 places each at a cost of nearly £6m. In addition, a small number of nursery classes, mostly in connection with voluntary primary schools, were planned.[150]

Immediately after the war the impetus towards increasing nursery provision continued as the Government mounted its programme of export-led economic recovery. The Ministry of Education requested that all possible assistance be given in connection with the recruitment of female workers.[151] Accordingly, the West Riding County Council took over many wartime nurseries as day nurseries, which were administered by the Maternity and Child Welfare Department with the aim of improving standards of child care. The Education Committee also approved the opening of schools for use as nurseries and play centres during school vacations.[152] By the early 1950s, however, the situation had begun to change dramatically: an industrial recession was under way; the post-war 'bulge' was beginning to move out of the infants' schools; there was a teacher shortage; a reduction in educational expenditure was implemented; attendances at nurseries were falling; and both Government and public opinion was moving in favour of mothers staying at home.[153] In November 1953 Sir Alec Clegg circularised a letter which stressed that the existing teaching staff should be employed first in the secondary schools and then in the primary schools. The education of children below compulsory age would have to be given a low priority. Head teachers were instructed that no children under five were to be admitted if this would entail the formation of additional classes or the appointment of extra staff. In short, only if it was absolutely essential were nursery classes to be formed, and only then if no additional cost would be incurred. The Authority also asserted that under no circumstances should a child be admitted to school before the start of the term in which it attained the age of five.[154]

By the mid-1960s the economic climate and public opinion were beginning to change once more, but the shortage of teachers persisted, and in 1964 the Ministry realised that married women teachers who had left the profession would only return if nursery facilities were available for their own children. As a result the West Riding, following the lead of the Ministry, permitted the formation of nursery classes if it could be shown that at least twice as many qualified women teachers would be released to the schools as the number actually employed in the nursery classes to be established.[155] Nonetheless, in September 1967 there were only five day nurseries operated by the County Council, and the ambitious proposals of the Development Plan had still not materialised.[156]

In the wake of the Plowden Report, and in response to the growing demand for nursery education, the Authority began to pursue a policy of expansion in the pre-school sector. From the mid-1960s onwards many voluntarily organised pre-school playgroups emerged. Neither the DES nor the LEAs had the power to provide direct financial assistance to individual groups, although the West Riding devised a scheme whereby groups could purchase essential materials and equipment at discount rates from the County Supplies Department.[157] In 1969 the Education Committee allowed children to enter school at the beginning of the school year in which they reached the age of five, and shortly afterwards use was made of the Government's urban aid programme to establish nursery units at schools.[158] Furthermore, the Education Committee agreed in 1972 that classrooms which were not in use and likely to be vandalised should be used for nursery classes.[159] Thus during the last few years of the Authority's existence there was a revival of interest in pre-school education and considerable progress was made. At this time the first purpose-built nursery units to be built since the 1939-45 war were erected, and by 1973 there were approximately twelve nursery schools and 126 nursery units attached to infants' schools.[160] Moreover, in October 1973 it was announced that £1.3m had been allocated to the Riding and its successor authorities for the nursery building programme 1974-6;[161] later, however, this budget was to be pruned as a consequence of the cuts in projected public spending.

# CHAPTER VII

# *The Butler Act and the Schools*

The outbreak of the Second World War inevitably caused some dislocation in the educational services. The West Riding was not an evacuation area; on the contrary, large tracts of the county were designated as reception districts. During the first few months of the war 16,000 elementary and 1,800 secondary school pupils from the cities were evacuated to the West Riding.[1] These children were distributed among 300 elementary and nineteen secondary schools. Double-shift systems were normally operated in the secondary schools concerned.[2] Once the readjustment to wartime conditions had been made, and the children from the evacuation areas had been absorbed into the school system, more persistent problems stemming from shortages of staff and the suspension of building programmes became evident. In the expectation of aerial attack, priority was given to air raid protection projects and all new educational schemes were shelved. Later, as supplies of labour and material became increasingly difficult to obtain, three partly constructed modern schools, which had been commenced before the war, had to be sealed off, in the hope that they would be completed after hostilities.[3] In these circumstances the process of reorganisation on Hadow lines was inevitably retarded. Nonetheless, despite the war the Authority succeeded in fully reorganising three new areas and adopted temporary measures to improve provisions in three further districts.[4] Throughout this period the accommodation in West Riding elementary schools proved adequate to meet the needs of the emergency. In many ways it was fortunate that the emergency occurred towards the end of a period of decline in the school population. In 1934 there were over 198,000 children on the registers of West Riding elementary schools, but by 1944 this figure had been reduced to about 150,000. Damage from bombing in the county was negligible, and adequate temporary buildings were obtained to house the increase in the elementary school population caused by evacuation.

Accommodation proved to be a much more intractable problem in the secondary schools. The number of pupils in these schools increased from 17,400 in 1938 to 22,400 in 1944. Although over five hundred more transfer scholarships, which enabled suitable pupils from senior elementary schools to move to secondary schools, were awarded in 1944 than in 1938, fee payers accounted for most of the increase. Between 1938 and 1944 the proportion of scholarship holders in the schools fell from 70 per cent to 61 per cent,[5] and there can be little doubt that both nationally and locally the modest increase in prosperity created by full employment made it possible for more people to pay for their children's secondary schooling. In these circumstances governors were often tempted to accept more pupils for their schools than the accommodation available justified.[6] In 1942 it was shown that five aided and seven maintained schools had more pupils than they could accommodate effectively,[7] and the Authority regularly received requests from governors for extensions and alterations. Under wartime conditions the Authority was in no position to comply with these requests, and Binns felt strongly that this tendency to overcrowd schools should be curbed.[8] Eventually the Committee agreed that in future governors should consult the Authority before numbers on the roll were allowed to exceed effective accommodation. Binns also sought the advice of the Board on this question.[9] Initially he received a noncommittal reply, but later the Board acknowledged unofficially that it was under heavy pressure from parents, governors and Members of Parliament to help authorities provide additional accommodation, and intimated that it might be able to assist with the provision of prefabricated huts in certain instances.[10] Binns, however, was reluctant to apply this solution on a large scale, as he feared that the existence of temporary huts after the war would be used as an argument by the Board for delaying the provision of new, permanent accommodation.[11] At about this time Keighley Girls' Grammar School asked for additional accommodation, but the Authority pointed out that its preparatory department was incompatible with Government policy as outlined in the White Paper on educational reconstruction, and suggested that this department should be closed to release existing rooms.[12] Eventually the governors agreed to phase out the preparatory division from 1945.[13] A few months later Binns informed the Board that he feared a violent collision[14] between the Committee and secondary school governors over preparatory departments. He felt that if the schools continued to admit pupils to these departments, the more radical members would try to abolish them at a stroke rather than phase them out gradually as the Board wished.[15] Binns, however, managed to avert a crisis, and it was agreed that after 1944–5 no children under eleven should be admitted to secondary schools.[16]

During the war years the mutual hostility between the head teachers and governors of secondary schools on the one hand and Walter Hyman, chairman of the Committee, on the other increased considerably. Hyman, who had never made a secret of his doubts concerning the value of a grammar school type of education, continued to criticise these schools both privately and in public. In 1943 he prepared a personal memorandum on educational reconstruction which was forwarded to the Board of Education,[17] and although he praised some aspects of the work of the grammar schools, the general tone of this part of the report is illustrated by the following passages:

> The [secondary school] system caters for about 10 per cent of our children. It has for long encountered strong criticism. It has been, till very recently, hamstrung to a vicious examination system, that was in its turn tuned to the needs of less than 10 per cent of its own numbers, who were destined to proceed to some form of university or advanced education. The obstructive role so long persisted in does not do credit to the influence on these schools obtained by the universities. The grammar school type of education, is in my view, even now ill adapted to the needs of a large percentage of its scholars.[18]

With regard to grammar school governing bodies, he claimed:

> Experience has not convinced me that so-called free governing bodies exercise benevolent influence on their schools. Indeed few governors know anything about their schools and never enter them, their activities being confined to monthly and quarterly meetings in the boardroom and to a seat on the platform on speech day.[19]

He concluded:

> The Spens Report estimates the needs of grammar school places as about 15 per cent. I think this mistaken and heavily overestimated in the light of a system of true secondary education for all – at the risk of some personal danger I have expressed with emphasis the view that we already have 33 per cent more grammar school places than we can justify.[20]

The Board official and the HMI who read these comments felt that they were not altogether fair. R. N. Heaton described this picture of governing bodies as 'wild exaggeration' and thought that there was some evidence to support the fears of some heads in the Riding that they might suffer from interference from the Education Committee and its officials in the future.[21] HMI Miss Hurford reacted rather more strongly. She felt that Hyman's 'ignorance of secondary schools enables him to make dangerous generalisations'. In general she praised the interest shown by governors in their schools, and pointed out that she found that the least useful members of governing bodies were often those nominated by the Authority. She acknowledged that there had always been some suspicion between heads and governors on the one hand and the

Authority on the other, but she attributed the recent increase in this mistrust almost entirely to Hyman's attitude towards secondary schools.[22]

Binns was well aware that Miss Hurford did not have much time for Hyman's views on secondary schools and feared that this divergence of opinion could be detrimental to the Authority's relationship with the Board. To avoid friction he advised the Higher Education Sub-Committee that HMIs should no longer be consulted about candidates for grammar school headships. He did not tell the Sub-Committee his main reason for giving this advice, but he explained his action in a confidential minute to one of his colleagues thus:

> I believe that if we go on consulting HMIs, Mr Hyman will continue to take exception to what they say, and unpleasantness between the Authority and HMIs will result. Having just got over, I hope, recent unpleasantness between Mr Hyman and Elementary HMIs I don't want the relations between the Board and the Authority to be further prejudiced in this way.[23]

Further strains were experienced in the spring of 1945, when Hyman reacted abruptly to the possibility that Ilkley and Ripon grammar schools might apply for direct grant status. When this matter was considered in sub-committee there was wide agreement that any such applications should be opposed, but Hyman argued forcefully that if these schools continued to charge fees during the period in which their applications were being considered the Authority should refuse to assist them.[24] Alderman Armistead, vice-chairman of the County Council, was strongly opposed to this course of action and Lady Houldsworth felt that it savoured of 'sharp practice',[25] but Hyman's view carried the day in sub-committee by a small majority.[26] Although this decision was reversed by the full Committee, Hyman did not relent and maintained that the governors of the schools should be told that they are 'muddleheaded and fundamentally uneducational'.[27] It was strange that Hyman should have felt it necessary to adopt such a forceful, even aggressive, manner over such a comparatively minor matter. The point in dispute was limited to the question of assistance for a transitional period of one term only; moreover, it was well known in the office that the governors of both schools wished to avoid conflict with the Authority.[28] In the event Ilkley did not even apply for direct grant status and Ripon's request was quickly rejected, but Hyman's posturing tended to make his relations with the grammar schools even more sour.

During the later years of the war the Authority was much concerned with post-war planning. The possibility of setting up a group to consider this issue was deferred in the autumn of 1942,[29] but Binns had already asked his staff to prepare draft proposals.[30] Later the Post-War Education Sub-Committee was appointed and one of its first tasks was to consider the West Riding response to the Government's White Paper. In general the proposals were given enthusiastic support, but strong objections were made to the suggestion that the dual system should continue. Eventually the Education Committee informed the Board that they wished 'to express their keen disappointment that instead of ending the dual system, the White Paper not only perpetuates but strengthens its position'. The Committee, therefore, urged that 'reconsideration be given to the whole question with a view to the abolition of the dual system'.[31] The Committee also resolved that 'the solution of the problem of the single-school area is vital' and stressed that 'all schools in such areas should in the new Act become "county" schools'.[32] Although these resolutions were couched in strong terms, there was no real possibility that the West Riding would react to the religious issue in the 1940s as it had done in 1902. Denominational fervour had subsided considerably since the beginning of the century, and even the members who supported these resolutions stressed that they did not wish to wreck the Bill.[33] Hyman, who was not committed to either side in the religious controversy, was determined that the West Riding should in no way endanger the Bill. He told those who were raising objections that 'if they imagined that by opposition they were going to change the views of the President of the Board and the Bill he was about to introduce they were living in a fool's paradise'.[34] These resolutions were not heeded by the Government and when the 1944 Act became law no more was heard of West Riding opposition. Instead the Authority tended to stress the problems which the dual system had created in the inter-war years and which had to be dealt with in the post-war period. It was pointed out that the voluntary school managers had retarded Hadow reorganisation in some districts, and that the buildings of some schools were by the 1940s well below the required standards, as the voluntary bodies had not been able to find the money for improvements and the Authority lacked the power to undertake such work. In preparing its Development Plan the Authority kept to its view that all schools in single-school areas should be local authority schools and insisted, moreover, that when it was necessary to replace an existing Church school the new building should be a county school. This policy aroused considerable opposition from the voluntary school interest, and no less than 140 of the 166 objections to the West Riding Development Plan concerned proposals to replace existing voluntary schools by county provision. Under the 1944 Act the Ministry of Education had to adjudicate in such cases, and in ninety-nine of the 140 instances judgement went against the Authority.[35] At this juncture the Committee accepted the Minister's decisions and amended its Development Plan accordingly. By the late 1940s the religious issue, which had so dogged the Authority in its early years, was virtually dead, but the urgent problem which remained was to improve the 'sorry condition'[36] of many of the voluntary schools which had opted for controlled status after the reforms of 1944.

The Government White Paper proposed that public education should be reorganised into three progressive stages, primary, secondary and further, and consequently the Authority employed these categories in its post-war planning. With regard to the primary sector it was anticipated that infant and junior schools would continue much as before, although it was acknowledged that class sizes needed to be reduced and buildings and equipment improved.[37] Hyman claimed, with some support form R. N. Heaton at the Board,[38] that the junior schools had become 'the Cinderellas' of the service[39] Hyman wanted to change this and proposed that in a large authority such as the West Riding there should be experiments in junior school design. He also urged forcefully that junior schools should have specially equipped craft rooms, but both Binns[40] and HMI L. G. Gibbon[41] doubted whether this idea was particularly sound.

The Committee realised that it would be concerned with selection at the age of eleven, but at this stage largely kept its options open. Hyman stressed the problems of continuing with examinations of the county minor type and predicted that the school record card, which was being introduced into junior schools, would play an important role in the future. He emphasised one aspect of the situation which was not always grasped by contemporaries in the early 1940s: 'I think that after some years of trial and error a satisfactory method will be evolved – possibly of record plus examination – but examination of every child for allocation to school and not for selection to one particular type of school.'[42] At this juncture the Council's Reconstruction Committee maintained that parents should have the final choice of the type of school a child would attend after leaving the junior.[43] More realistically, however, the Education Committee held that the ultimate power, at any event in the early stages, would have to rest with the Education Authority.[44]

Post-war planning for secondary education was carried out on the assumption that some form of secondary schooling would be provided for all children between the ages of eleven and fifteen. Although it was accepted that there would be different types of secondary schools, Hyman maintained that there must be equality of status between these different types. He did not underestimate the difficulties involved in this and asserted, 'Equality of status, if it is to be achieved, demands revolution in thought and outlook. . . . Tremendous obstacles exist. It is for that reason that I so earnestly plead a concentration of energy to that one end.'[45] He continued:

Only when all post-primary schools are accepted, especially by parents, as of equivalent status will the local education authority be in the happy position of being able to transfer the child to the school best suited to it, free from prejudice known as 'wishes of parents', wishes which while they must be taken count of will in the early years be based on anything but true values. . . . There can be no justification for higher standards of equipment, space, staffing in one secondary school than in another. . . . There can be no excuse for different quality of staffs.[46]

Many of these arguments were accepted at the Board in 1943,[47] and R. N. Heaton agreed with Hyman that 'it will require real devotion and imagination on the part of administrators and teachers to raise modern schools to the status which they should attain'.[48] Heaton stressed that 'there must be a levelling up rather than a levelling down', but HMI Miss H. E. Hurford, who was so strongly opposed to Hyman's views on grammar schools, replied, 'Unfortunately there is reason to suppose that his [Hyman's] remedy for inequality between the senior and the secondary school is to level down the latter.'[49]

The West Riding did not propose radical changes for its grammar schools,[50] for the Reconstruction Committee predicted, 'The grammar school will probably remain fundamentally the kind of school represented by the secondary school of today, but with a curriculum brought into line with modern ideas and requirements.'[51] Hyman's antipathy to these schools made it unlikely that they would be given priority after the war if he remained chairman, but Binns, on the other hand, made it clear at the time of the publication of the Spens Report that he respected the traditions and curricula of the grammar schools, describing them as 'the basis of a good education'.[52] With regard to the future of the other established form of post-elementary education – the modern schools – the Authority foresaw important developments. Hyman stressed, 'We shall have to concentrate all our energies on the modern type of school,'[53] and this sentiment was echoed in the report of the Reconstruction Committee, especially in the building programme.[54] The conception of exactly what secondary modern education would be remained vague and was couched thus: 'The modern school will be a post-war development of the existing senior elementary school, with community life, social activities and with staffing and equipment equal to the grammar school, but with a curriculum less academic, more practical and based on creative activity by the pupils.'[55]

The Spens Report recommended in 1938 that secondary technical schools should be developed, and this possibility was much discussed during the war years. In many ways this concept was not new to the West Riding, for even in the nineteenth century several technical colleges had developed day secondary departments, and scientific and technical studies were also well established in some West Riding grammar schools by the end of the 1890s. During the 1920s Hallam had attempted to strengthen this tradition in certain schools, and claimed:

> The selection of children for full-time attendance at secondary schools up to at least the age of sixteen is made at eleven or twelve years of age. In the absence of alternative courses, the curriculum offered to such children is uniform in type and leads to an examination which is, in its main feature, a university matriculation test ... it is desirable to regard the period from eleven to fourteen in the secondary school primarily as a testing period, and to offer at about fourteen some variation of the curriculum to pupils who are not of 'School Certificate type'. Experience has shown that where such alternative courses have been offered many of the pupils taking them have gained a revived interest in their school work generally and have grappled successfully not only with the new subjects but with others also.[56]

Courses on commerce, engineering, mechanics, textiles and agriculture were developed in boys' schools and syllabuses based on commerce and housecraft introduced into girls' schools. In the mid-1930s HMIs reported most unfavourably on several of these courses and implied that subjects such as engineering and textiles were not suitable for secondary schools. Hallam, who was by this time Director of Education, reacted sharply and a lengthy and acrimonious correspondence with the Board ensued.[57] Although it was never stated explicitly, it was made amply clear to the Authority that bilateral schools of the grammar/technical type were not acceptable to the Board.

During the 1930s the Authority also began to develop junior technical schools. These were normally situated in the premises of technical colleges and admitted pupils at the age of thirteen. By 1938–9 the West Riding had six junior technical schools attended by 682 pupils[58] and, in addition, sent scholars to similar institutions in neighbouring county boroughs. Hyman was on record as saying that advances in secondary education would be made in the junior technical rather than the grammar schools,[59] and during the war years there was a steady increase in provisions for junior technical education. By 1944–5 there were 1,939 pupils in attendance at eight schools within the county and about 1,100 others travelled to county borough institutions.[60] The Spens Report proposed that secondary technical schools should be provided on a much more extensive basis, and also suggested that the age of admission should be changed to eleven to bring secondary technical schools into line with other secondary schools. Binns felt that the curriculum in these schools for eleven to thirteen-year-olds should be similar to that of the

grammar schools, but after that boys should undertake much more specialised scientific and technical courses.[61] He pointed out that the Spens Report
had not contemplated any corresponding development for girls, but suggested that courses on housewifery, child welfare and nutrition should be
introduced.[62] Hyman accepted Binns's ideas concerning these schools, and
added, 'I trust we shall cease to look upon one type of school as more cultural
than another. . . . I refuse to see absence of cultural values in crafts or indeed
in any practical education and the specific trade school does not shock me as it
does some.'[63] Binns felt that the emphasis in junior technical schools had been
on instruction rather than complete education[64] and he wished to see
secondary technical education take on 'a more liberal atmosphere such as
that provided by a grammar school or a good modern school'.[65] He favoured
the development of bilateral grammar/technical schools, especially in industrial areas, and in a few cases where grammar school provision was in excess
of needs he thought that existing grammar schools might be converted into
secondary technical schools. He also wanted to see the setting up of bilateral
modern/technical schools, and during the war the Authority experimented
along these lines with its modern school at Bingley.[66] Binns felt that if the
leaving age was raised to sixteen most modern schools would have to develop
a more specialised technical side[67] but no specific proposals were made in this
field before 1945.

The other main type of secondary provision surveyed by the Spens Report
was the multilateral school, which was to be a combination of grammar,
technical and modern schools on a single site. In general this kind of school
was not recommended by Spens, although it was felt that it might have some
merit in country areas. Hyman, however, was much more sympathetic
towards this proposal and predicted, 'We will, I hope, in the West Riding,
experiment early in our programmme with what is known as the multilateral
school.'[68] He suggested that Tadcaster (where there was already a proved
need for both a new grammar and a new modern school) and Ripon might be
suitable districts for the early experiments. At the Board Heaton pointed out
the difficulties of providing multilateral schools on a wide scale[69] but felt that
experiments should not be ruled out. Miss Hurford was sceptical about
multilateral provisions at Tadcaster and Ripon, but her comments were not
particularly coherent because at the time of writing she clearly did not grasp
the difference between a multilateral and a secondary technical school.[70] The
question of a multilateral school at Tadcaster proved particularly interesting.
Binns and Walker thought this scheme worthy of serious consideration as
early as September 1942,[71] and the governors of the grammar school there
were also sympathetic. The Committee soon approved of the experiment and

more detailed planning, in which Hyman took considerable personal interest, commenced. In 1944 Binns told the newly appointed headmaster of Tadcaster Grammar School that the Committee favoured a multilateral scheme because it would solve the difficulties of selection for different kinds of secondary education and equalisation of standards in secondary education.[72] Binns, however, stressed to the Post-War Education Sub-Committee that he still regarded multilateralism as an experiment. He wrote:

> The Education Officer wishes to suggest to the Committee that they would be wise at this stage to keep an open mind about multilateral schools. He hopes that the multilateral experiment will figure in the Authority's development for post-war reconstruction, but he suggests that it should be regarded only as an experiment until its success is clearly proved, and that the Committee should be prepared to abandon the experiment after giving it a good trial, if it is eventually found to work out badly. He further suggests that buildings of multilateral schools should be so arranged that separate schools can be resorted to if that arrangement is eventually found necessary. Lastly, the Education Officer recommends that no attempt should be made, at this stage at any rate, to abandon a successful grammar school merely because its present site is not big enough to accommodate a multilateral school, and that no attempt should be made to crowd buildings for a multilateral school on a grammar school site which is really not big enough to carry them.[73]

This advice was accepted by the Committee, and it may well have been that Binns intended to leave no doubts in members' minds, perhaps not least Hyman's, about his position on this issue. Binns had made it amply clear that although he favoured experiments, he was not committed to multilateralism as a general solution to the problem of secondary school organisation.

1945 and 1946 were crucial years for West Riding education. In September 1945 Clegg succeeded Binns as chief officer, and in the spring of 1946 Hyman's position as chairman was strengthened by the local election results. Labour had been the largest party on the County Council since 1928, but in 1946 it won an absolute majority for the first time. By the end of the war Hyman had become a very powerful leader within the Labour group, and in many ways it was Hyman's strong political leadership in committees which enabled Clegg to go forward with his schemes for educational reform. Hyman and Clegg shared similar educational ideals. Both were suspicious of examinations at all levels and they placed emphasis on the aesthetic and expressive elements in the school curriculum. In general, they accorded a higher priority to the education of the emotions than to the development of the intellect, for both men felt that the former had been sacrificed to the latter for too long in English education.

At about the time that Clegg took over as chief officer, the Authority was in dispute with the Ministry over its draft articles of government for county secondary schools. Clegg saw that the heart of the disagreement was the procedures for 11-plus selection. He decided to approach A. E. Parsons at the Ministry unofficially to try to clarify matters. Clegg wrote to him:

> [The 1944 Act] says we must provide for children according to their age, abilities and *aptitudes*, and from this and from circulars and from other documents emanating from the Ministry we are given to believe that in the future we are not to take off the cream and send them to the grammar schools, but to allocate according to aptitudes, and that grammar and technical, if not modern, will each get some cream. . . . From whom can the Authority learn how to allocate children at the age of 11+ to schools appropriate to their aptitudes? . . . My own view is that whatever we do in the future we are for the moment bound by material conditions which have not altered one scrap as a result of the new Act. For the moment we have got to continue to take off the cream.[74]

Parsons discussed this issue with Clegg, but said, in effect, that he could not help.[75] He stressed that the West Riding was not alone in this difficulty and suggested that it might be taken up by the AEC or the CCA. He was clearly more concerned that the Authority should accept the Ministry's line about the articles of government, and in due course the Committee agreed to do this. Meanwhile, Clegg had submitted his question about aptitude selection to three leading contemporary educationalists who were much concerned with this issue:[76] Sir Fred Clarke (National Federation for Educational Research), Dr Charlotte Fleming (London Institute of Education) and Professor Godfrey Thomson (Moray House, Edinburgh), and their interesting replies, which have been preserved, were unanimous in declaring that it was not possible to detect special aptitudes in children of eleven and then to allocate the children to secondary schools accordingly.[77] Clegg pointed out to the Policy Sub-Committee that this verdict was completely in accord with Sir Cyril Burt's views as expressed in the *British Journal of Educational Psychology* for November 1943, for Burt had concluded that 'any scheme of organisation which proposes to classify children at the age of eleven or twelve according to qualitative mental types rather than according to general intelligence is in conflict with the known facts of child psychology.'[78]

In July 1946 Clegg put the subject of the future development of secondary schools before the Policy Sub-Committee.[79] Using the evidence which he had amassed concerning the difficulties of selection according to aptitudes, he argued that the Authority should be wary of a rigid tripartite division of secondary education and recommended experiment with all types of provision. He suggested that, where possible, multilateral schools should be set up, but he was not against segregation according to intellectual ability within them. Clegg realised that many areas (for example, Castleford) already had their full-complements of new and separate schools and that in these districts the pattern of secondary education would remain fixed for many years. In such areas Clegg was concerned about the future of the modern schools and foresaw one of the crucial problems which faced these schools in the next twenty years. He argued:

> The grammar school is perhaps the most vocational of all our schools. Parents know that it trains the black-coated worker. It gives a cachet of respectability and a promise of middle-class comfort. The technical school trains engineers and technicians, but the modern school is a meaningless name and is in the thoughts of the public devoid of vocational purpose. Wherever possible it should be combined with one of the other two types which are accepted at present and if it must stand anywhere in isolation a better name for it might be found.[80]

Clegg also knew that, despite his wishes, some modern schools would have to remain in isolation, and he stressed that in these circumstances they should be given some form of advanced work, as he felt that this was essential to achieve parity of esteem. Clegg's policy statement aroused no controversy in the Sub-Committee and was accepted by the various political groups.

Early in 1947 the organisation of secondary education in the West Riding became more controversial. Alderman B. Wilson, a Conservative from Tadcaster, quoted Hyman as saying that the Authority was going 'all out for multilateral schools',[81] and asked why in such circumstances the Council was concurrently being requested to approve of several new modern schools. Hyman replied in an evasive and aggressive manner stressing, 'We shall have no modern schools as such,'[82] but giving no explanation for this statement, and it was left to Clegg to provide Alderman Wilson with a satisfactory answer later. Because of the confusion Hyman eventually decided that a second policy statement should be put before the Education Committee and Clegg drafted one. Before this memorandum was considered, however, Clegg told Alderman Johns, the Liberal vice-chairman of the Committee, that he had endeavoured to make the statement as temperate in tone as possible to gain the support of a considerable number of members and not merely of one political party. Clegg felt that Hyman had been over-forthright in his expression and wanted to avoid false impressions of the Authority's policy from getting abroad. He pointed out that there were likely to be 160 secondary schools in the county of which only thirty-three were designated multilaterals. Clegg stressed that the Authority was not going completely multilateral and that an important number of grammar and modern schools would be continued. The Education Officer did not want this issue to become politicised, and in his efforts to avoid this he was prepared to emphasise different aspects of the scheme to different people. At this juncture Clegg achieved his aim, for the memorandum was accepted by the Committee with only one dissenting vote.[83] Lady Houldsworth objected because she felt that the institution of multilaterals should be an experimental rather than an established policy.[84] The Conservatives, led by Alderman Armistead, accepted the proposals, and for the Labour Party Hyman described the scheme as 'the best thing any authority has produced', although Alderman T. Tomlinson, chairman of the County Council, adopted a more cautious tone, observing that the scheme could be altered if it did not turn out to be successful.[85]

As part of its Development Plan the West Riding had to submit its views on the organisation of secondary education to the Ministry, and it was soon clear that serious disagreements had arisen.[86] The first bone of contention was secondary technical education. Using the evidence mentioned earlier in this chapter (p. 166), the Authority maintained that it was not possible to detect technical aptitudes in children of eleven. Consequently, few secondary technical places were included in the West Riding scheme and where such instruction was planned (largely in the former junior technical schools) it was proposed that the children would commence their courses at thirteen rather than eleven. The Ministry, however, was insistent that more places should be earmarked for secondary technical education and, under protest, the Authority increased the proportion of this type of provision to about 14 per cent of the total number of places. Similarly the Ministry insisted that selection for secondary technical education should take place at eleven. The West Riding recorded its disagreements with the Ministry over these issues in most forthright terms in the preface to its Development Plan.[87] The Authority claimed that although the present scheme was the most satisfactory possible within the Ministry's constraints, the Ministry should revise its policy at an early date. It was stressed that in such circumstances the Authority would amend its Development Plan accordingly.[88]

The secondary section of the Development Plan (excluding Keighley) provided for thirty-four multilateral schools, sixty-two bilateral schools, fifteen grammar schools and forty-seven modern schools. These proposals were accepted by all political groups on the Council but some Conservatives and Liberals were beginning to express their anxieties.[89] These fears were not alleviated by Hyman's statement that 'although he was interested in grammar school education, he was not interested in grammar schools as such, and

wanted them to disappear'.[90] Objections to multilateral schemes were forwarded to the Ministry from several localities, including Harrogate and
Ripon, which predictably wanted to preserve their grammar schools, but a
much more serious rift occurred between the Authority and the excepted
district of Keighley. In 1948 Keighley Borough Council, which contained
many Labour members, proposed a tripartite scheme for its area.[91] In a
forceful memorandum it was argued that multilateral schools had still to
prove themselves and it was maintained that Keighley was not a good
area for experimentation as existing traditions were well entrenched. It was
also mentioned that a recent meeting of the AEC had indicated that advo-
cates of multilaterals were still in a minority. This latter point was not
particularly tactful, as Hyman had moved the resolution in favour of multilaterals at that meeting and it must have been well known that he had been
heckled by other delegates before his motion was overwhelmingly defeated.[92]
The Authority, which had devised its own multilateral scheme for the
Keighley district, responded by forwarding a sarcastic and vituperative[93]
attack on the borough's proposals to the Ministry.

Before the Ministry's response to the Development Plan had been fully
considered, there were important political changes in the West Riding. In the
local elections of April 1949 the Labour Party lost seats and overall control of
the County Council. Nonetheless, Labour remained the largest single party
and retained the chairmanship of the Council. The chairmanship of the
Education Committee, however, proved to be an extremely controversial
issue which provoked strong clashes of personalities. After a long struggle
Hyman was ousted by the non-Socialists and replaced by the Liberal
Alderman W. J. Johns. Relations between Hyman and Johns remained
strained for some time, and Clegg found it difficult to keep the Education
Department out of the political wrangling. During 1950 Clegg was personally
accused by both major political factions of favouring their opponents and
during these bitter months the Education Officer seriously considered leaving
the West Riding altogether.

It was in this difficult context that the Authority reconsidered its Development Plan but, despite sharp differences, an amicable compromise was
eventually reached. The Minister suggested that the facilities for secondary
technical education should be more concentrated and asked why the com-
bined amount of grammar and technical accommodation varied from as little
as 25 per cent of the total in some mining areas to as much as 45 per cent in
certain other districts. The Ministry, which was under Labour political
leadership at this time, was also somewhat guarded in its response to
multilateral schemes:

The types of organisation necessitated by this conception are, of course, however, as the Authority are aware, still largely untried in this country. It may be that they will prove themselves; the Minister wishes only that they may. In the meantime, however, he cannot regard it as generally unreasonable that some whose intrests are in schools with long and tried traditions should be reluctant to contemplate at this time that the organisation which they know should be planned to be replaced by an organisation which so far they do not know.[94]

It was added that such considerations were particularly applicable in the case of Keighley. Eventually the newly elected Committee decided that it did not wish to make a wholesale revision of the Development Plan, but emphasised that all schemes in the Plan were not to be regarded as final. The Committee gave a pledge that local interests would be consulted fully again before any schemes were converted into 'bricks and mortar' and, with regard to secondary education, stressed the importance of diversity and flexibility. It was promised that full consideration would be given to local views and, in the light of local preferences, it was immediately agreed to drop the multilateral schemes for the Keighley, Harrogate, Goole, Pontefract and Spen Valley areas and to allow at least five grammar schools in other districts to remain outside the bilateral or multilateral arrangements which had been proposed.[95] The Education Officer felt that the practice of letting each area choose its own pattern of secondary organisation worked well and prevented continual changes in policy as political fortunes fluctuated in the county. The Development Plan was not finally approved until 1952, for the Ministry still felt that the facilities for secondary technical education needed to be more concentrated and suggested that there were too few proposals for grammar/technical schools and for separate technical schools.[96] At this late stage, at Clegg's suggestion, the Committee decided not to revise the whole Plan but agreed instead to note the Minister's criticisms in the preface and to re-examine, with the appropriate local bodies, all projects before implementation.[97] This procedure proved acceptable to the Minister.

The West Riding was one of the first LEAs to show serious and persistent interest in the development of multilateral schools. This came about partly because of Hyman's antipathy to grammar schools and his determination to find an alternative, and partly because of Clegg's early grasp of some of the most basic problems involved in selection at eleven-plus and tripartitism. In many ways Hyman's loudly proclaimed allegiance to multilateralism proved of dubious advantage to the cause, for it tended to drive his political opponents, somewhat reluctantly in some instances, into an opposing position. Clegg saw the dangers of this and resisted the process with some success, at least initially, but Hyman's rather extreme statements, coupled with his abrupt manner and the hardening of attitudes nationally, made conflict difficult to avoid in the long run. The compromise solution of 1949, however, was eminently sensible in an area which was politically so marginal and, to Hyman's credit, he praised his opponents for the way in which they dealt with the Development Plan at that time.[98] Divisional executives and district sub-committees exercised their rights of revision to the full during the next decade; consequently, by the 1960s the original Development Plan had been amended almost beyond recognition.[99]

Whatever the Authority planned for the future, in the short term it was obliged to operate the largely tripartite structure which it inherited from the pre-war period. During the late 1940s and early 1950s, moreover, the Ministry was unable to sanction the building of new schools on a large scale because of the national shortages of materials and skilled labour. In general, building projects were restricted to the provision of 'roofs over heads', and the increase in the birth rate immediately after the war meant that priority had to be given to the primary sector in the early 1950s. Nonetheless, as had been promised during the war, the school leaving age was raised to fifteen in April 1947, and this measure increased the number of pupils in West Riding schools by some 17,000.[100] An urgent programme was launched to provide accommodation for these children. Extra premises were rented and functional but ugly prefabricated huts were supplied by the Ministry of Works under the Huts Operation Raising School Age scheme (HORSA). In this programme, which was largely financed by the central government, ninety-six West Riding schools qualified for additional accommodation.[101] Wherever practicable this additional accommodation was used to reorganise 'through' schools into separate primary and secondary establishments. 'Through' schools were almost invariably former elementary schools which continued to educate their pupils throughout the whole of their school lives, and the elimination of such schools was regarded as a matter of urgency in the immediate post-war period; only the provision of 'roofs over heads' was given a higher priority nationally. Progress made with reorganisation in the West Riding in the inter-war years stood the Authority in good stead, for it was now faced with a rather less daunting prospect in this respect than many other LEAs. In 1948 there were nearly 9,000 children of secondary age still attending 'through' schools in the West Riding, but by 1954 this number had been reduced to under 4,000. It was shown in 1957 that most of the remaining 'through' schools were Roman Catholic, and that overall the West Riding had a considerably lower proportion of children in such schools than the country as a whole.[102] Most, if not all, of these few surviving 'through' schools were reorganised in the early 1960s and the last vestiges of pre-war elementary school organisation removed.

Immediately after the war a survey of the distribution of grammar school places throughout the Riding was carried out, and it was shown most clearly that there was a wide disparity between the north and the south of the county. There were acute shortages of places in the Adwick, Castleford, Hemsworth, Maltby, Thorne and Wath-upon-Dearne areas. In some of these mining areas there was only sufficient accommodation in grammar schools for about 12 per cent of the total secondary school age range, whereas in several of the agricultural and textile districts in the north and west of the county this proportion reached almost 40 per cent. The corollary of this was that the number of marks required by candidates to secure grammar school places in the county selection examinations varied greatly between different districts, and this was widely regarded as inequitable. Despite efforts to alleviate these disparities, they persisted well into the post-war period.

Hyman's attitude towards the grammar schools tended to obtrude into administration in the early post-war years. In 1946 Clegg felt that he had to justify to Hyman the inclusion of so many grammar schools in the first post-war schedules of jobs which went up to the Ministry, as he knew that Hyman firmly believed that priorities lay elsewhere.[103] About two years later Clegg admitted that he was sensitive to the criticism that the freedom of action allowed to grammar schools had been considerably eroded since 1944 and he indicated that he wanted to halt this trend.[104] Soon afterwards Clegg urged Hyman to change his attitude towards staffing policy.[105] Hyman felt that grammar schools were generously staffed by comparison with secondary modern and primary schools and insisted that restrictions should be placed on increasing grammar school staff whilst vacancies in other types of schools remained unfilled. Clegg argued, however, that the net result of this self-denying ordinance was that science and mathematics graduates were lost to the West Riding. He contended that these graduates had no interest in working in secondary modern or primary schools either in the West Riding or elsewhere, and if they were denied opportunities of working in West Riding grammar schools, they obtained posts in such schools with other authorities, which were often in the south of England. Hyman, however, remained unimpressed by these arguments.

By 1948 the pressure on accommodation in some grammar schools in the mining areas had become extremely serious. The large entries of pupils, which had been admitted in 1944 and 1945 when the Ministry was stressing the importance of increasing the number of potential teachers, were still passing through the schools. It was reported to the Policy Sub-Committee that there was already evidence at one school (Adwick) that overcrowding was inhibiting sound education,[106] and it was agreed that limitations on grammar school admissions would have to be applied from the school year 1948–9. During the year requests for increased accommodation were received from the Barnsley, Darfield, Mexborough and Wath areas. Mexborough Labour Party wrote to the Minister asking for more grammar school provision,[107] and pointed out that children in its area had to obtain sixty more marks in the selection examinations to secure grammar school places than those in more favoured districts. It was felt that this situation was contrary to both the principle of equality of opportunity and the spirit of the 1944 Act.[108] Early in 1949 attention was focused on the situation at Maltby Grammar School. This school admitted 150 pupils in 1946 and 120 in 1947 and 1948, but the Policy Sub-Committee was informed that, unless additional accommodation could be found, the intake would have to be reduced to ninety in 1949 and to sixty in 1950.[109] It was also stated that, if the intake fell to ninety in 1949, children in the Maltby area would have to obtain between sixty and seventy more marks in the selection tests than those in Otley to gain admission to grammar school. On the other hand, it was pointed out that efforts had been made with post-war building to increase provision in the mining areas. By 1949 Adwick, Ecclesfield, Pontefract and Wath had benefited in this way, but not Maltby. Although this detailed information was not available to the public at the time, Hyman was sufficiently concerned by the issue to make a special personal statement to the Education Committee, in which he stressed that important extensions and improvements had been made to grammar school premises.[110] He also strongly denied that he had any antipathy to the grammar schools.[111] One spokesman for the mining areas, however, Alderman A. Flavell from Hemsworth, persisted. He argued, with considerable justification, that the south of the Riding did not have its fair share of grammar school places.[112] In reply one of Flavell's political opponents contended that this was largely because during the period before the 1949 local elections priority had been given to modern schools and technical colleges rather than to extra grammar school places.[113] This, however, was in no sense a complete explanation, for, despite the fact that every grammar school in the south of the county was extended between 1945 and 1954, the Authority had to acknowledge in the latter year that there were still insufficient places in the mining districts.[114] In the county as a whole in the early 1950s nearly a quarter of the children in secondary age range attended grammar schools. This proportion was felt by the Education Officer to be too high[115] and, in his view, accounted to a considerable extent for the early leaving which the grammar schools experienced during this period. Clegg, however, saw no prospect of this proportion being reduced, for he felt that parental determination to avoid the modern schools was increasing every year and was 'almost frantic'.[116] He argued that parents could see a variety of ways out of the top of the grammar schools, and, until they could view the modern schools in a similar light, they would continue the pressure to get their children into the grammar schools.

In the post-war period secondary technical education in the West Riding, as in many other parts of the country, was not greatly extended. Between 1945 and the mid-1950s there were just under 3,000 West Riding children on the rolls of such schools, which were almost without exception former junior technical schools. Although in the early 1950s the Education Officer had hopes of building at least one brand-new secondary technical school which would take children of high ability while remaining outside the grammar school tradition,[117] this idea was dropped in 1955. In that year Clegg and his assistant, J. M. Hogan, presented a full report on technical education to the Education Committee.[118] The Education Officer had conducted an inquiry amongst firms of national repute concerning their views on vocational education and technical training in schools.[119] The replies expressed forcibly the opinion that schools should be concerned with the provision of a good general education rather than trade training. Consequently, the Education Officer advised the Committee to set up no more secondary technical schools, which anyway had proved to be the most expensive type of secondary schooling provided by the Authority. He also suggested that the existing schools should begin to recruit at the age of eleven, and should be converted in the long term, in effect, into grammar schools with a strong scientific and technical bias in their curricula.[120] These proposals were accepted by the Committee: in a way it was ironical that in the space of twenty years the Authority had turned almost full circle on this issue. During the inter-war years a technical bias was introduced into several grammar schools, to the obvious disquiet of the Board of Education. In the 1940s the Authority proposed few secondary technical and bilateral grammar/technical schools in its Development Plan, and was instructed by the Ministry to increase this type of provision. Finally, in the 1950s, the Authority reverted to the policy of the 1930s and made provision for technical instruction in selective grammar schools.

During the war Binns and Hyman had emphasised the importance of developing the secondary modern schools, and the possibility of introducing some more advanced work into these schools, perhaps through technical courses, had been mooted as early as 1944. Clegg agreed with these views and made sure that they were rehearsed in the preface to the Development Plan. In the post-war years Clegg was determined to try to raise the status of these schools, and the Ministry was asked whether it would be possible to develop advanced courses in a few modern schools so that some pupils could qualify for direct admission to teacher training colleges.[121] The response from the Ministry, however, was rather guarded. By the early 1950s Clegg was becoming increasingly concerned about the academic standards achieved in modern schools. He told Hyman that friendly and confident pupils were being produced but, in general, the schools lacked bite and drive. He felt that their most able pupils were not having their abilities stretched and that some of these young people who later attempted further education courses found themselves in difficulties.[122] The West Riding's own inspectors attributed these shortcomings to the fact that the schools had no clear aims and were consequently tending to drift. As early as 1951 the Authority reported to HMIs that it was receiving requests from secondary modern head teachers that some of their ablest pupils should be permitted to enter for General Certificate of Education (GCE) examinations, and advice was sought.[123] Although HM Inspectorate acknowledged that the Authority was not bound to refuse permission, it was of the opinion that such entries should be firmly discouraged and prevented if possible. A few months later, however, Clegg mentioned publicly that he was not against selected classes in modern schools taking GCE examinations in certain subjects.[124] The Education Officer, who never had a great deal of confidence in selection tests, consistently maintained that there was a good deal of overlap in intellectual ability between the bottom streams of the grammar schools and the top streams of the modern schools.[125] He also never doubted that there were many able pupils in the modern schools,[126] particularly in south Yorkshire, where in some districts there were grammar school places for only 12 per cent of the age range. This led him, throughout the period, to advise his Committee that, wherever practicable, facilities for courses of study beyond the age of fifteen should be provided in modern schools.

In the 1950s secondary modern governors and head teachers were left to make their own decisions about whether they wished to set up GCE courses in their schools. The Authority neither encouraged nor discouraged such developments, and as long as the Committee felt that a school had the staff and facilities to provide GCE courses without prejudicing the work of other pupils it did not interfere. The West Riding, led by the Education Officer, however, made it clear in 1956 that it was completely opposed to proposals for the introduction of a new secondary examination scheme which would be aimed largely at modern school pupils.[127] Several reasons were given for this decision, the most important of which were the fear that external examinations would cramp the exciting work being attempted in some modern schools, and the possibility that children who failed both the eleven-plus and the new examinations would be branded as failures for life.[128] About eighteen months later the Committee had to consider a different but similar kind of proposal. Keighley informed the Authority that it intended to set up a local leaving certificate.[129] This consisted of a series of examinations which could be taken by secondary modern school leavers in the Keighley area, and although it was recognised that it would be below GCE standard, it was hoped that the qualification would soon gain some standing in the locality. As Keighley was an excepted district, the West Riding could not prevent the setting up of this certificate, but it made it amply clear that in its view this innovation was contrary to the best interests of education.[130] Soon afterwards the Committee had to consider a very similar proposal from the Harrogate area, and the Education Officer clearly felt that it was time for the Authority to adopt a general policy regarding this question. He advised the Committee to institute a regulation that 'no scheme of examinations in secondary schools, other than normal internal examinations, shall be held without the express approval of the Authority',[131] and the Committee accepted this suggestion. A few months later the Harrogate proposals were specifically vetoed and at the same time Silsden Secondary School was prevented from continuing to enter pupils for the Keighley leaving certificate, a practice which had been allowed for an experimental period of one year.[132]

In the early 1960s Clegg, supported by the Committee, vigorously opposed the creation of the Certificate of Secondary Education (CSE). This was completely consistent with the attitude adopted towards external examinations and leaving certificates in the 1950s and, in general, the same objections were advanced. In 1962, however, it became clear that the Minister intended to set up a new national examination. At this juncture it was evident that further opposition was futile and there were discussions among the Directors of Education of several Yorkshire authorities about how the new examinations should be administered locally. Clegg and T. H. Tunn of Sheffield were particularly prominent in these negotiations, and it was eventually agreed, tentatively, that an attempt should be made to set up a CSE board for the region which was associated with the university Institutes of Education. At a meeting in September 1962 it was apparent that a number of the county boroughs did not take kindly to the idea of association with the Institutes of Education and wanted the administration to be conducted through the Yorkshire Council for Further Education.[133] Clegg was strongly opposed to this. He told Tunn that he did not wish to see technical education interests taking control of what was taught in the modern schools.[134] Eventually the two parties went their separate ways and two CSE boards were created in

Yorkshire. One of these was the West Yorkshire and Lindsey Regional Board,[135] which was associated with the Sheffield University Institute of Education. Clegg took a strong personal interest in the preparatory work of the Board, and he was determined that it should avoid what he regarded as the traditional defects of national examinations. He wanted emphasis to be placed on course work, and expressed the hope that the examination would have as little control as possible over the educational programmes of individual children.[136] He stressed how important it was that teachers could control examinations, and he argued that to achieve this aim effectively the detailed work involved in administering the examinations would have to be done not by a remote regional body but by representatives of schools working together in comparatively small groups.[137] The Board largely accepted these ideas, and during the 1960s and 1970s the school based forms of CSE assessment were taken up widely by West Riding teachers.[138]

The main types of secondary schools which existed in the immediate post-war period have been considered, and it is now time to examine the ways in which children were allocated to these various types of school. During the late 1940s the 11-plus selection procedures were based very largely on the old county minor examinations. In 1947, however, Moray House, Edinburgh, was commissioned to undertake an important experiment in this field. In 1947 pupils in their last year at primary school took not only the normal externally assessed selection examinations but also three standardised tests, which were set and marked in their own junior schools as part of their ordinary work. Moray House was asked to decide which of these two methods was the more efficient in predicting future ability, as shown by performance in secondary schools three years later. The conclusion eventually reached was that there was no significant difference between the two methods, but this information was not available until 1953. Meanwhile the Education Officer had become quite anxious about the effects of the 11-plus examinations. He was particularly concerned about their depressing effects on the work of the junior schools and about the pressures put on some children.[139] He also feared that many erroneous allocations were being made, and he felt that the public was becoming more and more agitated about the whole business. When the Moray House findings came out in 1953, Clegg immediately proposed that the externally assessed selection examinations should be replaced by internally administered standardised tests. He suggested that the new arrangements should operate in 1954 as 'an interim step towards a system of allocation based on junior school assessments scaled against an intelligence test'.[140] Hyman backed Clegg very strongly on this issue and carried the day in Committee. The Conservatives and Liberals were happy with the arrangements for 1954 but sought assurances, which were given, that there would be more discussion before further steps towards allocations on school assessments were taken.[141]

During 1953 Clegg discussed the possibility of creating a scheme of selection which was entirely free from tests with his brother-in-law, Gilbert Peaker, who was HM Staff Inspector for research. Eventually Peaker devised what came to be known later as 'the Thorne scheme' (as it was first operated in the Thorne district). The main aims of this scheme were to free the junior schools from examination pressures, to avoid cramming and to give junior school staffs more responsibility.[142] There is not space to describe the detailed workings of the scheme but, generally speaking, pupils were allocated to the type of secondary school which was felt to be most appropriate for them by their junior school staffs. All borderline children, however, were seen by small panels of teachers who took the final decisions in these cases. Clegg arranged for Peaker to explain his ideas to the Policy and Finance Sub-Committee and soon afterwards suggested that a shadow scheme should be tried experimentally in the Thorne area during 1955. The Education Officer stressed that the normal selection tests would also be given to the Thorne children and that the results of these would be used for the actual allocations. It was agreed that the shadow scheme should go ahead.

Early in 1955 Clegg told Peaker that Hyman was supporting this scheme enthusiastically and would probably wish to implement it widely throughout the county if his party won the local elections in the spring.[143] Both Peaker and HMI Barry advised Clegg that they were against rushing matters. In the event Labour lost control of the West Riding in the 1955 local elections and the situation was completely transformed. Initially Clegg thought that the Conservatives would insist on the Thorne experiment being dropped. Peaker, too, felt that this might be a consequence of Hyman's strong partisan support for the scheme, which had tended to set the other side against it.[144] Clegg approached J. Fuller Smith, the new Conservative chairman, but was told that the Tories would not accept systems of selection based on teachers' assessments. After a long discussion, however, Clegg persuaded him that the shadow experiment at Thorne should be allowed to continue. He also ascertained that if the Minister, Sir David Eccles, showed interest in this experiment, Fuller Smith was sure that his local party would be more sympathetic. Clegg hoped that the Minister, who was about to visit Ripon, could be persuaded to have an encouraging word with Fuller Smith about the Thorne experiment on that occasion, and there is evidence that this was arranged. The future of the experiment was thus assured and in September the Committee agreed to extend it to the Batley area.[145] By July 1956 the

Education Officer and the Committee were satisfied that the experiments had shown that the scheme could allocate children to secondary schools no less reliably than selection tests and it was agreed to use the scheme 'live' in the Thorne district during 1956–7.[146]

Over the next two years the Thorne scheme proved satisfactory in practice. The Education Officer felt, however, that Fuller Smith was never entirely happy with the scheme, and that many Conservatives remained suspicious because they feared that it was a comprehensive philosophy being introduced by the back door. From April 1958 the Authority again came under the leadership of Labour chairmen who were more enthusiastic about this method of allocation to secondary schools. In 1959–60 the Thorne scheme was extended to the Don Valley, Goole, Ripon and Swallownest areas and tried as a shadow scheme in Rothwell, Maltby and Keighley.[147] According to the Education Officer, the teachers in the Thorne area were thoroughly convinced of the soundness of the scheme and the allocations were accepted by parents with far fewer objections than had been normal under the old selection procedures.[148] During the next few years the Thorne scheme (or slight variants of it) was taken up widely throughout the county. The Committee did not force it on any district, and some areas rejected it in the erroneous belief that its acceptance might delay comprehensivisation[149] (the Education Officer was convinced that the rejection of the scheme in the Castleford, Normanton, Mexborough, Hemsworth and Wath areas could only be explained in this way).[150] Nonetheless, by 1964, excluding areas served by comprehensive schools, no less than two-thirds of the county operated schemes of selection without tests on Thorne lines.[151]

The West Riding was committed by its Development Plan to setting up some multilateral or comprehensive schools, as they were more commonly called from the 1950s. In the 1940s, however, there was little scope for school building, and it was not until January 1950 that the Authority was able to open its first comprehensive school, Calder High, at Mytholmroyd. The completion of a new school, which had been started before the war and which had been planned as a secondary modern, enabled the Authority to reorganise its provision in this area. Preliminary discussions were held amongst the staff at Wakefield during November 1948, and it was eventually decided, with the approval of the divisional executive, to create a comprehensive school, using the new building to accommodate the upper school and the buildings of the former Hebden Bridge Grammar School to house the pupils aged between eleven and thirteen years. Although, according to the headmaster, this two-site arrangement posed some problems in the running of the school,[152] its creation aroused little controversy in the Education Committee.

The Authority, however, did not open another comprehensive school for six years.

The Education Officer, nonetheless, retained his interest in comprehensives, and in December 1951 he told Hyman that the Authority should aim at setting up a brand-new, purpose-built comprehensive school as soon as possible. He felt that a project of this kind would enable the Authority to talk with some experience of the problems of organisation encountered by such schools. Clegg realised that it would be difficult to get the Ministry to sanction such a scheme when there were so many other pressing needs, but he already had in mind the names of several people whom, he believed, would make suitable heads for such a school. In April 1952 Labour was returned to power in the West Riding with a large majority, and plans were made for the construction of comprehensive schools in the Colne Valley, Penistone and Tadcaster. These schools had not been opened before a major political row over comprehensivisation occurred. Immediately before the 1955 local elections Councillor F. Morton alleged that the local Labour group had plans for large-scale comprehensivisation which involved 'the wiping out' of eight existing grammar schools.[153] At the March meeting of the Education Committee there were bitter exchanges between Morton and Fuller Smith, the Conservative vice-chairman, on one side and Hyman on the other. Morton first sought assurance that there would be full local consultation before the closing or building of a school took place, and secondly asked for a drastic revision of the Development Plan. Hyman reaffirmed his pledge on the first issue but described the second as 'arrogant impudence'.[154] He accused Morton of being 'as obstinate as a mule' and Fuller Smith of being 'completely ignorant of his job', adding that he had an 'appalling ignorance' of West Riding modern schools. The chairman of the County Council, Sir T. Tomlinson, took a much more conciliatory line, stressing that he did not wish to attack the grammar schools and expressing a hope that their conditions might be improved. Fuller Smith and Mrs Ryder Runton, however, made it clear that the Conservatives were completely opposed to a general policy of comprehensivisation, although they were prepared to experiment with such schools in exceptional circumstances.

Soon after this acrimonious meeting the Conservatives and their allies took control of the West Riding, winning the 1955 local elections with a majority of eight. Clegg did not think that this change would make much difference, but felt that it might save the Authority from running into the problems raised by too many ill-planned comprehensive schools. At a meeting on 10 May 1955 between Fuller Smith, the new chairman, Mrs Ryder Runton and Clegg it was agreed that the three projected comprehensives should be watched carefully but given every possible chance to succeed. Clegg believed that this was a noble gesture on the part of Fuller Smith. It was also agreed that in future proposals grammar schools were not to be obliterated but that there was no objection in principle to building a comprehensive school in an area where there was no grammar school.

During the three years of Conservative control, 1955 to 1958, the three comprehensives at Colne Valley, Penistone and Tadcaster were opened. Colne Valley was purpose-built and fully comprehensive in that it took all the secondary school children from its catchment area. On the other hand, Penistone and Tadcaster took all the secondary children from their immediate vicinities but also admitted selected ('grammar school-type') pupils from much wider areas. This form of comprehensive school was common in the West Riding during the 1950s and 1960s, for of the fourteen comprehensives set up by 1966 nine admitted selected pupils from comparatively large districts but took the non-selected children from only a part of their full catchment areas. In later years the Education Officer often made the interesting point that these four early comprehensive schools – Calder High, Colne Valley, Penistone and Tadcaster – were all opened when the Conservatives were in office in the county and they were all set up in districts which were not staunchly Labour. Between 1955 and 1958 Clegg felt that some Conservatives were suspicious of the comprehensive programme. He was convinced that some right-wingers took the view that the Education Officer was in Hyman's pocket and that he was dragging Fuller Smith half-way into it as well. Nonetheless, not only were three comprehensives opened in these years but planning on two others at Elland and Settle was also commenced. In addition, Clegg and L. W. K. Brown, who dealt with the more detailed planning of secondary school building, insisted that as far as possible new modern schools should have annual intakes of not less than 120 pupils. This ensured that the county was not peppered with small modern schools which, Clegg believed, would have been difficult to convert in any future comprehensive schemes.

During the early months of 1958 the Education Officer devised an ingenious new scheme for allocating children to secondary schools. It was not a comprehensive scheme, although local politicians tended to see it in terms of the comprehensive debate. Clegg had realised for some time that there was an important overlap of ability between the grammar and modern schools. He showed convincingly that there was little to choose between the old grammar school 'C' stream and the old modern school 'A' stream.[155] He also made the important point that at the margin children were allocated to different types of secondary schools on a distinction as fine as one mark in three hundred. It was estimated that of the 16,000 pupils whose parents wanted grammar school places 11,000 were refused them,[156] and in some districts some of these refusals were connected more with the shortage of places than the ability of certain of the children.

Clegg decided that it was important to think in terms of the length of the courses available in secondary schools. He suggested that there were pupils who were suited to courses which provided education to the age of sixteen and beyond and there were others who were more suited to shorter courses terminating at the age of fifteen. He proposed that parents of children in their last year at primary school should be asked whether they wanted their children to undertake a shorter or longer course at secondary school. Simultaneously junior school head teachers were to be asked which of the two courses they thought appropriate for individual children. In cases where the parents and the heads agreed (which, it was estimated, would account for about half the total) the children were to be allocated to grammar and modern schools accordingly. For the remainder allocation was to take place on the lines of the Thorne scheme. During their first years in either grammar or modern schools, however, the children were to commence the type of course chosen by their parents. The children continued on these courses except when experience showed that they had been misplaced, and in such circumstances parents were to be asked to agree to a transfer to the course (within the same school) which was regarded by the teachers as more appropriate. Clegg felt that this scheme avoided the problem of eleven-plus selection tests and enabled more children to be educated in accordance with the wishes of their parents. It was, moreover, a flexible scheme, in that it neither prevented the development of comprehensive schools nor made them essential to the removal of some of the most telling shortcomings which had been encountered in operating bipartite schemes. In many ways it was this very flexibility which tended to make the local politicians sceptical of the proposals.

Clegg showed this scheme to his chairman, Fuller Smith, in the spring of 1958, and Fuller Smith told him that although he did not like it, he would not oppose it. When Hyman, then vice-chairman, saw it, he reacted similarly. Clegg postponed action until after the local elections of 1958. In these elections Labour was returned with a majority of two in a Council of nearly 130 members, and Fuller Smith and Hyman reversed their positions. The scheme was eventually put to the Policy and Finance Sub-Committee in July. According to Clegg, the Labour members were not enthusiastic and the Tories raised no objections (Fuller Smith was unable to attend this meeting). It was agreed that the Education Officer would bring more detailed proposals to a later meeting. During August Clegg and Hyman had some heated discussions concerning comprehensivisation, which will be described later in this chapter, but at this juncture Hyman made it amply clear that the scheme could in no way be regarded as a substitute for comprehensivisation but should act as a complement to it in areas which worked bipartite schemes. In September the Policy and Finance Sub-Committee considered a more detailed proposal for the operation of a pilot scheme in the Cleckheaton and Ripon areas. At this juncture the scheme came under heavy attack from the Conservatives led by Fuller Smith. Several Conservatives felt that this was 'comprehensivisation by the back door', and others wondered why bipartite Conservative districts such as Cleckheaton and Ripon had been chosen for the pilot scheme rather than Labour strongholds on the coalfield which were also still bipartite in their organisation. Clegg maintained that these areas were chosen because he felt that the head teachers there would operate the scheme successfully. At this point Labour members, some of whom, according to Clegg, wanted to see the scheme defeated as they saw it as a threat to comprehensivisation, changed tack and argued that the Conservatives were denying the Education Officer a reasonable scheme. Eventually the Sub-Committee decided to defer the whole scheme, but soon after the meeting the Education Officer learned that Hyman intended to revive it and push it through as a one-party measure. Clegg warned Fuller Smith of this and asked him to reconsider his attitude, even suggesting that the scheme might be put before some arbiter at Conservative Central Office. Fuller Smith did not change his mind, and in December the scheme went through the relevant committees as a Labour measure. By this time there was an added difficulty for the West Riding Tories, for the Conservative Government's White Paper *Secondary Education for All – A New Drive* had appeared and welcomed experimental schemes which aimed at lessening the sharp division between grammar and modern schools. Clegg knew that senior civil servants at the Ministry were sympathetic to his scheme and when the Minister, Geoffrey Lloyd, visited Wakefield on 8 January 1959 he was already familiar with it and publicly commended the proposals.[157] This must have been a considerable embarrassment to the West Riding Conservatives, for less than a fortnight later they were opposing the scheme at a County Council meeting.[158] Although this scheme was put into operation in the Cleckheaton and Ripon areas, in the Authority in general it was soon overshadowed by comprehensive proposals. Nonetheless, it did have some impact, particularly on modern schools. The Committee accepted that GCE courses were not normally viable in small modern schools and hence resolved to avoid the creation of such schools where possible.[159] Between 1958 and 1960 the number of secondary modern schools providing 'O' level courses increased rapidly to thirty-five schools. By 1964 this number had grown to fifty-six, with over 1,000 candidates being examined, and three modern schools had retained some pupils until the age of eighteen and had entered them for 'A' levels.[160]

When Labour returned to power in 1958, the Authority was soon faced with considerable pressure from Labour-controlled divisional executives to devise comprehensive schemes for their areas. Clegg's initial response to this pressure was to stave off demands until the staff at Wakefield had had time to consider the schemes in detail, and in July he warned committee members that 'it was idle to believe that a pattern of comprehensive schools will evolve within the next twenty-five years'.[161] Perhaps partly as a result of this statement, in early August the Education Officer faced accusations from Hyman and C. T. Broughton, who later succeeded as chairman of the Education Committee, that he was deliberately making slow progress with comprehensive proposals, despite the wishes of the Committee. The Education Officer denied this, but during the next few weeks had several heated exchanges with Hyman. Clegg was particularly annoyed on a social occasion in Ilkley when Hyman asserted that if history were taught in a comprehensive school it would *ipso facto* be better taught than in a grammar or modern school. The Education Officer regarded this as complete nonsense, and had important general reservations about rushing into comprehensive schemes. First, he felt that if the Authority was hurried, it was likely to produce bad schemes which could provide the opponents of comprehensives with just the ammunition they needed; second, he was afraid that alarm would be caused amongst the grammar school teachers, and in a time of teacher shortage he held that it was particularly important that the Authority should not lose the services of good graduate staff; third, and perhaps most important, he was determined to avoid a situation in which a multiplicity of small sixth forms were created. He argued that with a small sixth form it was not possible either to offer a full range of subjects or to attract a well qualified staff. At a meeting on 14 August Clegg and Hyman thrashed out their differences and a procedure for the future was agreed. When a resolution requesting comprehensivisation was received from a division, it was to be taken to Committee and a resolution passed to the effect that the Education Officer be instructed to set out alternative ways of implementing comprehensivisation in the area. Details were then to be worked out by the divisional officer and the staff at Wakefield and eventually submitted to the Committee for discussion. Clegg made it clear, however, that he felt bound to oppose schemes involving any of the following: the union of buildings which were several miles apart; the federation of buildings which were in bad physical condition; or the combination of two or more schools under a mediocre head.

These disputes in August had largely been centred on a request for comprehensivisation from the Ecclesfield district. Clegg was not at all satisfied that the proposals which were coming from the districts were sound. He wrote to the divisional officer:

> My criticisms of your proposals are that they make no mention of the purely educational problems. There should be no difficulty about our carving up numbers and allocating to the schools in proper sequence. . . . What worries me, however, is that hitherto in the Ecclesfield area it has been possible, at any rate in theory and occasionally in practice, for any child of appropriate ability to get to Oxford or Cambridge. To withdraw this possibility in order to introduce a comprehensive school would damn the comprehensive school principle.[162]

Clegg tried to take this case steadily but was under continual pressure from Hyman to speed things up. Hyman accused the staff at Wakefield of creating unnecessary difficulties, and complained that he could not face his Labour friends from south Yorkshire until this matter was settled.[163] Clegg decided that his strategy would be to present two memoranda on this issue to the December meeting of the Policy and Finance Sub-Committee. He prepared what he described himself as 'a highly tendentious report' on the education of the gifted child in the comprehensive schools of the Yorkshire coalfield[164] and another concerned with specific proposals for Ecclesfield.[165] In the former he emphasised the manifold difficulties faced by children brought up on the coalfield, and claimed:

> A child has less chance of getting to a grammar school in the south than in the north and west [of the county]; when he gets there he is less likely to get to the sixth form; if he gets to the sixth form he is less likely to get an award; and if he gets an award it is less likely to take him to Oxford or Cambridge.[166]

The Education Officer concluded the report by saying that while graduate staff shortages persisted sixth-form work needed to be concentrated, and the Committee was also asked to make it known that it attached importance to the development of large sixth forms.[167] With regard to Ecclesfield there were several possibilities, but the one recommended was a compromise solution which involved the amalgamation of Ecclesfield Grammar School with two neighbouring modern schools.[168] The other modern schools in the district, however, were to continue for the time being to admit selected 'secondary modern-type' pupils, and, although several of these schools had already developed 'O' level courses, they were to transfer pupils at the age of sixteen to Ecclesfield Grammar School for sixth-form work. These recommendations were accepted by the Committee, and Clegg told a senior civil servant at the Ministry that he hoped very much that they would be approved by central government. The outcome was disappointing for Clegg in this respect, for the Ministry turned down the proposals, suggesting that the existing bipartite arrangements should be continued.[169] Despite this rebuff, the Education Officer had won the major battle some months earlier when he persuaded the Committee to avoid policies which involved spreading sixth-form work thinly over large numbers of schools.

When pressure for comprehensivisation increased in 1958, the Education Officer pointed out that the Committee ought to be prepared to consider schemes involving the establishment of junior and senior high schools, on the understanding that both types were non-selective. At this juncture he thought that pupils would normally proceed to the senior highs at the age of fourteen, but he predicted that the age of transfer would often be determined by the accommodation available. During 1959 consideration was given to the Leicestershire scheme but the Education Officer did not like certain aspects of these arrangements[170] (these objections will be discussed later), and it was decided not to follow the Leicestershire pattern. Clegg stressed, however, that if some districts wished to establish comprehensive schools for pupils from eleven to eighteen, the amount of new building involved would be very great indeed. He realised that the Ministry would only sanction such building in the very long term and emphasised that if these areas wanted comprehensives within a reasonable period of time, they would have to opt for arrangements other than conventional eleven to eighteen schools. In other schemes, especially those which divided secondary children by age, it was, of course, much easier to rearrange and adapt existing buildings. From the Education Officer's point of view, junior and senior high school systems also promised other advantages. The problems posed by sheer size in eleven to eighteen comprehensive schools were avoided, and it was hoped that the best current junior school methods would be introduced into the junior high schools.[171] In September 1959 it was suggested to the Hemsworth area that it might consider a junior/senior high school system,[172] as the large number of small modern schools in the district made reorganisation on eleven to eighteen lines extremely difficult. A similar suggestion was also put to Mexborough.[173] Mexborough, however, quickly rejected the proposal, as the division claimed that it wanted 'full-blooded comprehension',[174] and eventually comprehensivisation was arranged for this area in a rather different way. Hemsworth proved more amenable and early in 1960 accepted the Education Officer's suggestion.[175] By 1963 Castleford and part of the Don Valley had also accepted similar proposals and Keighley was considering whether to adopt a

Leicestershire scheme. In the schemes for Hemsworth, Castleford and the Don Valley in the early 1960s it was planned that pupils between the ages of eleven and fourteen would attend junior highs, and at the age of fourteen all would be transferred to senior highs for the remainder of their school careers. In 1963, however, the Education Officer added a new dimension to the situation which eventually transformed much of this planning.

As early as 1958, when the Authority was considering comprehensive proposals for the Ecclesfield area, Clegg became interested in the possibility of varying the age of transfer from primary to secondary schools. In reviewing a junior/senior high school scheme in 1958 he wrote, 'One interesting feature of this scheme is, of course, that it will enable us to juggle about if we want to do so with the age of admission to the junior high school.'[176] The Education Officer eventually adopted another approach to the Ecclesfield problem and for some years dropped the idea of changing age ranges because of the constraint of the definition of a senior pupil in the 1944 Act.[177] At the beginning of May 1963, however, he wrote to L. R. Fletcher at the Schools Branch of the Ministry thus:

> I am writing to you personally about a matter which has several times entered my head in recent years, but which I have discarded as being impractical. However, the idea is a persistent one, so I am writing to ask you if there is even a remote chance of getting it accepted if we put it forward officially. You must understand that I am not putting forward a properly though-out case, but merely flying a kite.[178]

Clegg proceeded to suggest that in some districts schools should be reorganised on a new basis which broke away from the conventional pattern of five to eleven primary and eleven to eighteen secondary schools. He proposed five to nine primary, nine to thirteen middle and thirteen to eighteen secondary schools. A few days later the Education Officer met Fletcher and Morrell from the Schools Branch in London. Initially, they did not think much of the scheme.[179]

The Education Officer did not abandon the idea, however, and worked on it through the summer. In October he presented a lengthy memorandum on the theme to the Policy and Finance Sub-Committee and set out his notions in some detail.[180] The three-tier proposals remained first and foremost a means for reorganising on comprehensive lines in areas where the existing buildings were unsuitable for adaptation into conventional eleven to eighteen patterns, but the Education Officer saw other important virtues in such a scheme. Perhaps one of its biggest attractions was that it could be used to introduce primary-school methods to the eleven to thirteen age range. This would give the less able children the security of more contact with class teachers and would keep the more able free from premature specialisation and examination pressures. In addition, he maintained that this form of reorganisation would remove pressure from primary-school accommodation and thus enable the primary sector to reduce class sizes and reintroduce nursery provisions. He was adamant that the age of transfer from middle to secondary school should be at thirteen rather than fourteen. He argued that it was essential for secondary schools to have three years to prepare for 'O' levels and CSE and he predicted that if secondary schools were given less time, pressure imposed by the schedules for external examinations would be felt in the middle schools. The wisdom of educating young children of eleven and citizens of eighteen in the same institutions was questioned, and it was pointed out that the public schools had always admitted pupils at thirteen rather than eleven. In conclusion Clegg stated that the West Riding could delay no longer. If the Ministry refused to allow reorganisation on these lines, the Authority would be forced to use a modified Leicestershire scheme in certain areas against its own better judgement. This memorandum was accepted by the Committee, and the issue aroused little political controversy at county level.

There is no doubt that Clegg pioneered the three-tier system of organisation in this country, but a note which was sent to D. B. Bartlett, Southend's Chief Education Officer, in 1963 suggests that the original idea itself may have owed much to the latter. Clegg wrote:

> Some time ago you made some bright suggestions to me about change of dates; I cannot think what they were, but I am pretty sure that they were something to do with this report [the memorandum on middle schools]. I told you that once I got a good idea I churned it over and turned it out as my own, and you will probably find that this is it.[181]

In October 1963 Clegg ensured that wide publicity was given to the three-tier proposals, for copies of the memorandum were supplied to the education correspondents of most national newspapers, to the chief officers of important LEAs and to many other leading educationists. During the next few months permission was sought from the Ministry on several occasions to transfer pupils at ages other than eleven. The Education Officer hoped to apply the three-tier scheme to divisions such as Hemsworth and Castleford, which had opted for junior/senior high school systems, but lack of progress made the local people 'restive and critical'.[182] At the end of 1963 Clegg asked Fletcher for a 'divine dispensation' for Castleford, and pleaded, 'Could you not wrestle with your conscience on this matter and persuade the Minister to wrestle with his? If you did, you would both of you, I am sure, come out victorious and education would take a leap forward in Castleford.'[183] In view of the existing law, civil servants could do little, but when the Minister, Sir Edward Boyle, visited the Don Valley in 1964, he told C. T. Broughton, the chairman of the Committee, that he hoped that an Act of Parliament would be passed enabling LEAs to try experiments of this kind. Before the Conservatives left office Boyle kept his promise: the Education Act was passed in 1964. The pioneering of the three-tier form of comprehensive reorganisation was probably the West Riding's greatest single contribution to national education in the post-war period. Without this innovation the unsuitability of existing buildings and the weakening economic position of the nation would, in combination, almost certainly have provided an insuperable barrier to comprehensive reorganisation in many areas in the later 1960s and 1970s.

In February 1965 the Authority's comprehensive proposals were with the new Minister of State, Reginald Prentice, and it was agreed that the three-tier scheme should be adopted in the Hemsworth area. The first stage of reorganisation was implemented in 1968 and an account of the preparations and early experiences was written up in 1970 as a DES pamphlet entitled *Launching Middle Schools*.[184] In contrast to Hemsworth, Castleford showed some determination to retain the junior/senior high school system which it had originally accepted in February 1962. During the autumn of 1963 a nine to thirteen scheme was devised for this division and on 4 May 1964 Clegg explained these proposals to the divisional executive. In July, however, Castleford rejected the nine to thirteen scheme and resolved to keep to the original proposals.[185] The Ministry had already intimated that it preferred a break at thirteen rather than fourteen in Castleford, and Clegg complained that, contrary to normal practice, Castleford was attempting to dictate the details of its reorganisation scheme. Clegg informed the Policy and Finance Sub-Committee that the Castleford scheme was likely to meet strong hostility from the teachers and predicted that if it was resubmitted to the DES, the Authority would be asked whether it now repudiated the arguments which it had advanced in favour of nine to thirteen schemes.[186] Eventually a deputation from the Committee met members of the divisional executive and tried to persuade them to adopt the nine to thirteen scheme. This proved of no avail because, according to the divisional officer, the nine to thirteen arrangements were regarded as Broughton's scheme. This officer believed that there was a strong anti-Broughton feeling, on strictly personal grounds, within the Castleford Labour group and consequently the whips were put on against the proposals. At this juncture Clegg said that he would make no further observations on the matter until the Authority was asked by the DES to declare its intentions for the future organisation of the area.[187] Later, in response to Circular 10/65, a five to eight, eight to twelve, twelve to eighteen scheme was recommended by the division and accepted by the Committee.

The West Riding came out as early as 1959 against certain aspects of the Leicestershire plan, but during the early 1960s the objections were more forcefully expressed. The Education Officer opposed the accelerated movement of groups of able pupils through the junior high schools, and felt that the senior highs needed more than two years to prepare for 'O' levels. His most serious objection, however, was concerned with the fact that not all children moved to the senior highs at the age of fourteen. Parental choice determined whether a child moved to the senior high or completed his education in the junior high, and Clegg questioned whether this could be regarded as genuine comprehensivisation. During 1963 the West Riding's senior inspector and a deputation of teachers visited Leicestershire schools, and adverse reports on the system were submitted to the Committee. The Education Officer predicted that the junior highs would become 'finishing schools for working-class children – or, put more crudely, "dumps" for the Newsom types'.[188] In November 1964 Clegg expressed amazement that some Socialists seemed prepared to accept the Leicestershire plan as a comprehensive solution, and submitted an article to the *Guardian* in which he attacked what he described to the editor as 'a bogus and spurious form of comprehensive education which could produce some schools which would be restricted almost entirely to certain occupational groups'.[189] The only part of the West Riding in which a Leicestershire scheme made much headway was the excepted district of Keighley. In November 1963 Keighley Education Committee decided in favour of a straight Leicestershire plan because it felt that this was by far the quickest way to abolish 11-plus selection in the borough. F. M. Pedley, Keighley's Education Officer, however, made it clear that he would have preferred a ten to thirteen middle school scheme.[190] In December Clegg met Pedley and reiterated the West Riding's objections to Leicestershire plans, and although these were explained to the Keighley Committee, the original proposals were retained. The West Riding continued to press Keighley to change its mind, and on 17 November 1964 Clegg, C. T. Broughton and Mrs L. Fitzpatrick met representatives of the Keighley Committee. These representatives stressed that their Committee ultimately wished to have breaks at ten and thirteen, with all children moving forward to the next stage at these ages, but were prevented from doing this in the near future because of lack of appropriate accommodation.[191] The West Riding continued to stall and the proceedings were overtaken by the appearance of Circular 10/65. This made it clear that Leicestershire-type schemes would be recognised by the DES only as interim arrangements for comprehensivisation and that eventually all pupils would have to be transferred to the senior high schools.[192] At this juncture the West Riding accepted Keighley's proposals as an interim measure. When Keighley later experienced serious difficulties in 1969, it was felt that the borough had only itself to blame.[193] The Education Officer wrote:

> My chairman (by this time Mrs L. Fitzpatrick [Conservative]) is likely to have little sympathy for any demand (beyond what the various pools can reasonably provide) for Keighley. She has vivid recollections of going to Keighley with me and of our failure to persuade Keighley not to go forward with what I considered then, and still consider, to be a botched scheme.[194]

Eventually in 1973 the West Riding approved a three-tier (five to nine, nine to thirteen, thirteen to eighteen) arrangement for Keighley which was to be implemented from September 1977.[195]

When the West Riding received Circular 10/65 it already had considerable experience of dealing with comprehensive schemes and this experience was soon put to good use. The Committee accepted the main requirement of the circular and agreed to supply the DES within one year with a statement of how it intended to reorganise its schools on comprehensive lines. Three areas – Colne Valley, Rother Valley and Hemsworth – were not greatly affected, as they were already committed to comprehensive patterns, but all other divisions had to prepare reorganisation schemes. It was accepted that representative working parties would be established in the divisions and that proposals would be fully discussed with local teachers' associations and appropriate bodies of parents. It was expected that the Education Officer and his staff would consult with divisional officers, attend meetings and give advice on the formation of schemes.

Early in 1966 the Education Officer was concerned about two aspects of Circular 10/65, but after informal discussions with Anthony Crosland, the Secretary of State, he was sure that the West Riding's needs would be accommodated. At one point Clegg was a little suspicious of the sentence in the circular which emphasised eleven as the normal age of transfer, and he also feared the reference to middle school 'experiments' might imply that only limited use was to be made of three-tier schemes. Nonetheless, he recalled that he told Crosland that, as far as the West Riding was concerned, the best scheme for each area would be produced and, regardless of whether it was a nine to thirteen scheme or a twelve to sixteen scheme, it would be sent up to the Minister.[196] If the Minister then decided that he required something which was educationally less sound and probably more costly, that was up to him.

It was made clear to the divisions that there were several features which in normal circumstances would not be acceptable in reorganisation schemes. These were: two-year eleven to thirteen schools; transfer at fourteen; selection for senior highs based on parental choice; and the creation of large schools in split premises which were widely separated. After consultation with experienced heads, it was decided that eleven to sixteen comprehensives needed minimum annual intakes of 180 pupils to ensure that adequate special facilities could be provided for 'O' level classes at one extreme and slow learners at the other. The minimum annual intake prescribed for eleven to eighteen schools was 240 pupils and although J. M. Hogan, the Deputy Education Officer, acknowledged that in one or two remote rural areas these minima had not always been achieved, in the exceptional cases it was hoped that the population would grow to make the school viable in the near future.[197] Clegg continued to stress the importance of having large sixth forms which could attract good specialist staff and could offer a wide range of 'A' level subjects. He maintained that the sixth formers in West Riding comprehensives should have the same opportunities as their contemporaries in public and direct grant schools, and he made it amply clear that he did not wish the Authority to repeat the experience of the small sixth form at Settle High School, where Latin by correspondence course had been requested.

By the spring of 1966 the Authority had received schemes from many divisions, and on 18 May 1966 Broughton moved a resolution in County Council that the Authority's schools should be reorganised on comprehensive lines. He paid tribute to the hard work which had been done at divisional level, and mentioned that although one or two divisions were most reluctant to prepare comprehensive plans, nearly all had now completed their tasks. He warned those divisions that wanted comprehensive education overnight that the Authority would not be rushed into providing schools with features which were as bad as or even worse than those which comprehensivisation aimed to remove.[198] The Conservatives opposed Broughton's resolution but were defeated by fifty-nine votes to forty-one.[199] On 19 July the bulk of the Authority's reorganisation schemes were submitted to the DES. In the preamble to the submission the Authority explained that the schemes emanated from the divisions and that in only a very few instances had the local proposals been modified and they had been radically altered in fewer still.[200] It was also mentioned that the West Riding had accepted eleven to eighteen schools, eleven to sixteen schools working in combinations with eleven to eighteen schools, and three different kinds of three-tier schemes: five to eight, eight to twelve, twelve to eighteen; five to nine, nine to thirteen, thirteen to eighteen; five to ten, ten to thirteen, thirteen to eighteen.[201]

The Conservatives did very well in the local elections in April 1967 throughout the country and they swept back into power in the West Riding with a comfortable majority. This political change made comparatively little impact on reorganisation in the county, but one important problem still had to be faced in a small number of divisions. It became clear in a few areas that the only means of abolishing selection within a comparatively short period of time was to amalgamate schools on different sites. The Education Officer had consistently opposed such amalgamations and the Committee had outlawed proposals of this kind when reorganisation schemes had been drawn up in 1965 and 1966. In 1969, however, Mexborough Divisional Executive proposed the amalgamation of the local grammar and secondary modern schools. Together these schools provided accommodation for over 2,000 pupils, but they were on sites about one mile apart.[202] On the recommendation of the Education Officer this suggestion was rejected in December 1969.[203] About a month later rather similar proposals from Normanton were considered.[204] Reorganisation in this area was being delayed because Normanton Grammar School provided places for a large number of selected pupils from outside its own area, and until reorganisation schemes in adjacent divisions were completed Normanton was stymied. In January 1970 there were vacant headships at both the secondary schools in Normanton and the Divisional Executive thought that this opportunity of amalgamating the two schools, which were about six hundred yards apart, should be taken.[205] At the meeting of the Policy and Finance Sub-Committee in February 1970 Clegg presented a memorandum on the general question of setting up comprehensive schools in split premises.[206] He pointed out that there was 'no wholly acceptable solution'[207] and stressed that there was a difficult choice to be faced between retaining selection or operating large comprehensives in split premises. With regard to the Normanton case, the Education Officer advised that the amalgamation should be permitted and asked that his views be recorded in the minutes.[208] The Policy and Finance Sub-Committee, however, refused the divisional executives' requests in both the Mexborough and the Normanton cases.[209] By this time the issue had become politicised, with Labour members supporting the Labour-controlled divisional executives and the Conservatives opposing large comprehensives on split sites. The political battle culminated in a censure motion on the policy of the Education Committee moved by C. T. Broughton, now vice-chairman, at a County Council meeting.[210] Broughton maintained that the Committee was ignoring local wishes, disregarding professional advice and continuing 'the unfair and inefficient system of education by selection'.[211] The Conservatives defeated this censure motion with a majority of twenty-one, and Mrs Fitzpatrick, the chairman of the Education Committee, stated that the West Riding branch of the NUT had expressed satisfaction at the fact that proposals to form comprehensive schools by amalgamating split premises were rejected.[212] The dispute concerning Mexborough continued, although it was eventually agreed to reorganise Normanton on a basis which did not include the amalgamation of schools on different sites.[213] In February 1971 it was decided that the Education Officer would consult the teaching staffs of the Mexborough secondary schools and report back to the Policy and Finance Sub-Committee.[214] In November Clegg reported that the Mexborough Divisional Executive and a majority of a working party composed of members of staff from both Mexborough secondary schools recommended that the two schools should be amalgamated so that comprehensivisation could be implemented in the town, and the Sub-Committee agreed in this instance to make an exception to their general principle concerning split premises.[215]

The question of secondary reorganisation in the Ripon division also attracted attention in the late 1960s and early 1970s. For some time the Authority experienced considerable difficulty in eliciting any response to the requirements of Circular 10/65 from this strongly Conservative area. Eventually a comprehensive scheme was submitted to the DES, but a large petition against it was also forwarded by a group of local people. Before matters were resolved there was a change of Government and the new Secretary of State, Margaret Thatcher, issued Circular 10/70, which invited authorities to re-examine any proposals submitted as a consequence of Circular 10/65, if they so desired. A special sub-committee of seven members was set up under the chairmanship of Mrs Fitzpatrick to deal with the situation which now arose in Ripon.[216] This group consulted the governors, managers and teachers of the schools concerned and met members of the public who wished to discuss the reorganisation scheme. Mrs Fitzpatrick described this question as 'the most complex matter I have had to deal with in many years on the Education Committee'.[217] After the consultations were completed, it was reported to the Policy and Finance Sub-Committee that opinion was 'sharply but fairly evenly divided'.[218] Ripon Borough Council came out against the comprehensive scheme but, according to the memorandum, 'most of the teachers in the area, either directly or through their associations, have argued in favour of ending selection at eleven'.[219] Clegg pointed out that part of the proposal was to extend the grammar school to take all the pupils between thirteen and eighteen in the area, and he added that he was in no doubt that 'this will ultimately be seen to have been the right way to deal with secondary education in Ripon'.[220] The Committee, however, decided otherwise and agreed that no change should be made to the status and character of Ripon Grammar School.[221] Mrs Fitzpatrick regarded this as a compromise solution which left the matter open for the future,[222] but by 1974 Ripon was alone in the West Riding in not having adopted at least tentative comprehensive proposals for its schools.[223]

During the 1960s the professional leaders of the West Riding education service took a strong interest in new experimental approaches to secondary schooling. Whilst the Education Officer was serving on the Newsom Committee he learned of new ideas for secondary school building being proposed by Mr and Mrs Medd of the Ministry's Architects Branch. Clegg arranged to meet the Medds and he soon became enthusiastic about their plans for developing special centres for older pupils in secondary schools. These centres were to be designed so that they could serve many purposes but emphasis was placed on facilities for informal activities such as group discussions and social gatherings. In essence it was hoped that they would make it possible to implement 'the Newsom idea of an extended and varied school day, with a blurring of the distinction between school and leisure activities'.[224] The Education Officer and his deputy, J. M. Hogan, felt that these centres could be used by adolescents and young adults outside school hours, along youth club lines.

In 1963 Clegg explained to Miss E. L. Sewell of the National Association of Youth Clubs that he would like to see such a centre incorporated in a new school built in a mining area.[225] The cost of such a project was well beyond the limits on expenditure for school building imposed by the Ministry, but Clegg hoped to tap 'one of the great charitable sources' for funds.[226] With the help and support of the National Association of Youth Clubs, the Authority sought aid from the Carnegie Trust. By December 1964 the Trust had agreed to make £30,000 available[227] and the West Riding decided that the experimental centre should be included in the proposed thirteen to eighteen school at South Kirby/Moorthorpe. Early in 1965 the Deputy Education Officer put the scheme to DES officials and although there was some initial criticism that the scheme was 'lavish' and too costly,[228] the proposals were eventually accepted. For several reasons there were long delays for the South Kirby/Moorthorpe project and, because of lack of progress, at one stage the Carnegie Trust considered transferring its grants to another LEA. This difficulty was overcome, and in February 1969 Minsthorpe High School and Community College (incorporating the Carnegie Centre) was officially opened. The West Riding maintained that Minsthorpe was not to be regarded simply as a secondary school with a youth club and an adult activities centre on the same site. It explained that this development was the product of 'a recognition that in so many ways the fundamental responsibilities of school and youth service should be regarded as synonymous'.[229] Many of the facilities were open to the public during the evenings, weekends and school holidays. Minsthorpe was soon to play a full part in the community life of the South Kirby, South Elmsall and Upton areas. Several of the features which were pioneered at Minsthorpe were later incorporated in the new West Riding secondary schools built in the early 1970s.

The West Riding also became involved in another experimental scheme in secondary education in the late 1960s – the Dartington Hall exchange project. Dartington Hall, Totnes, Devon, has been described as 'a progressive, co-educational, independent boarding school, beautifully equipped and generously staffed, well endowed and expensive'.[230] In January 1969 the headmaster of this school, Dr R. Lambert, suggested that there should be more contact between state schools and schools such as his own and proposed that exchanges of pupils might be arranged.[231] At about the same time M. J. Harvey, a member of the West Riding EPA project team, approached Lambert about setting up an investigation into working-class boarding education.[232] Soon afterwards the Education Officer took up this matter with Lambert and suggested that Dartington might become involved in an exchange scheme with some schools on the south Yorkshire coalfield.[233] Clegg had a long-standing interest in the possibility of the provision of boarding education for working-class children, and he felt that this scheme could widen the horizons of all the children involved in the experiment, as the pupils would come from markedly contrasting schools, locations and social backgrounds. In March representatives of Dartington visited the Mexborough area and agreed to participate in the project. The Dartington Hall Trustees purchased a house in Conisbrough known as 'The Terrace' to provide residential accommodation for groups of children from Dartington and from Mexborough Grammar School and Conisbrough Northcliffe Secondary, the two West Riding schools involved in the experiment. Children from the West Riding schools were also to board at Dartington.

Between July 1969 and March 1971 375 children from Yorkshire stayed at Dartington for short periods and took part in specially designed courses or projects. In return ninety-five children from Dartington (one-third of the school's pupils) visited Conisbrough and seventy-five staff from Yorkshire and thirty-eight from Dartington had participated in an exchange. By March 1971 twenty-two West Riding pupils, including six cases of severe need, were holding long-stay places at Dartington.[234] 'The Terrace', meanwhile, was also used by Northcliffe School to accommodate children in distress and as a base for rural studies, extra-curricular activities and short-stay residential work.[235] The progress and diversification of the project was lauded by all the parties in the scheme, and in 1971 the West Riding agreed to spend an additional £11,000 on the venture.[236] Indeed, partly because of the success of the experiment Lambert relinquished his post as headmaster to organise an 'alternative to school' project, backed by the Authority, involving ROSLA (Raising of the School Leaving Age) children in Conisbrough.[237]

Since 1944 developments in West Riding primary schools have attracted national attention. In the late 1940s, however, the West Riding, like other authorities, had to concentrate on the mundane but urgent problem of providing sufficient places for the rapidly growing child population. In 1948 the Ministry estimated that the number of children aged five to eight years in the country would increase by over 20 per cent between 1946 and 1952.[238] The West Riding concluded that it could not cope with an increase of such proportions, even if it rented all the available accommodation which was suitable for use as classrooms and increased class sizes to forty-five.[239] Eventually the Authority decided that it would have to launch its own hut-building programme along the lines of HORSA, which had accommodated the extra children in school after the raising of the leaving age in 1947. The programme to deal with the increased birth rate was soon nicknamed HENGIST, and between 1949 and 1954 this helped to house the extra 22,000 children in West Riding primary schools. On the advice of Hubert Bennett, the County Architect, it was decided that the huts provided in the HENGIST programme should be of a better quality than the prefabricated HORSA variety provided by the Ministry of Works. Although HORSA accommodation was less costly than that provided under HENGIST, the latter had a considerably better appearance than its forerunner and during the early post-war years the Committee, encouraged by Clegg and Hyman, made an effort to brighten up some of its drab primary schools. Dark browns and greens were replaced by lighter colour schemes, some of which were designed jointly by Bennett and Basil Rocke, the county's new art adviser.[240]

When Clegg arrived in the West Riding he was already convinced of the virtues of what he characterised later as 'the informal school'.[241] His previous experience, especially in Worcestershire, had persuaded him that one of the most important tasks which had to be undertaken after 1944 was to establish an identity for the new primary schools which was far removed from the traditional concept of the old elementary schools. In the late 1940s and early 1950s he consistently tried to reduce the influence of the 11-plus selection tests on the work of the junior schools, but he was also determined to bring about much more fundamental changes in the field of primary education. Although the three Rs were still regarded as important, more stress was placed on the aesthetic elements in the curriculum. More importance was attached to music, art and crafts, dance and movement, and to drama, creative writing and the spoken word in English lessons. Children were expected to be more active in school and they were to be given ample opportunities to express themselves. It was felt that there was a particular potency in artistic work[242] and that most children could succeed in this area of the curriculum in their own way. The importance of the development of children as 'individuals' was stressed, and expressive work was to be substantiated not in terms of the critical assessment of performance but 'through observing the children's growth in satisfaction, confidence and security'.[243] In general, local politicians made remarkably little public comment on these approaches, although in 1953 Fuller Smith, at that time vice-chairman of the Committee, stated in County Council that, 'since 1945 the advisers and educationalists had made guinea pigs of the children. Experiment after experiment had been tried out on them. In many of the schools spelling had been abolished and the old composition had been replaced by culture'.[244] This outburst was, however, completely contrary to normal practice, for the politicians usually left such matters almost entirely to the professionals.

The Education Officer believed that the best way to disseminate the policy of informal approaches to the primary schools in the county was through a dedicated team of advisers. He was satisfied that he inherited a good group of advisers from Binns but he attached great importance to strengthening this team as opportunities arose. Diana Jordan, who was an ex-pupil of Rudolph Laban's, the expert on movement and dance, became the first Warden of Woolley Hall. She followed Clegg from Worcestershire to the West Riding, as did Arthur Stone who came as an inspector in 1947. Clegg had known Stone from the early days of the war, when Stone had been the headmaster of Steward Street Junior School in a depressed area of Birmingham. Clegg retained a strong admiration for Stone's original work in that school and hoped that the example would be taken up in West Riding Schools. Later Stone's experiences were written up in Ministry of Education Pamphlet 14 entitled *The Story of a School*, which sold over 60,000 copies. During this period Basil Rocke, who had worked with Cizek, and Ruth Scriver, who knew Herbert Read well, were appointed as art advisers. At the end of 1951 Clegg told Hyman that he felt that the Authority had built up a fine advisory team and stressed that Stone ought to be released from some of his 'muck and rubble jobs' so that the could help more with purely educational matters over a wider area. The Authority regarded the in-service training of teachers as one of the main means of disseminating ideas throughout the area and the Bingley vacation courses and Woolley Hall were thought to be crucially important in this process. Emphasis was placed on innovation by example and changes were regarded as emanating from the vision and enthusiasm of charismatic leaders.[245] Clegg regarded the 1948 Bingley vacation course on junior schools as particularly seminal, and he has recalled that many of the people on it had just come out of the forces and wanted to be told how to teach. Instead they were asked 'to move, to paint, to write, in short, to face children's difficulties at first hand'.[246] The Education Officer felt that 'what they gained led directly to the kind of education which the Plowden Committee were to commend twenty years later'.[247]

It is not possible to quantify the impact made on West Riding primary schools by Clegg, his advisory team and their firm beliefs in informal approaches. Some schools were probably hardly affected at all; at the other extreme, some were completely transformed, and no doubt many steered a middle course. It is no part of the function of this book to pass judgement on these informal approaches to primary education as such; ultimately the issue

TABLE 7.1

*Numbers of teachers employed by the West Riding in primary and secondary schools,*
*1948–73*

| Year | Number of teachers |
|------|--------------------|
| 1948–9 | 8,104 |
| 1949–50 | 8,261 |
| 1950–1 | 8,332 |
| 1951–2 | 8,560 |
| 1952–3 | 8,483 |
| 1953–4 | 9,114 |
| 1954–5 | 8,857 |
| 1955–6 | 9,472 |
| 1956–7 | 9,630 |
| 1957–8 | 9,916 |
| 1958–9 | 10,178 |
| 1959–60 | 10,646 |
| 1960–1 | 10,678 |
| 1961–2 | 10,450 |
| 1962–3 | 10,915 |
| 1963–4 | 10,845 |
| 1964–5 | 10,982 |
| 1965–6 | 11,270 |
| 1966–7 | 11,574 |
| 1967–8 | 11,811 |
| 1968–9 | 12,213 |
| 1969–70 | 12,566 |
| 1970–1 | 13,587 |
| 1971–2 | 14,587 |
| 1972–3 | 15,674 |

*Source: Education Statistics*

is concerned with feelings and values rather than intellectual arguments. In essence they demand a response from the heart rather than the head, but the strong personal commitment to these ideas made by many of the professional leaders of the West Riding's education service in the post-war period was in no doubt. Their feelings were summarised succinctly in this sentence written by Alec Clegg in 1963:

> What I say only makes sense if one believes as I do that the fundamental educational issue of the next twenty-five years is whether the child-centred education of our primary schools is going to defeat or be defeated by the examination pressures which have since payment by results done such incalculable harm to our teaching.[248]

TABLE 7.2

*Numbers of pupils in West Riding schools 1948–73*

| Year | Number of pupils | | Number of pupils per teacher | |
|------|------|------|------|------|
| | Primary | Secondary | Primary | Secondary |
| 1948–9 | 160,378 | 63,004 | | |
| 1951–2 | 167,908 | 62,894* | 31 | 20 |
| 1954–5 | 181,363 | 73,378 | 32 | 23 |
| 1957–8 | 176,456 | 88,781 | 30 | 22 |
| 1960–1 | 159,940 | 104,297 | 28 | 21 |
| 1963–4 | 164,605 | 103,384 | 29 | 20 |
| 1966–7 | 177,526 | 104,139 | 28.6 | 19.4 |
| 1969–70 | 189,576 | 114,559 | 28.2 | 19.6 |
| 1972–3 | 204,224 | 126,501 | 24.3 | 17.4 |

\*  +5,337 in assisted schools
*Source: Education Statistics*

# CHAPTER VIII

# Education after School

On 30 October 1941 the Yorkshire Council for Further Education appointed a special committee to consider and report on post-war reconstruction in further education. The chairman of the Council at this time was the chairman of the West Riding Education Committee, Walter Hyman. It followed that the county's post-war aims in this area were worked out with characteristic vigour in the wider Yorkshire context. The special committee reported in the autumn of 1942. The report[1] assumed that from the end of the war the school leaving age would be fixed at sixteen; that there would be statutory arrangements for vocational guidance by LEAs and that the recruitment of school leavers to industry and commerce would be through their juvenile employment services; and that attendance at day continuation schools would be compulsory from sixteen to eighteen. These assumptions were entirely reasonable, given that they were based largely upon the suggestions made by Board of Education officials in the 'Green Book' which had been circulated to LEAs and others under confidential cover in July 1941.[2]

Following the suggestions from the Board, day continuation schools were seen as the centre piece of the provision for persons up to the age of eighteen, half of the report being devoted to it. The time spent in attendance was to be regarded as part of a young person's normal working week. The curriculum ought to meet vocational, social, physical and spiritual needs. Young people should no longer have to rely on evening classes for the basic knowledge they required to further their vocational interests. The report set out a detailed examination of the sort of teacher who would be needed to make continuation schooling a success and suggested a special course of training. The youth clubs and similar activities were seen as purely voluntary, making no demands which would conflict with day continuation schools. The report envisaged an expansion of higher technical education and urged the appointment of a committee at the national level to inquire into the future relationship between universities and technological institutions in order to avoid confusion and conflict. The question of whether the Council should have any more than an advisory function in sorting out possible conflicts between LEAs in Yorkshire proved difficult. The report affirmed that the Council was strongly opposed to any suggestion that LEAs should surrender any powers or duties to regional bodies. The statement in the draft report that when proposals for the building or substantial enlargement of institutions for further education were submitted to the Board of Education, the regional body 'should have a statutory duty to submit observations on the proposals to the Board' was changed to '. . . should have the opportunity to submit observations on the proposals'. At another point in the report, the chairman's marginal note against a deleted portion of the draft stated simply 'membership to be statutory, but decisions to be advisory – wording to be settled by Secretary'.

The attitudes shown here have been of some importance in their effect on the growth of technical education nationally during this century. The obvious and, in many ways, laudable anxiety of each authority to make its own technical college provision and to have sole control over it, or at least to make provision which others might share if there were insufficient demand from its own residents for more advanced or specialised facilities, has been an important influence in making the organisation and administration of much technical and further education cumbersome and inadequate. The very fact that the Yorkshire Council for Further Education had been set up and that it had achieved a good deal led the Percy Committee on Higher Technological Education to regard Yorkshire as something of a model area and to advise that rather similar bodies, to be known as Regional Advisory Councils, should be established to cover the whole country.[3] Yet even here the autonomy of the LEA in this regard was held sacred.

The clash between the local and national views came out clearly in the minutes of a Yorkshire Council conference held in 1944 in Leeds to consider the provision of the Education Act requiring consultation between LEAs, universities and other bodies in the preparation of schemes for further education. All the Yorkshire counties, county boroughs and universities were represented. The minutes record in successive paragraphs:

> In opening the conference the chairman [Hyman] emphasised that any action the Council could take would be in a purely advisory capacity and would not in any way impinge upon the autonomy of its constituent authorities.
> In opening the discussion Sir Robert Wood (Deputy Secretary, Ministry of Education) said that . . . centralised specialist departments would have to be provided; local patriotism within each authority was not enough.[4]

Towards the end of the war a good deal of time and thought was devoted to the problems involved in setting up the very many county colleges that would be necessary when part-time day continuation became compulsory up to the age of eighteen. Officials planned the sort of buildings that would be needed, the residential accommodation for rural areas, recruitment of staff, and so on. The Education Committee considered and approved the outline plans and made representations to the Minister and to West Riding MPs on the need to ensure that attendance at a county college should count as working hours for the purpose of payment of wages.[5] Yet, in the event, all this came to nothing and it was the more tardy LEAs who could congratulate themselves on not 'wasting' the energy of committee members and officials on such planning. In the years immediately following the war the Authority's provision for the further education of the majority of those school leavers who sought it remained in the traditional form of evening classes.

The wartime set-back to work in further education and the post-war revival may be seen in Tables 8.1 and 8.2. The overwhelming majority of students were still, of course, part-time. Out of the total of 90,195 in 1951–2 little more than 1 per cent were full-time – about 1,200. Part-time day students numbered 5,650; all the others attended classes in their spare time, usually in the evenings.[6]

The number of student hours worked in technical colleges and institutes increased more rapidly than did the number of students. This was due to the growth of the system of day-release in the post-war years. Before 1939 very

TABLE 8.1
*Total number of students enrolled*
*in further education classes, 1938–52*

|  | 1938–9 | 1940–1 | 1946–7 | 1951–2 |
|---|---|---|---|---|
| Art schools | 1,604 | 955 | 2,208 | 1,778 |
| Art classes | 319 | 144 | 887 | 563 |
| Technical colleges | 2,396 | 1,842 | 3,995 | 4,791 |
| Technical institutes | 9,938 | 6,901 | 12,907 | 14,451 |
| Evening institutes | 45,415 | 24,197 | 37,992 | 45,752 |
| Day continuation schools | – | – | 207 | 226 |
| Total in WR county institutions | 59,672 | 34,039 | 58,196 | 67,561 |
| WR students at county borough institutions | 12,530 | 7,044 | 15,492 | 22,634 |
| Grand total | 72,202 | 41,083 | 73,688 | 90,195 |

TABLE 8.2

*Student hours worked, 1938–52*

|  | *1938–9* | *1940–1* | *1946–7* | *1951–2* |
|---|---|---|---|---|
| Art schools | 227,056 | 146,193 | 231,615 | 199,622 |
| Art classes | 26,717 | 10,846 | 41,112 | 34,185 |
| Technical colleges | 229,912 | 136,181 | 361,691 | 533,793 |
| Technical institutes | 661,800 | 379,884 | 678,841 | 1,066,836 |
| Evening institutes | 2,116,231 | 902,481 | 1,465,244 | 1,993,922 |
| Day continuation schools | – | – | 27,810 | 34,542 |
| Total | 3,261,716 | 1,575,585 | 2,806,313 | 3,862,900 |

few were released during normal working hours to attend classes. In 1939–40 143 students were enrolled in day-release classes; by 1946–7 this number had grown to 2,906 and by 1951–2 4,035 young people were being released from employment for attendance at day classes. The great majority of these attended classes for vocational further education. The development of apprenticeship schemes in various industries did much to foster day-release classes. In the southern part of the county the implementation of the 'ladder plan' for juveniles entering the coal mining industry was particularly important. Under this scheme young entrants to coal mining spent half of their time in technical colleges or institutes and half at the mines for the first three months of their employment.[7]

Possibly the most influential new development in the whole field of the county's provision for education beyond school was the setting up of a residential adult college. The idea that the Riding should establish such a college was Walter Hyman's, while much of the detailed work of pushing the project along within the office fell to the Deputy Education Officer, John Haynes. The Education Committee gave its approval in principle to the scheme in October 1946. The aim then accepted was that ultimately the college should take about eighty adult students for courses lasting one year. Since such a college was a new venture it was recognised that it would have to create its own market, so that for the first year or two it might be necessary to fill up with short courses lasting only for a month or perhaps only for a weekend. The curriculum for the courses would be the humanities – modern history, geography, economics, government, philosophy and literature. Admission was not to be based on formal examination qualifications. There would be a test in the understanding of English and of the power of self-expression, and evidence would be required that a student had pursued a course of study after leaving school and that he had reached a level which would ensure he would benefit from a year's course. The permanent staff would comprise a Warden and eight full-time tutors. The Ministry of Education approved the scheme in principle and agreed to the acquisition of the Harlow Manor Hotel, Harrogate, for the purpose.[8]

The day after the scheme had been approved a letter arrived from S. Raybould, the Director of Extra-Mural Studies at Leeds University indicating that that body was also intent on setting up a residential college and asking whether there was a possibility of co-operation. Hyman was quite definite about this, and wrote to the Education Officer: 'I am *certain* however that it would be fatal to join up with Leeds University in anything approaching a joint scheme. It just would not work.'[9] The Ministry of Education raised the question of whether there was room for two rather similar establishments in the same part of the country. Haynes met Raybould to discuss this. At that time there were some 4,000 students taking tutorial extension or Workers' Educational Association classes in the Leeds region alone. Since the total of places in the two colleges would only amount to 120, or 3 per cent of this number, it was felt that the demand for places would be very keen. In its geographical sense (i.e. including the county boroughs) the West Riding had a population of 3,300,000 and persons from other counties might in any case be interested in coming to one of the proposed colleges. The Ministry accepted these arguments.[10]

By the early spring of 1947 it was becoming clear that the Harlow Manor Hotel would not, after all, be available. The Ministry of Works stated that it proposed to retain the building under a requisition order for an indefinite period for the use of the Air Ministry. The hunt then began for other premises that might prove suitable, including Wentworth Castle, Bawtry Hall and the Ben Rhydding Hotel at Ilkley. The solution to the problem came towards the end of July, when a Harrogate firm of estate agents wrote to the County Council offering Grantley Hall, near Ripon, for sale. The syndicate which had just purchased the 6,000-acre Grantley Hall and Brimham estates was anxious to sell off the Hall itself and its immediate grounds. Hyman, as chairman, inspected the premises as a matter of urgency and authorised the submission of an application to the Ministry of Education for approval in principle to its acquisition. The buildings were reported to be in good condition and little repair or renovation would be needed. The mansion itself would provide sleeping accommodation for up to sixty students. The County Council bought Grantley Hall for £13,500. It was estimated that £1,750 would need to be spent on adaptations and £11,000 was set aside for furniture and equipment.[11]

Arrangements went ahead for Grantley Adult College to open in May

1949. A governing body needed to be set up to deal with the necessary business and the Policy Sub-Committee considered the membership of this in January. A background paper provided by the Education Department pointed out that training college governing bodies consisted of nine members, eight from the Education Committee and the chairman of the local divisional executive. Such a pattern could apply at Grantley but, it was suggested, the nature of the developments expected here meant that there was much to be said for bringing in persons from outside with knowledge and experience of residential adult education. This would help to establish educational links for the college and to make it known, not only regionally but nationally. The paper suggested that in these circumstances the governing body should consist of eight members of the Education Committee and four co-opted members. Members of the Policy Sub-Committee were not prepared to follow the suggested course and resolved that the governing body should consist of nine members of the Education Committee. The question of co-opting any persons with knowledge or experience of residential adult education was left for further consideration.[12]

The college opened with D. M. Hopkinson as its first Warden and it quickly established itself as a centre for the provision of short residential courses. There can be no doubt about the success of Grantley in these terms. By 1953–4 there were eighty-two courses with 2,659 students; ten years later 125 courses were offered and about 3,900 students attended. During the last quarter of a century the value of a short period of residential study has come to be much more widely recognised and understood, but in its early years Grantley was a pioneering institution. It is perhaps worth recalling that the aim of taking a limited number of students for a year of residential study in the humanities has not been realised. The original concept of a northern Ruskin College was undoubtedly very ambitious, even though the first paper submitted to the Policy Sub-Committee put forward as an argument for setting up the college the demand for places at Ruskin ('There were 465 candidates from the whole country for fourteen vacancies at Ruskin College, Oxford').[13] A few months later arrangements were made for Haynes, the Deputy Education Officer, to visit Lionel Elvin, Principal of Ruskin College, to discuss the various problems and possibilities. One major difficulty lay in finding sponsors who would be willing to support students for as long as a year for this sort of course. Inquiries which Haynes made of such bodies as the Miners' Welfare Commission and the Carnegie United Kingdom Trust produced discouraging responses.[14] While the Authority itself could offer scholarships, the further question arose of what incentive there was likely to be for many people to take a year off work, the end of which was neither to improve their qualifications nor to prepare themselves for another and better job. Thus what was originally seen as a short-term policy of offering courses running for a weekend, a week or ten days in fact became the settled practice of the college.

Apart from such developments as the growth of day-release classes and the establishment of Grantley Adult College, there was a feeling that the general area of further education was not developing with the same vigour as other areas of educational work within the Riding in the years following the war. Indeed, it may be seen from Tables 8.1 and 8.2 that while the total number of students in evening institutes had just about recovered to the 1938–9 level by 1951–2, the number of student hours had actually fallen – and this in what was certainly the main instrument of non-vocational further education. The Education Officer believed that a necessary precondition for vigorous and successful development in this field was a reorganisation of administrative arrangements and responsibilities. From 1902 until the passing of the 1944 Act grammar schools, technical education and the rest of further education had all been categorised legally as higher education and this had naturally been reflected in the organisation of the Education Department where one man still had responsibility for these varied activities. When the man who had held this post for a generation left about five years after the war, it was clear to the Education Officer that his successor would have to give his full attention to meeting the needs of the schools. It would have been foolish to expect the new incumbent to do this work and to provide the driving force which was needed in further education. The difficulty could only really be overcome by appointing an assistant education officer especially for further education, whose status and remuneration would be equal to those of the persons dealing with primary and secondary schools. The situation was resolved after the Education Committee had agreed to the creation of the post and J. M. Hogan was appointed to it from Birmingham LEA. He became the principal architect of the new system of further education which was subsequently built up.

The existing evening institute system consisted of about 360 local centres based in day school buildings under the leadership of part-time heads. A paper considered and accepted by a special sub-committee of the Further Education Sub-Committee stated that, generally, 'West Riding Evening Institutes are somewhat narrowly conceived, unimaginative in direction and often depressing in level of attainment and atmosphere'.[15] Certainly the quality of the education offered by this system depended upon the energy and enthusiasm of people already committed to full-time jobs, few of whom could be regarded as expert in adult or further education. During normal working hours they were unable to meet employers or representatives of local organisations with whom they often needed to build up contacts because they were themselves teaching in day schools. Moreover, the large number of small institutes meant that there was a good deal of competition amongst them, a fact which militated against the rationalisation of specialised work among neighbouring institutes. The first major step was to persuade the Education Committee of the need to put some professional stiffening into the evening institutes by appointing full-time specialists in further education.

The Authority embarked cautiously on this policy in 1952–3, when it established its first two area institutes. One was in an area without a divisional executive, the Goole-Thorne district, which was organised from the Vermuyden Institute at Goole. The second was organised from the Rockingham Institute in the Wath-Swinton division, where the executive was helpful and sympathetic. The choice of these districts, one administered directly by the county and the other through an executive, enabled a useful comparison to be made. The importance of establishing an awareness of the further education interest on an appropriately constituted governing body soon became clear. The full-time Principals, J. Richardson and I. Lockyer, were able to establish good relations with local councils and other bodies and to set up an advisory board at each further education centre. In 1954 another area institute was established at Skipton, the aim of which was to move into, and gain experience of working in, an area which already had a technical institute and was also predominantly agricultural. The potential gain from this new system soon became apparent. In some places the number of enrolments doubled within a year or so. In view of this very satisfactory evidence, the Education Committee agreed to the creation of area institutes of further education for the greater part of the county in January 1955. New principals were to be appointed as soon as possible after 1 April so that they might take part in planning the next winter's programmes.[16] In some cases it proved beneficial to follow a policy of mixing vocational and non-vocational work. This was achieved at Shipley and in the Castleford-Pontefract district.

By this time the Authority attached great importance to its evening institute work becoming enmeshed and intermingled with the general social and cultural life of the community in the widest sense. It felt a responsibility to do what it could to encourage self-generated cultural activities, varying from brass bands to women's meetings. Thus at its meeting in January 1955 the Education Committee also agreed to introduce a scheme for the affiliation of voluntary societies with evening institutes. Those societies which affiliated would be able to enjoy the use of evening institute premises and equipment, or the services of specialist instructors, or both, on extremely advantageous terms. Whether they needed, for example, a hall for lectures, film shows or dramatic performances, a workshop for practical work or a gymnasium for boxing or badminton, the institute with which they were affiliated undertook to do all it could to meet their needs. In effect, the scheme offered a subsidy to voluntary organisations.[17] According to the official report:

> It seemed important that the institutes of further education should serve their local communities not only by providing classes in great variety but also by developing and strengthening a whole range of social, recreational and cultural activities that might best be pursued in organisations of people brought together on a voluntary basis.

There were initially some fears among members of voluntary organisations who valued their independence and did not want interference from local bureaucrats or councillors. The *Yorkshire Observer* reported: 'Individual members of the Education Committee, including Alderman W. M. Hyman (the chairman), are busy assuring the voluntary societies that such affiliation is no threat to their independence.'[18] The process of making known the value of the scheme to voluntary organisations and of reassuring them that their independence would not be lessened in any way went on steadily in the succeeding months and from time to time items appeared in local newspapers on this topic. Local party political organisations were not expected to seek affiliation and, perhaps more surprisingly, voluntary societies associated with the Churches were treated in the same way. The effect of this was to exclude a number of local societies in some areas from the benefits of the scheme.

By 1963 activity in the further education sector had increased to such an extent that area principals were clearly in need of assistance. This was provided through the appointment of heads of centres where this seemed to be justified; between seventy and eighty heads of centres were appointed in due course.

There must always be the possibility of some friction between teachers who work in a day school and use the premises and equipment most of the time and those who come in out of school hours and make use of the same workplace and equipment. Legally there was no difficulty, since the property was in any case that of the Authority in the case of county schools, but in practice, as schools came to be used increasingly for local music and drama groups and for social activities, a sensible understanding at the local level between the different users of the same accommodation and equipment became more important. When one difficulty did reach Committee level in 1961, the Authority decided that any future disputes about the use of premises for further education purposes should be referred to the chairman and vice-chairman of the Education Committee for decision. From 1956 the

TABLE 8.3

*Further education growth 1951–63*

| | 1951–2 | | 1962–3 | |
| --- | --- | --- | --- | --- |
| | *Students* | *Hours* | *Students* | *Hours* |
| Area institutes | – | – | 46,477 | 2,829,493 |
| Evening institutes | 45,752 | 1,993,922 | 7,866 | 356,962 |
| Art schools | 1,778 | 199,622 | 759 | 158,347 |
| Art classes | 563 | 34,185 | – | – |
| Day continuation schools | 226 | 34,542 | – | – |
| Technical institutes | 14,451 | 1,066,836 | – | – |
| Technical colleges | 4,791 | 533,793 | 9,471 | 2,141,137 |
| | 67,561 | 3,862,900 | 64,573 | 5,485,939 |

Authority adopted a policy of building further education units attached to new secondary schools and extensions to existing secondary schools. These were intended as a nucleus for evening institute and youth service activities and their furnishing was in every respect designed to meet the needs of adults.[19] So far as possible these units were sited in such a way as to lead naturally to those areas of school accommodation most likely to be used for further education purposes – hall, gymnasium and practical rooms. By 1974 further education units had been built at sixty-one schools and another eleven were in course of construction.

The last decade of the Authority's existence saw the growth in many parts of the Riding of linked courses which enabled secondary pupils to attend a local further education college during their last year or two at school (when they were usually between fourteen and sixteen) on a half-day-release basis for various purposes. Some attended careers 'tasting' or sampling courses, through which they might get to know more of the sort of work offered by local industry and commerce, and in this way the careers guidance offered through individual schools was strengthened. Gradually the emphasis moved away from work-sampling courses. Secondary pupils attended colleges in order to follow CSE or GCE courses in the more technical subjects for which their schools might not have adequate facilities. One college which had developed linked courses since 1962 was Whitwood Mining and Technical College. By 1974 about 1,800 pupils from schools were attending courses there. The majority were following CSE classes in such subjects as automobile engineering, building studies, carpentry, electrical installation, mechanical engineering, nursing studies, accounts, commerce, clerical duties and many others.

There had been some unease among further education staff at the possible impact of secondary school reorganisation on demand for their own courses for school leavers. The operation of linked courses and the setting up of liaison committees, on which college staff, heads of schools and area careers officers sat down together to decide the best way in which such provision should be made, helped towards co-operation and confidence in the arrangements.[20]

Another major development in the provision made for post-school education by the Authority was concerned with the youth service. The sort of needs which this service had come to meet had been satisfied to a limited degree by the initiative of such private voluntary organisations as the Young Men's and Young Women's Christian Associations, Girls Friendly Society, Boys Brigade and many others for almost a century. The outbreak of the Second World War and the accompanying break-up of families through mobilisation and evacuation, coupled with the blackout and the reduction in normal recreational facilities, led the Government to stimulate the rapid development of the youth service through the agency of LEAs. At the request of the Board of Education, the West Riding, along with LEAs generally, established a county Youth Committee in the early months of the war. Its chairman was the chairman of the Education Committee and it comprised eight other members from the Education Committee and twelve from various other organisations connected with provision for youth.[21] The main policy of the Committee was simply to reach as many young people as possible, to give them constructive ways of passing time and to keep them away from harmful influences. The registration of all youths from the age of sixteen and the official pressure subsequently exerted on them to join a youth organisation meant that the problem of coping with sheer numbers was always pressing. Grants were made to clubs without any very detailed investigation of the work they were doing and the Youth Committee itself did not define the standards by which clubs were to be judged when they applied for affiliation.[22]

At the end of the war there was inevitably something of a reaction against a service which had grown up in response to wartime needs and was associated in the minds of many with those wartime conditions which there was a widespread determination to cast off. In 1947 every youth group was asked to re-register with the county Youth Committee on terms that would, it was hoped, improve standards. The general impression of the immediate post-war years is that while the youth service reached fewer young people, there was a worthwhile effort to raise the standards of what the clubs and groups were able to offer. Arrangements were made in 1947 to appoint six area youth officers whose first task was to survey the actual position in the Riding. Youth groups and management committees were visited and the reports of the officers served to bring together a considerable store of information showing the actual state of the groups which had never previously been available. The advice they were able to give was welcomed by leaders and management committees. Their work included the investigation of applications for grant aid and the establishment of new clubs where it was considered that they were badly needed. It soon became clear that the advisory service the Authority was now offering was at least as important as grant aid. In 1947 short courses for part-time youth leaders were restarted after a break and in recognition of the need for more and better leaders.[23] Towards the end of 1948 there were 615 groups registered with the county Youth Committee; of these 469 had been granted full registration and 146 had been registered on a temporary basis, pending various improvements to bring them to the point where they could meet the standard required. A further 500 applications remained to be made.[24]

There would clearly be a good deal of overlapping between an active and well-run youth service and a further education service which took non-vocational education seriously. In the 1940s there had been little connection in the county between youth work and further education. The Education Officer felt that the youth service had tended to be run as a rather isolated appendage of the education system. The appointment of Hogan to the new post of Assistant Education Officer for Further Education in 1952 provided the opportunity to end this and to seek to integrate youth work much more closely with further education. In 1954 the county was divided into eleven (soon to be twelve) areas for youth service purposes, with a full-time area youth officer in each – a system rather similar to that which was being adopted for further education, with the appointment of area principals for the new area institutes. A youth committee was set up in each area with the area youth officer as its secretary, and a new Youth Council was established at county level, on which the area committees and voluntary organisations as well as the County Council were represented. Over the next four years the number of full-time leaders was also increased in order to stimulate development further.

The publication of the Albemarle Report[25] in 1960 gave further impetus to development and by 1962 it was possible for the county to agree to the introduction of a modified scheme of divisional administration which had the effect of basing the youth service on the divisions used for other aspects of the education service. It was hoped that a number of advantages would flow from this. The youth service would be seen as an integral part of the educational provision in the county rather than as something separate and different in purpose. Through delegation of control of the service it was hoped to stimulate more local interest. Finally, the scheme was designed to use the divisional offices to relieve the youth officers of part of their administrative load so that they might concentrate more on the advisory and organising role for which they had been trained. At the same time the opportunity was taken to appoint six assistant area youth officers in the six most densely populated areas. These were to be employed on a full-time basis and the existing total of part-time professional assistance was reallocated to the other six areas with their smaller populations.[26] In terms of committee structure, the existing eleven area youth committees were to be replaced by twenty-five divisional (or district) youth sub-committees. The new arrangements were put into effect during 1963.[27]

The success of a policy can sometimes be judged as much by the difficulties which it produces as by those which it removes. Some friction over the use of school premises by the youth service was likely to arise when that service had been integrated as a regular part of the education service with as much claim on the use of county-provided premises as any other sector of the educational field. In 1964 complaints over the use of day school premises by youth organisations were discussed by members of the Education Committee. In the divisions the procedure for settling conflicts was straightforward, since the minutes of a divisional youth committee were subject to confirmation by the divisional executive, which was therefore in a position to resolve any issue between a body of school governors and the youth committee. There was no such local mechanism for settling differences in county districts and when the problem was raised by Goole school governors, the Education Committee decided that special sub-committees should be established as required to settle these matters. The sub-committees were to consist of eight members – the chairmen and vice-chairmen of the secondary school governors, the further education governors, the district youth sub-committee and the district education sub-committee.[28]

The total establishment of full-time youth workers increased steadily. In 1965 it was increased from thirty-two to forty. Five years later twenty of these were employed as leaders at individual clubs, there were five district workers and there were fifteen youth tutors attached to secondary schools. The Authority then increased its establishment further to enable additional expansion to take place. Experience with youth tutor appointments in more than thirty schools showed that some redefinition of the responsibilities of head teachers, area youth officers, school governing bodies and divisional youth sub-committees was needed. The youth tutors found themselves responsible both to the head teacher and to the area youth officer and the respective committees that stood behind them. This cumbersome administrative arrangement had arisen as a by-product of the closer integration of the youth service with the education system. The raising of the school leaving age to sixteen and the development of some large secondary schools into institutions which increasingly tried to meet some of the cultural and social needs of their surrounding communities made it desirable that the heads of such institutions should, as far as possible, have responsibility for all that went on. Indeed, if there were a need for voluntary agencies to undertake this work outside the schools, this could be regarded as a reflection on the schools themselves. It was decided, therefore, that youth tutors should be responsible to the heads of schools, with area youth officers acting in an advisory capacity, and that day-to-day responsibility for youth work in a school should lie with the governors.[29]

The West Riding's strong tradition of placing emphasis on the importance of initial and in-service training for teachers in the schools penetrated further education during the last quarter of a century and, with closer integration, it became a marked feature of the youth service also. Following the recommendations of the Albemarle Report, the National College for the Training of Youth Leaders was set up and the county took into its full-time service a considerable number of persons who had been trained there. The training of part-time leaders was developed within the county and a West Riding Certificate was awarded to those who successfully completed the county's training course. Both for the youth service and for adult further education it became possible to require any staff who were not professionally qualified for the job to undertake a course of training for the Certificate. The training consisted of three elements: attendance at sessional and residential courses, reading and written work and supervised practical work in clubs or evening institutes.

The aim of maintaining and enhancing the quality of the service offered led the Authority to consider the provision of a residential course centre. This could be used for courses for youth leaders, for the staff of the youth employment service and for part-time teachers employed in further education. It would, in fact, serve those areas of activity in much the same way as Woolley Hall met the needs of other parts of the education service. In June 1960 the Education Committee appointed a group of its members to look over Arthington Hall, near Otley, which, it was thought, might be a suitable building for this purpose. At the same time the Committee decided to raise the question of the provision of a residential centre for the training of youth leaders with the Yorkshire AEC and to seek the views of the East and North Riding County Councils.[30] By the end of the year it was clear that if any action were to be taken, the West Riding would need to move on its own. The Policy and Finance Sub-Committee considered a further paper at its December meeting. This contained a series of forceful arguments in favour of making a decision to acquire a suitable property and showed that if one were acquired, it would be very fully used. The Sub-Committee approved the proposals in principle and authorised negotiations for the lease of the property.[31] In the event the attempt to lease Arthington Hall failed because by the time the county had reached a firm decision, the owners had already agreed to lease it to another party. Various other properties were considered before Bramley Grange, Thorner, was acquired in 1965 at a cost of £27,000. After alterations and extensions had been completed, it was hoped that it would accommodate up to about forty persons. The warden was responsible for the overall running of the establishment, but most of the courses were to be directed by members of the county's advisory and inspectorial staff.[32]

Through the clubs and agencies supported by the youth service young people came to take part in an enormous variety of leisure-time activities which there is not the space to describe at all fully here. But two of these might, perhaps, be taken as examples: attendance at Outward Bound schools and the Duke of Edinburgh's Award Scheme. The Outward Bound Trust established its first school at Aberdovey in 1941 and centres were subsequently opened at other places, including Eskdale and Ullswater. The residential courses were designed to present boys with the conditions necessary to discover themselves, conditions demanding self-discipline, teamwork, adventure and some risk. The Authority agreed in principle to give support to a few boys to attend Outward Bound courses in 1947. The amount of assistance granted was increased from time to time. The scheme came to include girls as well as boys, those still attending secondary schools and those who had left. In 1965 the Authority decided to reserve a minimum of twelve places, which should be distributed in the ratio of 75 per cent for those at work and 25 per cent for those still at school, the allocation of places between boys and girls being decided on the basis of merit only. By the 1970s the county was taking about twenty-five places on Outward Bound courses each year.[33]

The Duke of Edinburgh's Award Scheme offered other opportunities to meet and overcome challenges and the Authority gave vigorous support to it. In 1956 the West Riding was invited to become one of the 'experimenting authorities' during the initial phases of the scheme and experiments took place in a number of grammar and secondary schools as well as in youth service organisations. As early as 1959 a considerable number of bronze and silver awards had been gained both by school and youth group participants. Other awards were won by local youth group members whose clubs operated the scheme with the national voluntary youth organisation to which they were affiliated as the experimenting authority – the Harrogate Youth Club through membership of the National Association of Boys Clubs, for instance. The scheme developed tests suited to girls as well as boys and increasing numbers were attracted to it. In due course operating groups came to be established in less likely places – day schools for educationally sub-normal children and approved schools. The appointment of an officer to look after the scheme indicated how important it had become. Industry took a lively interest in the advantages to be gained from the scheme and a number of firms operated it for their younger employees through the West Riding Operating Authority. One of the requirements of the scheme was that participants should undertake some public service and an inquiry made in 1967 showed that the most popular forms of service being undertaken were the St John's Ambulance, life saving and the Fire Service.[34] In many ways the response to the Duke of Edinburgh's Award Scheme typified what the Riding was attempting to achieve generally through its increased provision for the youth service. In the words of the Education Committee's report in 1964: 'The object of all the increased concern, effort and expenditure is, of course, to ensure that very many more are appealed to with equal success.'

The policy of regionalising and centralising much of the senior and more advanced technical education which had been developed through the Yorkshire Council for Further Education between the wars became accepted national policy in the post-war years. In some ways this meant that at the administrative and advisory level the West Riding was free to concentrate more of its efforts on more general post-school educational work. Most students undertaking advanced work in the Riding attended the large technical colleges situated in the county boroughs.[35] The county met the full recoupment costs on the agreed inter-authority scale. While the total expense was considerable, it was a good deal less than the probable cost of trying to run the advanced courses in institutions provided by the county. Further education institutions in the Riding catered for candidates studying for qualifications up to Ordinary National Certificate and Higher National Certificate levels but no higher. The actual policy of 'free trade' was applied without restriction even to non-vocational and non-advanced part-time courses until the later 1960s. Here too the student attended the institution of his choice and the county paid the economic cost of his course to the providing authority.

The development of technical education for the mining industry before 1939 has already been described. A considerable amount of 'fairly advanced work' in mining continued to develop in the county's technical colleges at

Whitwood, Dinnington and Mexborough. After nationalisation the National Coal Board asked the West Riding to carry out the training of apprentices and the Board's other employees up to the level of shot-firers and deputies. Additional facilities were provided by the county and paid for by the Coal Board.[36]

The county continued to rely on the large technical colleges in Bradford and Huddersfield for the more advanced work in textiles. The amalgamation of the technical institutes in Batley and Dewsbury produced a college to serve the heavy woollen textile manufacturing area under a joint management committee consisting of members drawn from the West Riding and from Dewsbury County Borough. Keighley Technical College had for many years made provision for some advanced work in textiles and it continued to make a useful contribution. The county also continued to provide instruction to a reasonably advanced level in a number of the smaller technical institutes in the textile area, including Todmorden, Morley and Shipley.

Immediately after the war there were still full-time art students in institutions maintained by the county at Batley, Harrogate, Keighley, Selby and Skipton. The county's policy was to centre art education on Harrogate where the School of Art was very successful, judged by most criteria – it gained more than its share of admissions to the Royal College and to the Slade, for instance. The recommendations of the Summerson Committee in 1961 led to the loss of advanced courses and a fall in the volume of work at the Harrogate School of Art, since the new diploma in art and design courses were to be located in some of the larger regional colleges. In 1964 the Education Committee decided to combine the School of Art with the Institute of Further Education to form Harrogate College of Further Education. Full-time courses in art were then limited to pre-diploma study, after which students had to move on to regional colleges. A new vocational course in graphic design was started, as was a course of general education through art and design.[37]

The Industrial Training Act of 1964 had an important influence on the work of technical colleges in the county and indeed in Yorkshire generally. The Act was designed to increase the amount of training, to improve its quality and to distribute training costs more equitably. As training boards were established in different industries it became clear that many industries lacked sufficient training facilities. The Authority was approached by a number of industries, including shipbuilders at Selby, engineering companies, companies in the construction industry, the National Coal Board and, to a lesser extent, textile employers and others. The West Riding was pleased to participate in this work, partly because it meant that technical college facilities would be used more extensively over forty-eight weeks of the year. Moreover, as colleges and industries worked closely together it became clear that many young people were attaining considerable standards of skill more quickly than before. Among other consequences, the work of the industrial training boards stimulated the demand for further education and demonstrated the need for training in teaching for lecturers and tutors – a need that was met to some extent by seconding staff to Huddersfield College of Education (Technical) for training.[38] The costs of courses provided at the request of particular industries were divided, so that industry paid for the training element while the West Riding met the cost of the educational element.

The expansion of higher and further education in the 1960s, against a deteriorating national economic and financial background, led to restrictions on the policy of 'free trade'. About 77,000 full- and part-time students were attending West Riding institutions of further education and about 40,000 those of other authorities, the latter arrangement involving payments from the county of the order of £2,500,000 annually. From September 1968 the prior approval of the Authority was needed in respect of the attendance of West Riding students at the non-vocational classes and courses of other LEAs and a system of permits was brought into operation. In 1966 the National Advisory Council on Education for Industry and Commerce, with Sir Harry Pilkington as chairman, reported on making the most effective use of resources in further education institutions. The committee recommended the following normal minimum enrolments for further education classes: full-time – twenty-four students; part-time day, involving a large element of workshop practice – fifteen; other part-time day courses – twenty. Principals of West Riding institutions and the Authority's officers feared that the enforcement of these recommendations would produce considerable difficulties if the policy of 'free trade' were continued. The Education Committee, therefore, agreed that from 1969 all West Riding students under nineteen years of age wishing to enter a full-time or part-time course at craft or technician level should be required to apply to the Principal of the West Riding institute of further education covering their area. The Principal would then advise the student whether the course was being provided in a county institution; if it was not, he would arrange to issue the necessary permit for the student to take a course in an institution of another authority. It was hoped that this policy would ensure the viability of courses in the Riding's own institutions, while not denying the opportunity to a student to follow a course elsewhere if necessary. The issue of a permit committed the county to meeting the recoupment charge involved.[39]

When the Education Officer reviewed the position for the Committee after the new scheme had operated for three years, he was able to report that there was no doubt as to the effectiveness of the new policy in increasing the viability of courses and classes in West Riding institutions. It had also brought significant savings in recoupment payments to the county boroughs. The agreed rates of recoupment on a per capita basis for 1972–3 are set out in Table 8.4, which makes clear the considerable scope for continuing savings. The policy did lead to a certain amount of strain in the relationship between the county and some of the county boroughs. Its obvious effect was that county borough institutions lost students and income, and this was most serious in the case of small county boroughs with only one college which had to depend on a catchment area a good deal larger than their own small populations could provide. Wakefield, for instance, lost £30,000 in one year.[40]

TABLE 8.4
*Recoupment costs 1972–3*

| Standard of work | Full-time | Part-time day 8 hours per week | Part-time 2 hours per week |
|---|---|---|---|
| School (up to 'O' level) | £506 | £132.48 | £33.12 |
| Intermediate (between 'O' and 'A' level) | £594 | £155.52 | £38.88 |
| Advanced (post 'A' level or post Ordinary National Certificate) | £803 | £210.24 | £52.56 |

Certain other policy decisions at this time added to the strain over further education with some county boroughs. The Riding investigated the relationship between advanced art courses and employment and discovered that 40 per cent of students completing specialised art courses did not take up employment in any related field. The Education Committee, therefore, reduced the number of grants awarded for art courses and this naturally meant some contraction in the number of county students who went to the county boroughs for further education. Moreover, in some further education colleges in the boroughs a number of disparate vocational courses were devised to meet the needs of employees under the Industrial Training Act for which the employers paid nothing. The West Riding refused to support students taking such courses unless employers paid for the 'training' component – usually about 60 per cent of the total cost – and insisted that it was proper for an LEA to bear only that cost which could be attributed to continued education. This again reduced the number of West Riding students undertaking further education in the county boroughs and contributed to ill-feeling on occasions. Bradford Technical College, for instance, apparently advised its students to protest about the Authority's policy. It is, perhaps, of some interest that there were deputations from medical practitioners and from farmers who wanted their secretaries trained without charge by the county. The Authority, however, continued to offer facilities and awards for secretarial courses so that students could acquire the necessary skills of shorthand, typewriting and so on, 'but the application of that knowledge to particular fields of work such as medicine or farming had not been a financial responsibility that the Committee consider should be carried by West Riding rate payers'.[41]

Agricultural education for many years stood apart from the rest of further education. For half a century the Yorkshire Council for Agricultural Education (YCAE) had been responsible for much of this work but the conflict between the West Riding on the one hand and its partners in the YCAE, the East and North Ridings and Leeds University, on the other helped to prevent active development for some years. The Ministry of Agriculture wished the work of the YCAE to continue and opposed the West Riding's attempt to withdraw and go its own way in the early years of the war. When the county started to appoint organising staff for agricultural education the Ministry made it clear that there would be no grant aid towards their salaries. It was against this background that the Education Committee took its decision to appoint a senior organiser of agricultural education and a head instructress in rural domestic economy in 1941.[42] Much of the confusion in the situation was bound to continue until the position of the Yorkshire Institute of Agriculture was cleared up. Although its buildings at Askham Bryan were largely complete in 1939, the army took over the premises until 1943, when the National Institute of Agricultural Engineers moved in and stayed until 1947. The first courses for students at the institute under the auspices of the YCAE started in September 1948. Although the institute was situated in the West Riding, it was largely administered through the East Riding at this stage, and Sir John Dunnington Jefferson – a landowner and prominent educationist in the East Riding – took an active part in its affairs as chairman of the YCAE. The eventual outcome of these years was an agreement that the Askham Bryan Institute should be taken over by the West Riding when the East Riding had established an institute of its own. This it did at Bishop Burton. From 1954 Askham Bryan was transferred to the sole ownership of the West Riding and the YCAE was formally dissolved. The North Riding continued to share the annual running costs and to make use of Askham Bryan until 1960, when a new arrangement was agreed.[43]

Administrative arrangements at national level also made the integration of agricultural education with the rest of the county's further education difficult. As part of the educational reconstruction embodied in the 1944 Act, the Board of Education sought to take over responsibility for technical education for agriculture in the same way as it already had responsibility for the rest of that service. The Ministry of Agriculture resisted this, since it was unwilling to trust LEAs to make adequate provision. It was only willing to pass responsibility over if the Board of Education itself undertook to run agricultural education directly. R. A. Butler wrote to his Permanent Secretary, after discussing the matter with the Minister of Agriculture, 'I said we operated through local education authorities, and that I could not sit in my room and run a lot of institutes. He said he thought I had better, otherwise I would not get them.'[44] In the event he did not get them. The framework for future arrangements was spelled out in a joint circular from the two Ministries in 1945. The Ministries would be jointly responsible for agricultural education. The Ministry of Agriculture kept responsibility for the sufficiency and suitability of instruction in the theory and practice of agriculture, and continued to give grant aid under the Board of Agriculture Act 1889 for the provision and maintenance of farm institutes and part-time courses. Courses forming part of the normal arrangements of a school or institution grant-aided by the Ministry of Education were to be taken into account for purposes of grant from that Ministry. A condition of grant would be the establishment of a separate sub-committee by a local authority to manage farm institutes and the nomination of a proportion of its members by the Minister of Agriculture.[45] The effect of this national compromise was to cause some local organisational difficulties. In the West Riding the Agricultural Education Sub-Committee and the School Management Sub-Committee had potentially conflicting jurisdictions in such a matter as rural studies in schools where there was some difficulty in 1953. A further defect of the arrangements was that the farm institutes, which ought to have been research and advisory centres for the farmers in any district where teachers and lecturers were in contact with the farming community and its problems, were in fact divorced from the farms in this respect by the National Agricultural Advisory Service.

With obstacles such as these it was hardly surprising that further education in agriculture did not develop rapidly in the years just after the war. In 1950 the Education Officer was only too keenly aware of the contrast between the vital role part-time further education was playing in many industries and its negligible contribution to the farming industry. Considerable efforts were made to establish part-time classes in both agricultural and horticultural subjects. By 1960 there had been an increase in the number of part-time day-release students attending these classes to 350 from only thirty-five six years earlier. One of the major obstacles to development was removed by the publication of the De La Warr Report in 1958, which led to the transfer of central government responsibility for agricultural education from the Ministry of Agriculture to that of Education.[46] A scheme of nationally recognised qualifications was established which enabled young people entering the industry to qualify for admission to the Institute of Agriculture. By 1962 the three centres for day-release courses existing in 1954 – Skipton, Knaresborough and Castleford – had been joined by seven others – Ripon, Otley, Snaith, Askham Bryan, Wath-on-Dearne, Settle and Grassington. Within two years another seven centres were to be added. Successful students taking the appropriate City and Guilds Stage I examinations at these centres could move on to one of four centres – Skipton, Knaresborough, Castleford and Sherburn-in-Elmet – to take Stage II courses in crop husbandry, animal husbandry or farm machinery operation and care. A number of further developments were planned, including the provision of Stage III courses at Skipton, Castleford and Askham Bryan. Other developments were being pushed forward in the early 1960s in horticultural education.[47]

During the Authority's last twenty years Askham Bryan Institute came to play an increasingly significant part in the county's provision. When the county took over the administration of Askham Bryan on 1 April 1954 there were sixty students. The West Riding was responsible for forty of these and the North Riding for twenty. One recommendation of the De La Warr Committee was that no further residential institutes should be set up, so that the North Riding's hopes of eventually establishing its own institute were dashed. The North Riding continued to be represented on the governing body and to make use of the facilities offered by Askham Bryan on a recoupment basis.

After the Ministry of Education took over responsibility for agricultural education, a period of vigorous expansion of the Institute began. While the Ministry of Agriculture had remained responsible, HMIs were in a weak position and their recommendations were unlikely to carry much influence. But after the Ministry of Education took over they became more active and were, of course, particularly concerned with the educational side of the work. The Ministry of Agriculture had not shown much sign of being 'educationally minded' and there was little opportunity for capital expenditure. This situation was now transformed. Very substantial sums were spent on buildings and equipment after 1960. In that year a major expansion scheme was agreed by the County Council which was designed to increase accommodation to cater for 140 students by the building of a new hostel block of seventy-six study-bedrooms, as well as to provide additional teaching and laboratory facilities.[48]

The Pilkington Report on agricultural education was published in 1966. It recommended the adoption of the same terminology as that used in other industries when referring to types of courses and the introduction of the sandwich-course principle, whereby periods of full-time education alternated with supervised experience in an industry. A consequence of these recommendations at Askham Bryan was the setting up of courses for Ordinary National Diplomas in agriculture and horticulture. Once these were running it was hoped to set up Higher National Diploma courses. The latter were eventually introduced after some difficulties with the DES, which insisted that they should be taught in a joint arrangement with Leeds Polytechnic. The growth of new courses and its general development led the county to seek the approval of the DES in 1967 to change the Institute's title to 'Askham Bryan College of Agriculture and Horticulture'. During the West Riding's last year 216 full-time and forty-four sandwich-course students were enrolled, while the total staff now numbered seventy-four.[49]

During the 1960s the county's agricultural education came to be centred increasingly on Askham Bryan. In October 1960 the Education Committee agreed to appoint three staff who would work in the North Riding. Frank Barraclough, secretary to the North Riding Education Committee, considered that without a farm institute it would be very difficult to attract suitable staff to teach day-release classes and to undertake the visiting, lecturing and organisational work that would be necessary to operate such a scheme. Moreover, the farming community in the southern part of the North Riding tended to look to Askham Bryan as their centre for agricultural education. Accordingly, the Principal of the farm institute became responsible for organising agricultural education in the North Riding and supervised resident staff in different parts of that administrative county.[50]

In the West Riding itself the Education Officer believed that the development of agricultural education had now reached the point at which it had either to be pulled much more closely into the existing further education framework or to be operated largely through Askham Bryan. In fact the latter course was followed and events ripened sufficiently for important decisions on reorganisation to be taken by the Education Committee in 1968 and 1969. The effect of this was to abolish the post of County Adviser in Agricultural Education and to appoint an agricultural liaison officer on the staff of Askham Bryan College 'with an understanding that he should be required to give such advice and supervision on agricultural education, other than that provided by Askham Bryan College, as the Education Officer might require'. Part-time studies in agriculture and horticulture in the North and West Ridings were to be co-ordinated from 1 January 1969 and the head of the North Riding Department at the College was to become head of an expanded extra-mural department covering the two Ridings.[51]

While aid to students attending universities and other institutions of higher education increased greatly during the Authority's last thirty years, grants to universities as such became much less important. After the war the total sum granted to Leeds and Sheffield Universities represented the product of a penny rate less the economy cuts of 1930 and 1931, which had not been restored. The total available was divided between the two universities every three years in proportion to the population and rateable value of the West Riding areas regarded as served by Leeds and Sheffield respectively and the number of county students from these areas at the two universities. In 1948 both universities approached the county with a request for an increase in the grant. The arguments in favour of increasing the sum in both cases were that the number of West Riding students had doubled and the cost per head to the universities had more than doubled. Moreover, during the previous twenty years the Treasury grant had quadrupled. Over this period the grant expressed as an amount per West Riding student had fallen in the case of Leeds from £65 to £25, in the case of Sheffield from £95 to £51. In 1925–6 Leeds University had received 11.4 per cent of its income from the West Riding County Council; in 1946–7 this had fallen to 3.1 per cent. In the same years Sheffield University had received 8.1 and 2.0 per cent respectively of its income from the county's grant. The outcome of the discussions which followed this approach was a decision to increase the annual grant to Leeds by £11,000 and that to Sheffield by £5,000, the total sum granted to the two universities for 1949–50 being £43,900.[52]

In the spring of 1963 the Vice-Chancellors of both Leeds and Sheffield approached the clerk to the County Council with submissions seeking an increase in the annual grant to universities. During the thirteen years since the level of grant was fixed both universities had become more than half as large again and their expenditure in inflated money terms had increased by over 300 per cent. The applications were rejected on the grounds that the estimates for the coming year had been agreed.[53] In the autumn the Vice-Chancellor of Leeds, Sir Charles Morris, had further discussions with the Clerk to the County Council, Sir Bernard Kenyon, to see if anything could be done for the next year. Kenyon reported that many in the county felt universities had now become a national financial responsibility and wanted to leave the university grant at its present level. He stressed that there was little point in reopening the question while the composition of the County Council remained as it was.[54]

The foundation of a new university at York and the upgrading of Bradford College of Technology to university status led to a reallocation of the total grant. From the late 1960s the individual grants were based on the total number of students in each university and the population of the counties or county boroughs which might be expected to contribute in view of their geographical position. Thus for Leeds and Bradford there was the relevant county borough; for Sheffield, the county borough and Derbyshire; for York, the county borough and the other two Ridings. These factors produced the following ratios for the division of the total grant (£47,481) in the last year of the Authority's existence: Leeds 15, Sheffield 8, Bradford 6, York 4. The specific grants for extra-mural classes and the like were additional to these formula payments.[55]

Until 1960 there were complaints that the West Riding offered proportionately fewer awards to students to attend universities than did neighbouring authorities. Before the end of the war Binns wrote to Hyman proposing that the existing system should be changed: 'At present, as you know, seventy are awarded each year but it seems to me that a fixed number is wrong. I should like to recommend that the number of scholarships each year should be decided by the number of candidates who qualify that year.' The Joint Matriculation Board suggested annually how many candidates taking Higher School Certificate qualified for awards in their opinion, and this was always in excess of the number of scholarships offered. After discussion with the Secretary to the Joint Matriculation Board, Binns wrote further to Hyman that in each of the last few years the Joint Board had recommended about ninety candidates for awards. He added:

I must confess that the Secretary of the Matriculation Board astonished me by pointing out that the West Riding provision of university scholarships has in the past been considerably less generous in relation to the population involved than has the provision made by most of the West Riding county boroughs. He says it is a definite handicap to a candidate to be resident in the county rather than in a county borough in this respect.[56]

In the next year or so the Education Committee continued to offer a specific number of major awards – 115 in 1946. Clegg was anxious to see more attention paid to personal factors in making awards and the Education Committee came to adopt a system by which the awards were no longer made solely on the basis of Higher School Certificate results. For some years candidates were interviewed by a panel of two assessors and an independent chairman, along with some members of the Education Committee. The less favourably boys and girls impressed the panel, the higher was the standard of performance required in the 'A' level examinations. Although no specific limitation was imposed on the number of awards each year, the effect of this procedure was to ensure that the West Riding continued to be a good deal less generous in the number of awards it offered than English counties as a group or LEAs as a whole. There was repeated criticism of the Authority at this time and in 1955 unsuccessful candidates took the matter up with the Minister of Education. The Ministry wrote to the West Riding and made explicit the extent of the shortfall in the county's provision. Its letter contained an analysis of the proportion of awards to certain year-groups of the school population for the previous four years, which showed that the county was only giving about two-thirds as many awards as it would have done if it had kept in line with English counties as a whole. The emphasis placed on personal-quality assessments certainly had a drastic effect on the number of awards granted in these years. In 1955, for instance, out of 973 applicants no fewer than 600 were put into categories C and D by the interviewing panel. This meant that they would only get awards if they obtained three passes at GCE 'A' level, with an aggregate mark of 165 and at least sixty marks in one subject.[57]

The growth in the number of applicants for awards was making the task of the Education Committee panel which interviewed them all an almost impossible one, and in the face of the Ministry's critical attitude the system was modified so that not all candidates were interviewed. The Authority was still anxious to avoid making awards simply on the basis of examination results and the offer of a place, and still wanted to exercise its own judgement on the personal qualities of future students. Thus awards were now to be granted automatically to candidates who gained 155 marks in three 'A' level passes or 120 in two such passes. The panel interviewed the other likely and borderline candidates for awards in September, retaining the principle of requiring a lower examination performance where it awarded a higher personal-quality assessment. In 1956 the Authority also agreed to consider taking over responsibility for the cost of the remainder of the course at university in cases where a student who had failed to get an award nevertheless entered a university at his own expense. Any applicants would be interviewed by the Appeals Sub-Committee.[58] In passing it should, perhaps, be added that while the involvement of committee members in the business of interviewing would have been very unusual in many counties, it was entirely in keeping with the tradition of their involvement in the minutiae of the Authority's business which was a notable feature of West Riding administrative arrangements.

In the following year the Ministry of Education approached the Authority about its practice of making loans to students and charging interest on the sums advanced. At one time many authorities made such loans, although by no means all of them charged interest. The West Riding made its first advance in 1911 and from then until 1957 had advanced a total of £397,958, on which it had charged £58,045 as interest. The county explained that it had retained loans for use at the margin of its award scheme to enable students to pay for expensive equipment on medical or dental courses or to undertake a repeat year after an examination failure. The Ministry was unconvinced and replied that 'The general policy recommended by the Minister since the war is that loans are in general an undesirable form of assistance to students'. In the case of state scholars the Ministry gave additional grant to cover the cost of expensive equipment and stated that if a 'scholar is good enough to stay up at the university at all we are prepared to consider seeing him through even if a repeat year is involved'. While not wishing to press an authority which felt that a marginal use of loans still had a valuable part to play in its provision, the Ministry felt very uneasy about the interest charged by the West Riding for its loans, since the Authority was apparently the only one which retained this practice. The West Riding agreed not to charge interest on loans granted after July 1957.[59]

Some dissatisfaction over the Authority's policy on university awards continued to be felt until the report of the Anderson Committee led to the implementation of a uniform national structure. In December 1958, for instance, the Mexborough Governing Body for Grouped County Secondary Schools sent forward to the county a resolution 'that in every case where a pupil obtains three Advanced level passes in the GCE and is accepted for admission to a university, the award of a county scholarship should be made automatically'. When the Policy and Finance Sub-Committee considered this it was also told that twenty-nine of the candidates who had been interviewed but were not given awards the previous September were accepted by universities, and fifteen of these had actually taken up their places in spite of having no award. That summer 662 awards had been made to 1,088 applicants. The Sub-Committee decided to take no action on the Mexborough resolution.[60]

The recommendation of the Anderson Committee was that awards should be given to all students admitted to degree courses at universities who had two GCE passes at 'A' level, and from October 1960 this recommendation was accepted by the West Riding. Following this report, the Government reviewed the scale of parental contributions and of standard grants. The West Riding paid grants in accordance with the new scale from 1961, at an additional annual cost of £300,000. Shortly afterwards legislation was enacted which made mandatory the payment by local authorities of student grants on the lines recommended by the Anderson Committee. This, of course, still left a great deal of scope for local initiative in the field of awards and grants for courses of further study apart from first degrees or their equivalents. The actual number of awards increased greatly in the 1960s with the rapid expansion of higher education. 3,401 major awards were made by the county in 1969 – a dozen years earlier the figure had been 624 – and 8,277 were currently tenable. At the same time 2,614 other intermediate awards were held by students attending institutions of further education.[61]

Within the West Riding the differences in social desires, prevailing ideas and ambitions were illustrated in an analysis which the Education Officer prepared for his committee in 1962. The number of university awards given in the Hemsworth, Don Valley, Staincross, Mexborough, Wharncliffe and Rother Valley divisions, which constituted the southern part of the county, were compared with the number given in the remaining divisions in the north and east. The comparisons per thousand of the relevant age group were:[62]

|  | The south | The rest |
|---|---|---|
| Students entering university with WR awards | 12.4 | 28.4 |
| Students obtaining state scholarships | 1.5 | 4.8 |

It was against this background that the Education Officer set about planning what came to be called 'the Oxbridge scheme'. The very small number of boys and girls from maintained grammar schools in the county – and particularly from those in the southern divisions – who went to Oxford and Cambridge was very striking. In 1958 the Education Officer had gathered views on this from the heads of grammar schools in the county in connection with his work as a member of the Central Advisory Council for Education.[63] In statistical terms the maintained grammar schools in the West Riding constituted 4 per cent of the country's maintained schools, yet provided fewer than 0.5 per cent of the students at Oxford and Cambridge. Of those who did go, there was a marked shortage of children with parents employed in groups 3, 4 and 5 of the Registrar General's classification of occupations.[64]

There is not space here to give a reasonably full account of this scheme, which was the fruit of remarkable individual enterprise on the part of the Education Officer, but, briefly, he persuaded a number of colleges at both Oxford and Cambridge to set aside places to be filled outside their normal arrangements by nomination from West Riding schools. The colleges for their part were always anxious to secure the most able entrants that they could for their places and were prepared to try a new source. The selection was as far as possible confined to the sons of the less well-to-do – textile workers, miners, shop assistants, and so on. Before taking 'A' level they were selected by the West Riding from among those whom the heads thought were capable of making use of the opportunities at Oxford or Cambridge. Those chosen were to make a break between school and university, working or undertaking voluntary service overseas. This complete break from earlier background (instead of a third year in the sixth form) was extremely important as a way of enabling boys from a limited and possibly rather narrow environment to learn to pick their way amid totally different circumstances, so that the transition to yet another different world at Oxford or Cambridge was greatly facilitated. The first boys to go to university under this scheme went up in 1964.[65]

By 1970 it became clear that the scheme could not continue, as the situation had changed. Of the four boys nominated by the interviewing panel that year, only one was offered a place for October 1971. Pressure on places at Cambridge appeared to have become more intense than before. The extension of the arrangements under the Universities Central Council on Admissions made it more awkward for colleges to operate special entry schemes which were not in phase with the normal entry system. Moreover, there seemed to be a shortage of suitable candidates in the Riding who were willing to spend a year away from school and university. Those wishing to go to the ancient universities were more interested in applying for entry immediately following two years in the sixth.[66] Perhaps it was inevitable that a special scheme which depended so heavily upon the personal attention of the Education Officer and senior staff would have only a limited life. At the same time, it may not have been coincidental that the number of West Riding students who gained entry at Oxford and Cambridge by the normal methods almost doubled during the period in which the scheme was operative.

# Epilogue

In the introduction we commented on the uniqueness of the event which made this study possible – the passing of a large county education authority. It is hardly possible to conclude without noticing that the local government system which was introduced in 1974 was intended to change the style as well as the areas of local educational administration. Whether the type of administration which was exemplified in the West Riding will survive is not clear.

The arrangements which came into force in April 1974 marked the first occasion on which a nation-wide system of local government had been designed so as to create units which would fit the needs of educational administration. The minimum population required for an education authority was assumed by the legislators to be 250,000, although nine of the new authorities in the north had smaller populations than this. The former system based on historic counties, along with county borough administrations in the larger towns, had its immediate origin in the legislation of 1888, the era of the school boards, and education was subsequently grafted on to that system – most notably by the Education Act of 1902. In order to ensure that the interests of the education service were not overlooked, the statute required both the creation of education committees composed partly of expert, non-Council members and the delegation to such committees by counties and county boroughs of their educational powers. This pattern survived with little fundamental change for three-quarters of a century. The most serious effort to change it was made during the Second World War. The Ministry of Health – then responsible for local government – wanted to create much larger units by fusing two or three existing counties into one. It believed that a post-war health and hospital service could only remain under the jurisdiction of local government if the latter had much enlarged units. The Ministry approached the Board of Education for support. The Board felt that such fundamental change was likely to be impossible in wartime and pressed ahead with its own scheme for quite minor modifications (abolition of Part III authorities and creation of divisional executives) within the existing counties, while the Ministry of Health eventually went for regional hospital boards outside the local government structure.

In 1974 the interests of education played some part in determining the size of the new local government units, and the administration of education should, it was thought, lose much of its statutory and practical autonomy within local government. Originally the reformers believed that there should be no statutory requirement to have education committees. Pressure from education interests, however, led to second thoughts and the statutory requirement for education committees survived the reforms. Even so, the practice of corporate management has led in some authorities to the determination of educational policy by persons who have neither experience nor understanding of, nor contact with, the school system. Opponents of the new approach argue that the emphasis has come to be placed upon local government for its own sake and no longer on the quality of the individual services it provides, that education is no longer seen as a *national* service administered locally. It is certainly a fact that although statutory education committees have survived, many of them were made to withdraw from their national organisation, the Association of Education Committees, so that that organisation has come to an end. It will be the task of future historians to assess the impact of these events.

# *Notes and References*

ABBREVIATIONS IN REFERENCES

| | |
|---|---|
| AEC | Association of Education Committees |
| *AR* | *Annual Report* |
| CCR | County Council Report |
| Elem Ed S-C | Elementary Education Sub-Committee |
| FE S-C | Further Education Sub-Committee |
| FGP S-C | Finance and General Purposes Sub-Committee |
| H Ed S-C | Higher Education Sub-Committee |
| NAPTSE | National Association for the Promotion of Technical and Secondary Education |
| P and F S-C | Policy and Finance Sub-Committee |
| PRO | Public Records Office |
| RCLG | Royal Commission on Local Government |
| RCSE | Royal Commission on Secondary Education |
| RSMO | Report of the School Medical Officer |
| S S-C | Special Sub-Committee |
| *TES* | *Times Educational Supplement* |
| WR | West Riding |
| WRCC | West Riding County Council |
| WREC | West Riding Education Committee |
| WRTIC | West Riding Technical Instruction Committee |
| YCFE | Yorkshire Council for Further Education |
| *YO* | *Yorkshire Observer* |
| *YP* | *Yorkshire Post* |

Memoranda considered by committees are referred to by title and date. Where items of correspondence are referred to, the original file classification is cited where it could be ascertained. Most correspondence has not been listed or catalogued in a record office. All memoranda and many of the Minutes of sub-committees are unpublished.

## CHAPTER I

1. WRCC, Minutes, 7 Nov 1889.
2. The NAPTSE was responsible for putting the sustained pressure on the Government which had resulted in the passing of the Technical Instruction Act, 1889.
3. Later Sir John Brigg, Member of Parliament for Keighley. For some years Brigg served as vice-chairman of the WRTIC.
4. Swire Smith was a Liberal woollen manufacturer from Keighley. He initiated important pioneering work in technical education at Keighley Mechanics' Institute from the early 1870s. He served as a member of the Royal Commission on Technical Instruction (1881–4) and wrote several important papers on education. His influence on the early work of the WRTIC was to be considerable.
5. WRTIC, Minutes, 6 Dec 1889.
6. J. W. Davis was a prominent member of the Yorkshire Union of Mechanics' Institutes. He lived in Halifax, and had a strong interest in science and science education.
7. A. H. D. Acland was, at this juncture, secretary to the NAPTSE and Member of Parliament for Rotherham. He was a member of the Cabinet during Gladstone's fourth ministry (1892–5) and held office as Vice-President of the Committee of Council on Education. In the early 1890s Acland lived in London, but after the turn of the century he moved to Yorkshire and played an important role in the work of the WRTIC and WREC (see pp. 78–81).
8. For the origins and importance of these grants, see P. R Sharp, *Journal of Educational Administration and History*, I, 1 (Dec 1968), pp. 14-21, and IV, 1 (Dec 1971), pp. 31–6.
9. Local authorities were given the option of either spending these grants on technical education or devoting them to rate relief.
10. WRTIC, Minutes, 3 Dec 1890.
11. This was particularly important in West Yorkshire where so many important educational institutions were situated in the county boroughs.
12. WRTIC, Minutes, 7 Jan 1891.
13. *Ibid.*, and S-C, Minutes 31 Dec 1890.
14. 54 and 55 Vic., c.4, The Technical Instruction (Amendment) Act, 1891.
15. 'An Educational Experiment in Yorkshire', *Blackwood's Magazine* (Feb 1872); *Educational Comparisons*, Yorkshire Union of Mechanics' Institutes, 1873; 'Technical Education and Foreign Competition', *Westminster Review* (May and Aug 1887). He also wrote several important pamphlets for the NAPTSE.
16. *Blackwood's Magazine* (Feb 1872), p. 225.
17. See p. 77.
18. WRTIC, *Directory*, Feb 1892, p. 10.
19. *Ibid.*
20. *Ibid.*
21. *Ibid.*, p. 6.
22. *Ibid.*
23. Yorkshire Union of Mechanics' Institutes, Reports, *passim*.
24. RCSE, 1895, IV, Q 15,072, evidence of W. V. Dixon.
25. Yorkshire Ladies Council of Education, Minutes, 27 July 1892.
26. WRTIC, Minutes, 22 Mar 1893.
27. The forerunners of Leeds and Sheffield Universities respectively.
28. See p. 99.
29. WRTIC, Minutes, 24 June 1891.
30. RCSE, 1895, IV, Q 14,524, evidence of J. Brigg.
31. *Ibid.*, Q 14,528, evidence of W. V. Dixon.
32. Chapter IV.
33. RCSE, 1895, IV, Q 14,989, evidence of W. V. Dixon.

34. *Ibid.*, Q 14,986.
35. *Ibid.*, Q 14,421, evidence of J. Brigg.
36. Calculations based on material in P. R. Sharp, *Journal of Educational Administration and History, op. cit.*
37. RCSE, 1895, IV, Q 14,550, evidence of W. V. Dixon.
38. WRTIC, *AR*, 1899, p. 14.
39. WRTIC *AR*, 1901, p. 16.
40. £3,600 was transferred from the county rate to the technical instruction fund in 1901–2.
41. The county boroughs and urban sanitary authorities made much wider use of their rating powers under the Act than the county councils.
42. NAPTSE, *AR, 1900–1*, p. 22.
43. WRTIC, *Report to County Council*, 8 Apr 1891, p. 7M.
44. WRTIC, Minutes, 29 May 1891.
45. *Ibid.*, 24 June 1891.
46. RCSE, 1895, IV, Q 14,428, evidence of J. Brigg.
47. WRTIC, *Directory*, 1896, p. 13.
48. RCSE, 1895, VII, report by A. P. Laurie, p. 209.
49. *Ibid.*
50. See p. 93.
51. WRTIC, *AR*, 1898, p. 8.
52. WRTIC, *AR*, 1900, p. 27.
53. See p. 78.
54. For examples, see WRTIC, Minutes, 17 Dec 1895, and 26 Feb 1896: resolutions relating to Goole School Board, Cleckheaton Mechanics' Institute, Liversedge Technical School and Rotherham School of Science and Art.
55. WRCC, *Lines for the Guidance of Teachers in Elementary Schools who take up Science*, Wakefield, 1893.
56. P. R. Sharp, 'The Work of the Technical Instruction Committees (with special reference to the West Riding, Lancashire and Northamptonshire)', unpublished M. Ed. thesis, Leeds University, 1969.
57. WRTIC, Minutes, S-C, 31 Dec 1890.
58. WRTIC, Minutes, 26 Feb 1892.
59. RCSE, 1895, IV, p. 199, statement submitted by the WRTIC.
60. P. R. Sharp, M. Ed. thesis, *op. cit.*, pp. 87–90.
61. RCSE, 1895, IV, Q 14,449, evidence of J. Brigg.
62. WRCC, petition to the Vice-President of the Committee of Council on Education, 12 Apr 1893; also NAPTSE, *The Record*, Oct 1896, p. 559.
63. P. R. Sharp, M. Ed. thesis, *op. cit., passim.*
64. WRTIC, *Directory*, 1892, p. 15.
65. RCSE, 1895, IV, Q 14,399, evidence of W. V. Dixon.
66. WRTIC, *Directory*, 1892, p. 40.
67. *Ibid.*
68. WRTIC, *Summary of Reports of District Committees*, 28 Feb 1893.
69. Bradford, Halifax, Huddersfield, Leeds and Sheffield.
70. WRCC, Statistics submitted to the Royal Commission on Secondary Education, 1894, Table A.
71. WRCC, petition to Vice-President of the Committee of Council on Education, 12 Apr 1893; WRTIC, *Report to County Council*, 13 May 1896, p. 81.
72. WRTIC, Minutes, 25 June 1897, and WRTIC, *Report to County Council*, 8 May 1901, p. 1K.
73. WRTIC, *Report to County Council*, 13 May 1896, p. 8I, and *ibid.*, 8 Jan 1902, p. 1H.
74. These are discussed in more detail on later chapters.

## CHAPTER II

1. WRTIC, Minutes, 17 Dec 1901 and 15 Apr 1902; WRCC, Minutes, 8 Jan 1902.
2. WRCC, Minutes, 8 Oct 1902.
3. Hansard, HC, vol 110, col 1269 (9 July 1902). The County Councils Association had voted in favour of the proposal, with only seven exceptions among the counties.
4. Hansard, HC, vol 97, col 510 (15 July 1901), where John Brigg (Keighley) expounded this view.
5. Hansard, HC, vol 110, cols 351 and 403 (30 June 1902), J. M. Duncan and J. Brigg.
6. R. G. Neville, 'Problems of Financing Higher Education, 1902–1918: A West Riding Perspective', *Journal of Educational Administration and History*, IX, 2 (1977) pp. 14–25.
7. WRTIC, Minutes, 14 Jan 1903.
8. *Ibid.*, 16 Jan 1903.
9. WRTIC, Special S-C Minutes and accompanying schedules, 29 Jan 1903.
10. WRCC, Minutes, 11 Mar 1903.
11. Board of Education, Circular 470 (1903); P. H. J. H. Gosden, 'The Origins of Co-optation to Membership of Local Education Committees', *British Journal of Educational Studies*, XXV, 3 (1977) pp. 258–67.
12. Representation was sought by the Church of England, the Roman Catholic Church and the North Central Wesleyan Association.
13. WRCC, Minutes, 11 Mar 1903.
14. WRTIC, Minutes, 16 June 1903.
15. WREC, Minutes, 14 July 1903.
16. WRTIC, Minutes, 14 Jan 1903.
17. WRTIC, Special S-C, Minutes, 21 Apr 1903; WRTIC, report of Special S-C on position and duties of the clerk to the Education Committee, 28 Apr 1903.
18. WRCC, Minutes, 10 May 1903; WRTIC, Minutes, 6 July 1903.
19. FGP S-C, Local Government S-C's papers, 18 Sep 1903, is an example of this.
20. *YP*, 'West Riding Education Difficulties, Resignation of the Director', 2 June 1904.
21. WREC, Special S-C in connection with the resignation of the Director, 31 May 1904.
22. WRCC, Minutes, 10 May 1905.
23. WRTIC, Minutes, 24 Feb 1903.
24. WRTIC, Minutes, 16 June 1903.
25. WREC, report of the Local Government S-C, 3 Nov 1903; Board of Education, *Report of the Consultative Committee upon the Question of Devolution by County Education Authorities*, 1908 [Cd 3952], p. 73.
26. WREC, Minutes, 12 Mar 1904.
27. Board of Education, *op. cit.*, p. 74; WREC, Minutes, 24 Oct 1905.
28. WREC, Local Government S-C, Minutes, 17 Nov 1903.
29. *YP*, 27 Dec 1941, p. 6.
30. *TES*, 12 May 1928, p. 209.
31. *YP*, 16 July 1936, p. 6; *TES*, 24 Dec 1938, p. 468.
32. *Education*, 29 Mar 1957.
33. Chapter VII.
34. PRO, ED 136/351, Bosworth Smith to Holmes, 1 Feb 1943; PRO, ED 136/359, Maude to Maxwell, 19 Apr 1943; Holmes to Butler, 1 May 1943.
35. P. H. J. H. Gosden, *Education in the Second World War: A Study in Policy and Administration*, 1976, pp. 297–300.
36. PRO, ED 136/255, Federation of Part III Education Committees, Statement of Policy adopted on 10 June 1942.
37. *TES*, 5 Feb 1927, p. 71.
38. Ministry of Education, Circular 1, 15 Aug 1944.

39. WR correspondence, H3, Claims for Excepted District Status, Town Clerk of Todmorden to Ministry of Education, 7 Sep 1944; Clerk to County Council to Ministry of Education, 31 Oct 1944.

40. *Ibid.*, Town Clerk of Pudsey to Ministry of Education, 13 Sep 1944; Clerk to County Council to Ministry of Education, 31 Oct 1944.

41. *Ibid.*, Binns to Clerk to County Council, 16 Sep 1944; Clerk to Education Officer, 27 Sep 1944.

42. *Ibid.*, Town Clerk and Mayor of Harrogate to Ministry of Education, 28 Sep 1944; Clerk to County Council to Ministry of Education, 31 Oct 1944.

43. *Ibid.*, Town Clerk of Keighley to Minister of Education, 4 Aug 1944; Clerk to County Council to Ministry of Education, 26 Oct 1944.

44. Shipley's claim to excepted-district status did not arrive at the Ministry until 3 October 1944. The Minister refused to consider it on the grounds that it had arrived after the closing date, 1 October – A. E. Parsons (Ministry of Education) to Clerk to Shipley Urban District Council, 5 Oct 1944.

45. WR correspondence, G77, Binns to Gittins, 2 Mar 1944; circular letter to clerks of West Riding Part III Education Authorities from Chief Education Officer, Mar 1944.

46. WREC, Minutes, 17 Jan 1945.

47. Ministry of Education, Circular 5, 15 Sep 1944; WRCC, Divisional Administration Scheme, 1945.

48. Post-War Ed S-C, 19 Dec 1944. NUT claim on teacher representation; G77, Binns to Bishop of Sheffield, 22 Nov 1944; NUT (WR) to Binns, 13 Jan 1945.

49. *Ibid.*, Education Officer to H. Player (secretary, WR Teachers' Association), 6 Jan 1945; Deputy Education Officer to H. Player, 26 Mar 1945.

50. WR correspondence, H3, R. N. Heaton (Ministry of Education) to County Clerk, 7 Mar 1945; W. A. B. Hamilton (Ministry of Education) to County Clerk.

51. *Ibid.*, Kenyon to Secretary (Ministry of Education) 20 Mar 1945; Heaton to County Clerk, 21 Mar 1945.

52. WREC, Minutes, 28 May 1946; WREC, *The Final Ten Years 1964–74*, 1974, p. 109; oral evidence Sir Alec Clegg.

53. Ministry of Education, Circular 90, 8 Mar 1946.

54. Policy S-C, Minutes, 18 Nov 1947 and accompanying memorandum. Section 86 of the Local Government Act 1933 stated that 'no costs . . . exceeding £50 shall be incurred by a County Council except upon a resolution of the Council based on an estimate submitted by the Finance Committee'.

55. P and F S-C, memorandum, 5 July 1968.

56. WREC, *West Riding Education: Ten Years of Change*, 1954, p. 135.

57. Policy S-C, Minutes, 27 Sep 1949.

58. *Ibid.*, 27 May 1952.

59. *Ibid.*, 23 Dec 1952; WREC, Minutes, 21 Jan 1953; P and F S-C, Minutes, 26 Feb and 14 May 1957.

60. P and F S-C, Minutes, 10 July 1962 and 14 Sep 1965.

61. FGP S-C, Minutes, 14 Mar 1950; P and F S-C, Minutes, 11 June 1963; 9 Feb and 5 Apr 1966. Thus the teachers' panel included one member from each of the Joint Four, the ATTI and the NAS, and ten NUT representatives.

62. Ministry of Education, Circular 210, Oct 1949.

63. P and F S-C, Minutes, 6 Dec 1955; *TES*, 27 Apr 1956, p. 538.

64. P and F S-C, Memorandum, 11 Sep 1956; WREC, *Education 1954–64*, 1964, p. 162.

65. E. W. Cohen, *Autonomy and Delegation in County Government*, 1952, and T. L. Reller, *Divisional Administration in English Education*, 1959, discuss fully some of the broader issues involved in this method of administering local education services.

The apportionment of powers and duties between divisional executives, managers and governors in the West Riding at this time is set out in Table 2.8, pp. 46–7.

66. 6 and 7 Eliz. II, c.55.
67. WREC, *Education 1954–64*, 1964, p. 161; P and F S-C, Minutes, 5 Nov 1958.
68. Cf. D. E. Regan, *Local Government and Education*, 1977, p. 212: 'Education looms so large in the spectrum of local government service in terms of cost, public interest and general importance, that its needs have invariably been given great weight in any scheme for local government reform.'
69. WRCC, Legal and Parliamentary Committee, Minutes, 13 Jan 1904; 10 Mar and 12 May 1909; 1 Mar 1911; 10 Jan 1912.
70. *Ibid.*, 8 May 1912.
71. *Ibid.*, 14 May and 9 July 1913; 14 Jan 1914.
72. *YP*, 16 Mar 1922, p. 5.
73. RCLG, 1924, Part III, Minutes of Evidence, p. 568.
74. *Ibid.*, p. 679.
75. WRCC, Law and Parliamentary Committee, Minutes, 18 July 1956.
76. *Ibid.*
77. P and F S-C, memorandum and comments from the Education Officer, 9 Sep 1969.
78. *TES*, 19 Mar 1971, p. 2.
79. P and F S-C, memorandum on local government reorganisation, 9 Mar 1971.
80. P and F S-C, 5 Dec 1972 and 3 Apr 1973.

## CHAPTER III

1. WREC, *1st AR*, 1905, p. 4. This figure includes pupil teachers also.
2. *Ibid.* p. 5.
3. *YP*, 15 May 1913.
4. *Ibid*, 17 Mar 1904.
5. *Ibid.*
6. *YP*, 12 May 1904.
7. *Leeds Mercury*, 11 May 1905.
8. WREC, Minutes, 27 June 1905.
9. *YP*, 13 July 1905.
10. *Ibid.*, 12 Oct 1905.
11. FGP S-C, Minutes, 16 Feb 1904.
12. *YP*, 17 Mar 1904.
13. PRO, ED 24/1907/8746.
14. *YP*, 12 Oct 1905.
15. By this time a Liberal Government pledged to introduce new educational legislation was in power.
16. Elem Ed S-C, Minutes, 18 Apr 1906.
17. *YP*, 25 Apr 1906.
18. WREC, Minutes, 24 Apr 1906.
19. *Leeds Mercury*, 12 July 1906.
20. *Ibid.*
21. *Ibid.*
22. *YP*, 10 Jan 1907.
23. Hansard, HC, vol 169, col 1453 (26 Feb 1907).
24. Hansard, HC, vol 175, col 326 (3 June 1907).
25. WREC, Staffing and Salaries S-C, Minutes, 6 Nov 1906.
26. The deputation consisted of Alderman M. T. Kenworthy, Councillor P. R. Jackson and Mr Horne, Inspector for Elementary Education.

27. Elem Ed S-C, Minutes, 20 Nov 1906.
28. School Management S-C, Minutes, 5 Feb 1907.
29. Elem Ed S-C, Minutes, Letter from Board of Education, 19 Mar 1907.
30. Hansard, HC, vol 186, col 1024 (23 Mar 1908).
31. PRO, ED 16/340, notes on Garforth Case by R. L. Morant.
32. *Ibid.*, Morant to Tabor, 12 July 1907.
33. WREC, Special S-C on the Garforth case, Minutes, 18 Feb 1908.
34. WREC, report, Schedule I, Memorial of Roman Catholic Managers' Association, 13 Jan 1909.
35. *YP*, 9 July 1908.
36. *YO*, 18 Feb 1913, article by P. H. Booth.
37. *YP*, 9 July 1908.
38. *Ibid.*, 15 Oct 1908.
39. *Ibid.*, 9 July 1908.
40. WREC, *9th AR*, 1913, p. 46.
41. WRCC, Reports of Inspection of the Public Elementary Schools by the West Riding Architect, 1904, p. 783.
42. *Ibid.*, p. 2.
43. *Ibid.*, p. 26.
44. WREC, *1st AR*, 1905, p. 41.
45. WREC, *3rd AR*, 1907, p. 52.
46. *YO*, Article by P. H. Booth, *op. cit.*
47. *Ibid.*
48. WREC, *1st AR*, 1905, p. 44
49. WRCC, By-laws, approved by Board of Education, 4 Aug 1905.
50. WREC, Accommodation and Attendance S-C, memorandum, 3 Nov 1908.
51. *Ibid.*
52. WREC. *8th AR*, 1912, pp. 56-7.
53. WREC, report, 12 July 1911.
54. *YP*, 14 Mar 1912.
55. It is interesting to note that during the last year in which these exemptions operated (1921-2) 9,691 out of a total of 9,745 were granted for good attendance records.
56. See p. 58.
57. WREC, *1st AR*, 1905, p. 43.
58. WREC, *4th AR*, 1908. p. 83
59. *Ibid.*
60. School Management S-C, Minutes, 4 Apr 1911.
61. *Ibid.*, 30 May 1911.
62. WREC, Special S-C (Elementary), Minutes, 31 Oct 1911.
63. See p. 55.
64. WREC, *ARs*.
65. WREC, *12th AR*, 1916, p. 25.
66. *Ibid.*
67. Elem Ed S-C, memorandum on school attendance by-laws, 11 Apr 1916.
68. *YP*, 11 Jan 1917.
69. Elem Ed S-C, Minutes, 13 Mar 1917.
70. WREC, *19th AR*, 1923, p. 39.
71. Elem Ed S-C, memorandum, 5 June 1923.
72. *YP*, 25 July 1923.
73. *Ibid.*
74. Elem Ed S-C, memorandum, 3 Feb 1931.
75. WREC, *22nd AR*, 1926, p. 12.
76. Elem Ed S-C, memorandum, 7 May 1929.

77. *Ibid.*, 8 July 1932.
78. *Ibid.*, 3 Feb 1931.
79. *Ibid.*
80. *Ibid.*
81. *Ibid.*, 31 Mar 1931.
82. *Ibid.*, 7 July 1931.
83. *Ibid.*, Minutes, 7 July 1931.
84. *Ibid.*, Minutes, 7 June 1932.
85. *Ibid.*, Minutes, 5 July 1932.
86. PRO, ED 136/45, P. R. Jackson to O. Stanley, 2 Dec 1935.
87. See p. 57.
88. *YO*, 11 Feb 1913.
89. *YP*, 11 Jan 1917.
90. *Ibid.*
91. WREC, Special S-C on Education Act, 1918, Minutes, 20 Jan 1919.
92. *Ibid.*
93. *Ibid.*
94. *Ibid.*, 17 Feb 1920.
95. *YP*, 15 July 1920.
96. *Ibid.*
97. WREC, *17th AR*, 1920, pp. 1–2.
98. *TES*, 22 July 1920.
99. *Ibid.*
100. WREC, *16th AR*, 1920, p. 25.
101. Elem Ed S-C, memoranda submitted by CCI E. M. Briggs, 4 Dec 1921 and CCI A. J. Jay, 5 Dec 1922.
102. WREC, *16th AR*, 1920, p. 20.
103. *Ibid.*, p. 25.
104. WREC, *21st AR*, 1925, p. 33.
105. WREC, Special S-C on the Education Act, 1918, Minutes, 23 Mar and 18 May 1920.
106. *Ibid.*, 23 Nov and 21 Dec 1920.
107. The views of the Education Committee on the recommendations of the Economy Sub-Committee were not reported to County Council until 10 Jan 1923.
108. WRCC, report of Economy S-C, presented to Finance Committee, 4 Oct 1922 and County Council, 11 Oct 1922.
109. WREC, report of Education Committee, 10 Jan 1923.
110. WREC, *19th AR*, 1923, p. 37.
111. WREC, *23rd AR*, 1927, pp. 15–16.
112. WRCC, report of Economy S-C, *op. cit.*
113. *Ibid.*
114. Elem Ed S-C, Minutes, 7 Nov 1922.
115. WRCC, report and memorandum submitted by Education Committee, 10 Jan 1906; *YP*, 11 Jan 1906.
116. *TES*, 9 Dec 1922.
117. WREC, *19th AR*, 1923, p. 37.
118. Elem Ed S-C, memorandum on arrangements for the most advanced children in elementary schools, 19 Jan 1923.
119. *Ibid.*
120. *Ibid.*
121. This designation is somewhat confusing in the light of the subsequent development of '9–13 middle schools' in the 1960s. There was no connection between these two types of 'middle school'.
122. Special S-C on the Provision of Middle and further Secondary School Accommodation, Minutes, 27 Feb 1923.

123. *Ibid.*, 9 Sep 1924.
124. WREC, *23rd AR*, 1926, p. 23.
125. Special S-C on the Provision of Elementary, Secondary and Technical Education, Minutes, 28 Oct 1924.
126. *Ibid.*
127. *YP*, 25 July 1923.
128. *Ibid.*, 15 Jan 1925.
129. *TES*, 14 Apr 1923.
130. AEC, Annual Meeting, 18–20 June 1924, President's Address. Geddes was chairman of the Committee on National Expenditure which first reported in 1922 and which recommended drastic economies in the public services.
131. *Ibid.*
132. WREC, notes on Board of Education Circular 1371 prepared by the inspectors and submitted to FGP S-C, 8 Dec 1925.
133. WREC, *24th AR*, 1928, p. 24.
134. WREC, *25th AR*, 1929, p. 25.
135. *Ibid.*
136. WREC, *27th AR*, 1931, p. 12.
137. WREC, *ARs.*
138. WREC, *26th AR*, 1930, p. 6.
139. PRO, ED 24/1514/8746.
140. Elem Ed S-C, memorandum on religious instruction in council schools, 11 Feb 1919.
141. *Ibid.*
142. WREC, *25th AR*, 1929, p. 27.
143. Special S-C on the Education Act 1918, Minutes, 20 May 1919.
144. *Ibid.*, 17 June 1919.
145. *Ibid.*
146. E. Phipps to W. Vibart Dixon, 15 Aug 1919, quoted in full in Special S-C on the Education Act, 1918, Minutes, 18 Nov 1919.
147. Elem Ed S-C, memorandum on Queensbury Schools, 6 Dec 1921.
148. See p. 69.
149. *YP*, 13 July 1922.
150. WRCC, Minutes, 11 Jan 1922.
151. Elem Ed S-C, memorandum on Queensbury Schools, 30 May 1922.
152. *YP*, 13 July 1922.
153. PRO, ED 24/1514/8746.
154. *Ibid.*
155. Elem Ed S-C, memorandum on transfer of non-provided schools, 15 May 1925.
156. *Ibid.*
157. *YP*, 21 Jan 1926.
158. *Ibid.*
159. *Ibid.*
160. *Ibid.*
161. WRCC, Minutes, 20 Jan 1926.
162. *YP*, 30 Apr 1930.
163. Elem Ed S-C, memorandum on reorganisation of elementary schools, 3 Sep 1929.
164. *Ibid.*
165. *Ibid.*
166. *Ibid.*, Board of Education to WREC, 18 Feb 1929.
167. *Ibid.*, memorandum, 3 Sep 1929.
168. The five dioceses of York, Ripon, Wakefield, Sheffield and Bradford were represented on the Committee.
169. In 1930 the Government introduced a White Paper to bring about a national solution to this problem.

170. WREC, J. H. Hallam to A. B. Byne, 9 Jan 1933.
171. *TES*, 16 Jan 1932.
172. WREC, *30th AR*, 1934, p. 4.
173. Elem Ed S-C, memorandum on raising the school leaving age, 6 Mar 1934.
174. *Ibid.*
175. Hansard, HL, vol 93, cols 484–98 (11 July 1934).
176. *YP*, 21 Oct 1937.
177. Board of Education, Administrative Memorandum 135, 23 July 1935.
178. Board of Education, Circular 1444, 6 Jan 1936.
179. *YP*, 21 Oct 1937.
180. *Ibid.*
181. WREC, *ARs*.
182. Board of Education, *Education in 1938*, 1939, p. 5.
183. Board of Education, List 49, Reorganisation of Public Elementary Schools in England and Wales, 1937–38 (1939).
184. *YP*, 26 Apr 1939.
185. *Ibid.*, 21 Apr 1937.
186. *Ibid.*, 29 June 1938.
187. *Ibid.*
188. *Ibid.*, 21 July 1938.
189. *Ibid.*
190. WRCC, Minutes, 18 Jan 1939.

## CHAPTER IV

1. See p. 5.
2. WRTIC, *11th AR*, 1903, p. 3.
3. WREC, Report on Secondary Schools, 1904, p. 26.
4. WRTIC, *Directory*, 1896, p. 9.
5. WRTIC, Minutes, 20 Oct 1902.
6. WRTIC, Minutes, 17 Dec 1901.
7. A. H. D. Acland and H. Llewellyn-Smith, *Studies in Secondary Education* (1892), pp. 306–7.
8. WRTIC, Minutes, 9 Dec 1901.
9. *YP*, 8 Oct 1903.
10. H Ed S-C, Minutes, 14 Feb 1905.
11. Board of Education, Regulations for Secondary Schools, 1907.
12. H Ed S-C, Minutes, 9 Nov 1909.
13. WREC, Report on Secondary Schools, 1904.
14. *Ibid.*, p. 59.
15. *Ibid.*, p. 60.
16. *Ibid.*, p. 2.
17. WRTIC, *1st AR*, 1892, p. 7.
18. WREC, Report on Secondary Schools, 1904, p. 2.
19. *Ibid.*
20. *Ibid.*, pp. 3–4.
21. WREC, *Handbook*, Section VIII, Secondary Schools, 1906, p. 358.
22. Secondary Education (Provisions) S-C, Minutes, 11 July 1905.
23. WREC, statement of A. H. D. Acland at WRCC meeting, 11 July 1906.
24. WREC, County Boroughs S-C, Minutes, 24 and 31 July 1906. This settlement

was revised in 1922, and the distinction which Acland insisted upon in 1906 was abolished. From 1922 a reciprocal arrangement was made with most neighbouring local education authorities that the authority in whose area the pupil resided paid to the authority financing the school attended an annual grant of 80 per cent of the maintenance cost plus £1 per head per annum towards capital expenditure.

25. PRO, ED 53/269, Swallow to Morant, 9 Dec 1905.
26. WREC, account of Conference, 30 Oct 1906, containing copy of letter Halifax County Borough Council to Board of Education, 5 Sep 1906.
27. WREC, reply to statement of West Riding District Councils' Association, 16 May 1907.
28. *Ibid.*, p. 1.
29. *Ibid.*
30. *YP*, 15 Mar 1906, 14 July 1910.
31. See p. 85.
32. *YP*, 13 Apr 1907.
33. WREC, reply to statement of West Riding District Councils' Association, 16 May 1907, p. 6.
34. *Ibid*; also *YP*, 27 Apr 1907.
35. Inside the Council chamber their leading spokesman was Major J. W. Dent (Moderate). Outside, R. Garnett, a farmer from the Skipton area, provided a lively and often amusing leadership.
36. *YP*, 14 Mar, 13 Apr, 27 Apr 1907, 12 Jan, 4 Mar 1911. *YO*, 22 Apr 1907.
37. *YP*, 27 Apr 1907.
38. Secondary Education (Provisions) S-C, Minutes, 24 Mar 1908.
39. Board of Education, Report on the Experiment in Rural Secondary Education conducted at Knaresborough, 1915.
40. Chapter I, p. 00.
41. F. H. Swift, *The Financing of Grant-Aided Education in England and Wales* (1939), p. 717.
42. WRCC, *Reports*, 11 Jan 1911, p. 2H.
43. *Ibid.*
44. WREC, *10th AR*, 1914, p. 22.
45. *YO*, 18 Feb 1913.
46. B. Simon, *The Politics of Educational Reform 1920–1940* (1974), p. 363.
47. WREC, *ARs.*
48. WREC, *15th AR*, 1919, p. 4.
49. WREC, *ARs.*
50. H Ed S-C, Minutes, 11 Mar 1919.
51. WREC, *ARs.*
52. H Ed S-C, Minutes, 11 and 23 June 1910 and 29 Nov 1911.
53. Report of Special S-C on Age of Admission to Secondary Schools, submitted to H Ed S-C, 1 Feb 1921.
54. *Ibid.*
55. *YP*, 23 Feb and 23 Mar 1921.
56. WRCC, Minutes, 13 July 1921.
57. *YP*, 23 Mar 1921.
58. WREC, *17th AR*, 1921, p. 9.
59. WREC, *18th AR*, 1922, p. 10.
60. Calculations based on statistics in WREC, *ARs.*
61. H Ed S-C, Minutes, 7 Mar, 4 Apr, 2 May, 5 Sep 1933.
62. WREC, Minutes, 28 Mar 1939.
63. WREC, *8th AR*, 1912, p. 16.
64. H Ed S-C, Minutes, 6 Sep 1921.
65. *YP*, 1 Mar 1922.
66. WREC, *20th AR*, 1924, p. 34.

67. *YP*, 11 May 1922.
68. *Ibid.*
69. WRCC, Minutes, 10 May 1922.
70. H Ed S-C, Minutes, 2 and 30 May, 4 July 1922.
71. *Ibid.*, 3 Oct and 7 Nov 1922.
72. WREC, *20th AR*, 1924, p. 38.
73. RCLG, 1924, II, Qq 10, 929-31, evidence of P. R. Jackson.
74. H Ed S-C, Minutes, 6 Sep 1921.
75. *Ibid.*
76. *Ibid.*, 7 Feb 1922.
77. *YP*, 1 Mar 1922.
78. H Ed S-C, Minutes, 2 Dec 1924.
79. RCLG, *op. cit.*, Q 10,928.
80. H Ed S-C, 9 June 1925.
81. H Ed S-C, memorandum, 6 Sep 1927.
82. H Ed S-C, memorandum, 6 Mar 1928.
83. WREC, *22nd AR*, 1926, p. 67.
84. WREC, *ARs.*
85. *Ibid.*
86. *YP*, 24 Feb 1932.
87. WREC, *29th AR*, 1933, p. 6.
88. H Ed S-C, Minutes, 2 Feb 1932.
89. H Ed S-C, memorandum, 6 Sep 1927.
90. H Ed S-C, Minutes, 2 Feb 1932.
91. *YP*, 24 Feb 1932.
92. *Ibid.*
93. Simon, *op. cit.*
94. *YP*, 26 Oct and 21 Dec 1932.
95. H Ed S-C, memoranda (including copies of letters from Board of Education), 7 Feb and 7 Mar 1933.
96. H Ed S-C, memorandum, 7 Nov 1933.
97. *Ibid.*
98. H Ed S-C, Minutes, 7 Nov 1933.
99. *YP*, 17 Oct 1935.
100. Board of Education, Circular 1444, 6 Jan 1936.
101. H Ed S-C, memorandum, 11 Feb 1936.
102. S77, memorandum of interview at Board of Education, 19 Jan 1939.
103. S50/181, Board of Education to WREC, 28 Apr 1939.
104. S77, Binns to Walker, 11 July 1939.
105. Chapter III, p. 72.
106. *YP*, 2 Feb 1938.
107. *YP*, 17 Oct 1935.
108. WREC, *1st AR*, 1905, p. 34.
109. WREC, *ARs.*
110. WREC, *21st AR*, 1925, p. 76.
111. These appointments did not prove permanent and both had lapsed by 1915.
112. WREC, *5th AR*, 1909, p. 28.
113. *TES*, 5 Aug, 9 Sep, 23 Sep, 7 Oct and 2 Dec 1920.
114. WREC, *17th AR*, 1921, p. 14.
115. WREC, *ARs.*
116. H Ed S-C, memorandum, 30 May 1922.
117. *Ibid.*
118. WREC, *19th AR*, 1923, p. 24.

119. *Ibid.*
120. WREC, *25th AR*, 1929, p. 99.
121. *Ibid.*
122. WREC, *35th AR*, 1939, p. 12.
123. H Ed S-C, memoranda, 7 Mar, 2 May, 5 Dec 1933, 10 Apr, 5 June, 3 July, 4 Sep, 6 Nov 1934, 8 Jan 1935.
124. *Ibid.*, 5 June 1934.
125. *Ibid.*, 6 Nov 1934.
126. H Ed S-C, memorandum, 6 Dec 1927.
127. Conference of Yorkshire Local Education Authorities, The Guildhall, York, 30 Apr 1928, *Minutes of Proceedings*, speech of Ald. E. Talbot *inter alia*.
128. *Ibid.*, speeches of Sir Percy Jackson and A. Abbott.
129. Board of Education, *Co-operation in Technical Education*, 1937.
130. Yorkshire Council for Agricultural Education, Minutes and Memorandum, 17 Sep 1918.
131. *Ibid.*, Minutes, 11 June 1919.
132. WREC, *Report to County Council*, 8 July 1925.
133. WREC, *Report to County Council*, 15 Mar 1939, Appendix – Memorandum submitted by Vice-Chancellor, University of Leeds.
134. *Ibid.*, Memorandum submitted by W. H. Hyman.
135. *YP*, 19 Mar 1942.
136. WREC, *Report to County Council*, 15 Oct 1941.
137. *YP*, 19 Mar 1942; see also p. 100 of this book.
138. H Ed S-C, Minutes, 14 Jan 1919.
139. WREC, *17th AR*, 1921, p. 15.
140. WRTIC, Minutes, 29 May 1891.
141. This subject is dealt with at greater length by P. R. Sharp, 'Finance', in P. H. J. H. Gosden and A. J. Taylor (eds), *Studies in the History of a University*, 1975, pp. 83–131, and in A. W. Chapman, *The Story of a Modern University*, 1955, pp. 339–49.
142. Gosden and Taylor, *op. cit.*, p. 93.
143. *Ibid.*, p. 212.
144. See p. 83.
145. Leeds University, Central Filing Office, 130 F 30.
146. Gosden and Taylor, *op. cit.*, p. 110.
147. *Ibid.*, p. 117.
148. Leeds University, Central Filing Office, 130 F 30.
149. WREC, *ARs*.
150. Royal Commission on the Civil Service, Third Report, 1913, pp. 315–16; replies of the Council and Senate of the University of Leeds.
151. *Ibid.*, Fourth Report, 1914, Appendix 1.
152. See p. 97.
153. *YP*, 19 Mar 1942.
154. Leeds University, Central Filing Office, 137 F 16.

## CHAPTER V

1. Board of Education, *General Report on the Instruction and Training of Pupil Teachers*, 1907, p. 22.
2. WREC, report concerning the supply of elementary school teachers, Dec 1908; WREC, summary of the facilities offered for entrance to the teaching profession, Jan 1909.

3. WRCC, report from Education Committee, 12 July 1911. R. G. Neville, 'Problems of Financing Higher Education 1902–1918: A West Riding Perspective', *Journal of Educational Administration and History*, IX, 2, 1977, pp. 14–25, gives an account of the difficulties experienced by the West Riding and other Part II county authorities in financing teacher training and 'higher' (i.e. non-elementary) education generally.

4. Elem Ed S-C, supply of teachers, 16 Dec 1913.

5. WREC, Minutes of a Special Meeting, 25 Jan 1916; WRCC, report from the Education Committee, 10 Mar 1920.

6. WRCC, printed letter to parents, 'Teaching Profession. Prospects and opportunities for training', July 1921.

7. H Ed S-C, conditions of award of maintenance allowances, 3 July 1923.

8. H Ed S-C, Bingley Training College – admission of students 1922, 5 July 1921.

9. WREC, Special S-C, suggested abolition of the student teacher system, 29 June 1926.

10. Secondary Education Provision S-C, 13 Sep 1904.

11. H Ed S-C, 14 Mar 1905, memorandum by the chairman.

12. H Ed S-C, training college provision, 10 Apr 1905; Secondary Education Provision S-C, 31 July 1906 and 23 July 1907; WREC Minutes, 22 Oct 1907.

13. WREC, notes with regard to training college provision (undated, late 1907); WREC, Minutes, 28 Jan 1908; WRCC Minutes, 14 Oct 1908; WRCC, *Speeches on the occasion of the laying of the foundation memorial stones, Bingley Training College*, 29 May 1909.

14. WRCC, Minutes, 10 July 1912.

15. WREC, *8th AR*, 1912, p. 5; H Ed S-C, Minutes, 7 June 1921.

16. Board of Education, Circular 1301, 20 Mar 1923.

17. Board of Education, *Full Inspection Reports on Training College, No. 5*, Nov 1924, Bingley Training College.

18. H Ed S-C, Bingley Training College, 13 Apr 1920.

19. 16 and 17 Geo. V, c.9, Economy (Miscellaneous Provisions) Act, 1926. Comparisons of grants receivable by a voluntary college and by Bingley figure in committee memoranda of the later 1920s and 1930s. In 1934, for instance, the West Riding would have received £964 more in grant if Bingley had been treated as a voluntary college and representations were made on this again to the AEC – H Ed S-C, 10 Apr 1934.

20. WRCC, *Handbook of the Education Committee*, Section XI, Courses for Teachers, 1908.

21. H Ed S-C, *Report on Vacation Courses*, 1908.

22. H Ed S-C, *Report on Vacation Courses*, 1913; WREC, *Twenty-First Bingley Vacation Course*, 1934; H Ed S-C, Report of Board of Education on Bingley Vacation Course, 1932, T 50 M/131.

23. Gosden, *Education in the Second World War, op. cit.*, pp. 124–5; Ministry of Education, *Challenge and Response. An account of the emergency training scheme for the training of teachers*. Pamphlet No. 17, 1950. Board of Education, Circular 1652, 15 May 1944.

24. Staffing and Salaries S-C, Minutes, 11 Jan 1944; Further Education S-C, provision of emergency training colleges, 3 Sep 1946; Further Education S-C, Minutes, p. 104, 2 Dec 1947; Policy S-C, Minutes and memorandum: Harrogate Training College – Extension of life, 19 Oct 1948.

25. Ministry of Education, Administrative Memorandum 529 (22 May 1944); Staffing and Salaries S-C, release of selected teachers to serve on staffs of emergency training colleges, 23 Jan 1945.

26. Staffing and Salaries S-C, Minutes, 28 May 1946; WR correspondence, G71, Binns to Clegg, 21 June 1946; G71 Ministry of Education to Chief Education Officer, 27 June 1946; Staffing and Salaries S-C, Minutes, 23 July 1946.

27. Policy S-C, Minutes, 15 June 1948; Emergency training of teachers–probationers, 19 Oct 1948; *TES*, 26 Jan 1962, p. 133.

28. G77, Clegg to Hyman, 15 Nov 1945.

29. Post-war Education S-C, training of teachers; provision of additional training places in the county, 19 Feb 1946.
30. G77, Clegg to G. N. Flemming, Ministry of Education, 3 May 1946.
31. Policy S-C, Minutes, 14 Dec 1947.
32. G77, Clegg to T. R. Weaver, Ministry of Education, 9 Apr 1946.
33. G77, Clegg to B. Kenyon, 25 Oct 1946; Clegg to Col. Langdon, Earl Fitzwilliam's Estate Office, 1 Nov 1946.
34. G77, Flemming to Clegg, 1 Nov 1946.
35. Policy S-C, training college provision Wentworth Woodhouse, 21 Jan 1947; proposed physical training college for women, 16 Sep 1947.
36. G77, Flemming to Clegg, 23 Feb 1949.
37. G77, Clegg to HMI Miss Briant, 16 Mar 1949; Clegg to Woodall (Ministry of Education) 25 May 1949; Policy S-C, provision of a college in the County for the Training of Domestic Science Teachers, 24 May 1949; Further Education S-C, Minutes, 31 May 1949.
38. G77, Flemming to West Riding Education Authority, 22 Sep 1949; Policy S-C, Minutes, 27 Sep 1949; G77, Clegg to Secretary, Teachers Branch, Ministry of Education, 29 Sep 1949.
39. YP, 19 Oct 1950, p. 6.
40. P and F S-C, Wells House Ilkley, proposed training college for teachers of domestic science, 28 Mar 1950.
41. Sunday Express, 16 Mar 1952; YP, 20 Mar 1952, p. 3, and 22 Mar 1952, p. 4.
42. A77, Clegg to George Taylor, CEO Leeds, 25 Apr 1958.
43. M77, W. H. J[ones] to Clegg, 7 Jan 1960; Clegg to L. G. Cook, Ministry of Education, 15 Jan 1960.
44. M77, office note, Clegg to Hogan and Petty, 29 Feb 1960; 78 A/J, Clegg to Dodd, 3 Aug 1960; 78 A/B, L. G. Cook, Ministry of Education, to the West Riding Authority, 7 Nov 1960; South Yorkshire Times, 7 Jan 1961, Letter from C. T. Broughton, chairman, WREC.
45. P and F S-C, Swinton Day Training College, 11 Sep 1962; P and F S-C, Minutes, 2 Apr 1962.
46. DES, College Letter 7/65, 3 July 1965. The paper submitted to the P and F S-C with this letter must have contained erroneous figures, for it said that 'of the 2,000,000 teachers required nationally in 10 years' time, some 80,000 will be required in the West Riding'. The number currently being employed was under 11,000.
47. P and F S-C, problems of teacher recruitment in the West Riding, 12 Oct 1965.
48. Post-war Ed S-C, refresher courses for teachers and youth leaders, 16 Oct 1945.
49. G77, County Education Officer to Ministry of Education, 14 May 1946; Education Officer to Clerk to County Council, 3 June 1946.
50. P and F S-C, Woolley Hall and Minutes, 12 July 1960.
51. DES, Children and their Primary Schools, 1967, I, p. 947.
52. P and F S-C, the county council inspectorate and the advisory staff working in schools and technical institutes, 9 Feb 1954; the county council inspectorate and the advisory staff, 7 Feb 1956.
53. P and F S-C, the county council inspectorate and the advisory staff, 6 Apr 1965.
54. P and F S-C, the advisory service, 8 Oct 1968.
55. P and F S-C, Minutes, 22 Oct 1968; county advisory staff, 9 Dec 1969; County advisory staff, 13 Jan 1970.
56. P and F S-C, advisory teachers and Minutes, 7 May 1968; advisory teachers, 10 Feb 1970.

## CHAPTER VI

1. *Report on Metropolitan Soup Kitchens and Dinner Tables*, 1871, p. 58.
2. *Report of the Committee on Physical Deterioration*, Cd 2175, 1904.
3. 6 Edw. VII, c.57.
4. CCR, 9 Jan 1907.
5. CCR, 13 Oct 1908 and 13 Jan 1909.
6. WREC, *5th AR*, 1909, p. 83.
7. WREC, Report to Board of Education, 21 Dec 1909.
8. CCR, 8 May 1912; WREC, *8th AR*, 1912, p. 73, and *9th AR*, 1913, p. 73.
9. 4 and 5 Geo. V, c.20.
10. Chief Medical Officer of the Board of Education, *AR* for 1913 (1914) p. 249 *et seq.*
11. CCR, 14 July 1915.
12. FGP S-C, 14 June 1921.
13. CCR, 18 Mar 1925; *YP*, 19 Mar 1925, p. 6.
14. Chief Medical Officer of the Board of Education, *AR* for 1933 (1934) p. 28.
15. H Ed S-C, survey of school dinners in WR secondary schools, 4 Nov 1924.
16. PRO, ED 138/60, Sep 1944, Paper by E. D. Marris, war history of school meals and milk.
17. Board of Education, Circular 1484, 21 Nov 1939; WREC, Canteen S-C, 5 and 12 Dec 1939.
18. PRO, ED 50/215, War Cabinet, Food Policy Committee Papers 7 June to 9 July 1940; Board of Education, Circular 1520, 22 July 1940.
19. Gosden, *Education in the Second World War, op. cit.*, Chap. 9.
20. Canteen S-C, 2 Sep 1941.
21. *Ibid.*, 31 Mar 1942.
22. CCR, Mar 1942 to Feb 1943, supply of milk to school children.
23. Canteen S-C, 11 June 1943.
24. Ministry of Education, Circular 96, 28 Mar 1946.
25. Ministry of Education, Circular 97, 12 Apr 1946; WREC, Canteen S-C, 9 July 1946; oral evidence Mr H. Haigh, 3 Mar 1975.
26. P and F S-C, 14 Sep 1971.
27. Report of the Inter-Departmental Committee on Medical Inspection and Feeding of Children Attending Public Elementary Schools, I, *Report and Appendices*, 1905 [Cd 2779], p. 2.
28. *Ibid.*, Appendix I, pp. 89–99 and Vol II, *List of Witnesses, Minutes of Evidence, Appendices, and Index* [Cd 2784], Appendix VII, p. 284.
29. *Ibid.*, medical officers for educational purposes had been appointed by six counties, thirty-five county boroughs, thirty-one boroughs and thirteen urban districts – Vol I, *op. cit.*, p. 13.
30. WREC, *2nd AR*, 1906, pp. 48–9.
31. 7 Edw. VII, c.43; WREC, First Report of the Medical Officer on the Medical Inspection of School Children for the Year ended 31 Dec 1908, p. 6, presented to School Management S-C May 1909.
32. *Ibid.*, pp. 6–7.
33. *Ibid.*
34. *Ibid.* pp. 1 and 7–8; cf. B. M. Barrows, *A County and its Health: A History of the Development of the West Riding Health Services 1889–1974*, Wakefield, 1974, p. 25.
35. WREC, First Report of the Medical Officer on the Medical Inspection of School Children, *op. cit.*, p. 7.
36. *Ibid.*, p. 8.
37. Barrows, *op. cit.*, p. 42.
38. WREC, *5th AR*, 1909, p. 71.

39. WREC, 1st Report of the Medical Officer on the Medical Inspection of School Children, *op. cit.*, pp. 74–5, viz. copy of memorandum by the County Medical Officer concerning proposed ameliorative measures; cf. Barrows, *op. cit.*, pp. 26–7.

40. See, for example, WREC, *4th AR*, 1909, p. 60.

41. WRCC, reports 11 Mar 1914 to 13 Jan 1915; report of the WREC presented to WRCC on 13 May 1914, p. 5J; WREC, *7th AR*, 1911, p. 49.

42. WREC, *10th AR*, 1914, p. 48.

43. See, for example, WREC, 8th RSMO for 1915; cf. Barrows, *op. cit.*, p. 25.

44. WREC, 8th RSMO, p. 7.

45. There were twenty-two provided secondary schools and twenty-four endowed secondary schools aided by the WREC at this time. H Ed S-C, memorandum submitted by CCI J. H. Hallam, 10 Mar 1914; WREC, *11th AR*, 1915, p. 17.

46. Elem Ed S-C, memorandum submitted by the Tuberculosis Officer, T. Campbell, 8 May 1917; WRCC, reports 14 Mar 1917 to 9 Jan 1918; report of the WREC presented to WRCC on 11 July 1917; report of a conference of representatives of the WREC with the Tuberculosis S-C of the West Riding Public Health and Housing Committee, 16 July 1917.

47. WRCC, reports 13 Mar 1918 to 8 Jan 1919; report of the WREC presented to WRCC on 10 July 1918, p. 3B.

48. 8 and 9 Geo. V, c.39. *The School Health Service 1908–1974 Report of the Chief Medical Officer of the DES and Presenting an Historical Review by Dr Peter Henderson, Principal Medical Officer of the DES from 1951–1969*, 1975, pp. 6–7.

49. Barrows, *op. cit.*, p. 66.

50. Henderson, *op. cit.*, p. 11; Barrows, *op. cit.*, p. 62–4.

51. *Ibid.*

52. See, for example, WRCC, reports 12 Mar 1924 to 14 Jan 1925; report of the WREC presented to WRCC on 8 Oct 1924, p. 4D.

53. WRCC, reports 10 Mar 1926 to 19 Jan 1927; report of the WREC presented to WRCC on 21 July 1926, p. 14E.

54. *Ibid.*

55. WRCC, reports 9 Mar 1927 to 18 Jan 1928; report of WREC presented to WRCC on 20 July 1927, p. 4B; WRCC, reports 14 Mar 1928 to 16 Jan 1929; report of WREC presented to WRCC on 14 Mar 1928, p. 5E.

56. *TES*, 11 June 1932, p. 225.

57. *Ibid.*

58. Barrows, *op cit.*, p. 66. The West Riding appointed an educational psychologist in 1951 and child guidance clinics were subsequently established at Rawmarsh, Skipton and Wakefield. After 1955 the Regional Hospital Boards provided the Authority with part-time psychiatrists and the West Riding also appointed a part-time psychiatric social worker.

59. For a full consideration of the school medical service during the Second World War, see Gosden, *Education in the Second World War, op. cit.*, Chap. 8.

60. WRCC, reports 18 Mar 1942 to 16 Feb 1943; Report of the Public Health and Housing Committee presented to WRCC on 15 July 1942, p. 50.

61. Gosden, *Education in the Second World War, op. cit.*, p. 175.

62. WRCC, reports 15 Mar 1939 to 17 Jan 1940; Report of the Public Health and Housing Committee presented to WRCC on 18 Oct 1939, p. 72.

63. Henderson, *op. cit.*, p. 7.

64. *Ibid.* and Barrows, *op. cit.*, p. 210.

65. *Ibid.* pp. 214–16.

66. P and F S-C, memorandum relating to Food and Sweets in School, 6 Dec 1960; cf. P and F S-C, memorandum, 7 Mar 1961.

67. Barrows, *op. cit.*, pp. 217–18.

68. 62 and 63 Vic., c. 32; D. G. Pritchard, 'The Development of Schools for Handicapped Children in England During the Nineteenth Century', *History of Education Quarterly*, III (Dec 1963), p. 221.

69. *Royal Commission on the Care and Control of the Feeble-Minded, Appendices to the Minutes of Evidence*, V, 1908 [Cd 4219], p. 232, statement by W. H. Brown, Inspector of Elementary Education in the West Riding; WREC *1st AR*, 1905, p. 54.

70. *Royal Commission on the Care and Control of the Feeble-Minded, op cit.*, p. 232.

71. WREC, *2nd AR*, 1906, p. 35.

72. 4 and 5 Geo. V. c. 45. Pritchard, 'The Development of Schools for Handicapped Children', *op. cit.*, pp. 221–2.

73. WREC, *11th AR*, 1915, p. 42.

74. 8 and 9 Geo. V, c. 39.

75. WREC, *2nd AR*, 1906, pp. 54–5.

76. WREC, *9th AR*, 1913, pp. 62–3; *12th AR*, 1916, p. 24.

77. WREC, *4th AR*, 1908, p. 79; *5th AR*, 1909, p. 77.

78. WREC, *5th AR*, 1909, p. 77.

79. WREC, *17th AR*, 1921, p. 18; *35th AR*, 1939, p. 24; WREC *24th RSMO*, 1932, Table III, p. 47.

80. D. G. Pritchard, *Education and the Handicapped 1760–1960*, 1963, p. 188.

81. From 1 July 1928, however, the Mitchell Memorial Home at Rawdon was utilised by the WR Public Health and Housing Committee for the treatment of children crippled by tuberculosis. WRCC, reports 14 Mar 1928 to 18 Jan 1933; report of the Public Health and Housing Committee, 14 Mar 1928, p. 45. The Education Act 1944 substituted the term 'educationally sub-normal' for 'mentally defective'.

82. D. G. Pritchard, *Education and the Handicapped*, 1760–1960, *op. cit.*, pp. 188–9.

83. See, for example, P and F S-C, Minutes, 27 Sep 1949; memorandum relating to special schools – Existing Provision and Development Plan Proposals, 27 Sep 1949.

84. WREC, *West Riding Education: Ten Years of Change, 1954, p. 69.*

85. *Barrows, op. cit.*, 213–14; WREC, *Education 1954–64*, 1964, pp. 81–3.

86. WREC, *The Final Ten Years 1964–1974*, 1974, p. 77; Barrows, *op. cit.*, p. 213.

87. P and F S-C, minutes and memoranda relating to transfer of responsibility for handicapped children, 13 Oct, 10 Nov and 8 Dec 1970; 9 Feb and 11 May 1971.

88. 56 and 57 Vic, c. 42. D. G. Pritchard, 'The Development of Schools for Handicapped Children', *op. cit.*, p. 221.

89. WREC, *1st AR*, 1905, p. 9; *14th AR*, 1918, p. 3.

90. See, for example, WREC *4th AR*, 1908, p. 46.

91. 10 and 11 Geo. V, c. 49. For full details of the West Riding's scheme under the Act, see WREC, report of the Special S-C re Blind Persons Act 1920, presented to FGP S-C on 13 Dec 1921; WRCC, reports 12 Jan 1921 to 11 Jan 1922; report of the WREC to be presented to the WRCC on 11 Jan 1922, pp. 8H–18H; WREC *18th AR*, 1922, pp. 15–16; *20th AR*, 1924, p. 60.

92. P and F S-C, Minutes, 17 June 1947 and 27 Sep 1949; P and F S-C, memorandum re special schools – Existing Provision and Development Plan Proposals, 27 Sept 1949.

93. WREC, *Education 1954–64*, 1964, p. 81.

94. 9 Edw. VII, c. 7.

95. 10 Edw. VII, c. 37.

96. Juvenile Employment Inquiry, Report to the Prime Minister by the Rt. Hon. Viscount Chelmsford, 23 July 1921.

97. WREC, Minutes, 13 Oct 1920.

98. Board of Education, Circular 1233, 11 Oct 1921.

99. FGP S-C, memorandum on Board of Education Circular 1233 and Lord Chelmsford's report, 8 Nov 1921.

100. WREC, Minutes, 12 Mar 1924.

101. H Ed S-C, provision of courses of instruction for unemployed boys and girls, 10 Apr 1934; Ministry of Labour, Circular AC1, 12 Mar 1934; H Ed S-C, juvenile unemployment centres – report on classes at Doncaster, 1 Sep 1925.
102. H Ed S-C, junior instruction centres and classes, estimates 1936–7, 11 Feb 1936.
103. Policy S-C, establishment and location of juvenile employment bureaux, 16 Mar 1948.
104. Policy S-C, Minutes and memorandum on juvenile employment service, 21 Oct 1947; *ibid.*, Minutes, 20 Jan 1948; *ibid.*, Minutes and memorandum on appointment of County Juvenile Employment Officer, 17 Feb 1948; *ibid.*, Minutes and memorandum on establishment and location of juvenile employment bureaux, 16 Mar 1948.
105. 11 and 12 Geo. VI, c. 49.
106. Policy S-C, Minutes and memorandum on preparation of model scheme, 21 Sep 1948.
107. Policy S-C, Minutes and memorandum on youth employment service – revision of scheme, 27 Nov 1951.
108. Policy S-C, Minutes, 27 Sep 1949.
109. P and F S-C, county youth employment service, 9 May 1967; *ibid.*, development of the youth employment service, 19 Sep 1967; *ibid.*, Minutes, 10 Oct 1967.
110. P and F S-C, Minutes, 6 June 1972.
111. WRCC, Minutes, 20 Oct 1948.
112. P and F S-C, memoranda, 5 Apr, 6 Dec 1966; 7 May 1968; 11 May, 12 Oct 1971; 11 June, 7 Nov, 5 Dec 1972; 1 May, 4 Sep 1973.
113. WREC, *Education 1964–74*, 1974, p. 65.
114. A. Clegg and B. Megson, *Children in Distress*, 1968.
115. P and F S-C, memorandum, 3 Dec 1968.
116. *Ibid.*
117. WREC, report, The West Riding Educational Priority Area Project, 5 July 1971.
118. P and F S-C, Minutes, 11 May 1971.
119. P and F S-C, memorandum, 12 Oct 1971.
120. WREC, *Education 1964–74*, 1974, p. 66.
121. P and F S-C, memorandum, 11 Jan 1972.
122. A. H. Halsey, *Educational Priority*, vol I, HMSO, 1972.
123. This section provides only a brief history of the project and readers are directed to the following sources for a full consideration: G. Smith (ed.) *Educational Priority, vol 4: The West Riding Project*, HMSO, 1975; *Red House Early Education Programmes, Progress Report* (Red House Education Centre, Denaby Main, Doncaster), 1972 – prepared by several members of the project team; a series of ten working papers prepared by the Red House Team under the general title *West Riding Educational Priority Area Project*; a brief survey is to be found in *The Final Ten Years, op. cit.*, pp. 79–81; see also WREC P and F S-C memoranda: Educational Priority (3 Dec 1968), The Educational Priority Area Project (11 Mar 1969) and Red House, Social Education Centre, Denaby (10 Nov 1970).
124. WREC, The West Riding Educational Priority Area Project, 5 July 1971, p. 4.
125. *Ibid.*, p. 10.
126. *Ibid.*, p. 5; A. H. Halsey, *Educational Priority*, vol I, *op. cit.*, p. 83.
127. WREC, The West Riding Educational Priority Area Project, 5 July 1971, p. 5.
128. *Ibid.*, p. 6.
129. *Ibid.*, p. 10.
130. P and F S-C, Red House, Social Education Centre, Denaby, 10 Nov 1970.
131. *Ibid.*
132. *Ibid.* An additional social worker was appointed to work at Red House in 1971 (see P and F S-C, Minutes, 13 July 1971) and subsequently the Authority further increased the staff establishment. The Authority also took advantage of the DES allocations for building projects in EPAs – see, for example, P and F S-C, School Building in Educational Priority Areas, Circular 11/67, 7 May 1968, and P and F S-C, Minutes, 7

May 1968. It is interesting to note that in many cases the local education authorities recognised more schools as EPAs than were designated nationally. In the West Riding out of a total of more than 1,000 primary schools only thirteen were recognised by the DES as EPA schools, although the Authority itself recognised over 100.

133. WREC, The West Riding Educational Priority Area Project, 5 July 1971, p. 10.
134. P and F S-C, The Social and Educational Implication of Immigrant Children in West Riding Schools, 12 Sep 1967.
135. Correspondence files: Sir Alec Clegg to Sir Herbert Andrew, 11 Nov 1968.
136. P and F S-C, Minutes and memorandum, Special Education Provision for Indian/Pakistani Children in Batley, 12 Jan 1965.
137. Ibid.; P and F S-C, The Social and Educational Implications of Immigrant Children in West Riding Schools, 12 Sep 1967; WREC, The Final Ten Years, p. 72.
138. P and F S-C, Minutes, 10 May 1966 and 11 July 1967.
139. P and F S-C, The Social and Educational Implications of Immigrant Children in West Riding Schools, 12 Sep 1967.
140. P and F S-C, Minutes, 12 Sep 1967; WREC, The Final Ten Years, pp. 72–3.
141. P and F S-C, Minutes, 12 May 1970 (the camp was organised by the students and staff of the Bingley College of Education as part of the Government's urban aid programme). P and F S-C, Immigrant Pupils in West Riding Schools, 2 Apr 1968; WREC, The Final Ten Years, p. 73.
142. See, for example, P and F S-C, Minutes, 2 Apr 1968; WREC, The Final Ten Years, 1974, pp. 72–3.
143. WREC, The Final Ten Years, 1974, p. 73.
144. For an account of the history of pre-school education nationally, see N. Whitbread, The Evolution of the Nursery-Infant School: A History of Infant and Nursery Education in Britain, 1800–1970, 1972 (which contains a useful bibliography).
145. WREC, 33rd AR, 1937, p. 7; correspondence files: A. L. Binns to W. M. Hyman, chairman of the Education Committee, 16 Jan 1943; cf. office minute, Post-War Reconstruction Nursery Schools and Classes, 14 Jan 1943.
146. Correspondence files: A. L. Binns to W. M. Hyman, 16 Jan 1943.
147. Whitbread, op. cit., p. 100.
148. Elem Ed S-C, Minutes, 23 Dec 1941.
149. WREC, Ten Years of Change, 1954, p. 12.
150. Correspondence files: data for Mr Holmes, MP, 5 Sep 1947.
151. Policy S-C, women workers – provision of nursery school and other accommodation and meal facilities for children during holidays, office files, office minute, Women in the Textile Industry, 24 May 1949; nursery schools and classes, 23 May 1949; correspondence files: L. R. Fletcher, Ministry of Education, to Clegg, 3 May 1949.
152. Policy S-C, Minutes, 24 May 1949.
153. P and F S-C, day care of children under five, play groups, etc., 12 Sep 1967; WRCC, West Riding Health Committee, Care of Mothers and Young Children and Nursing Services Sub-Committee, 20 Mar 1967; report of County Medical Officer, Day Care for Children under Five Years of Age.
154. Office memorandum, Clegg to V. Gordon, CCI, nursery classes, 23 Nov 1953; WREC Circular D.O. 53/1357, 22 Dec 1953, re nursery classes; P and F S-C, conditions for admission of children under five to maintained primary schools, 7 Dec 1954; P and F S-C, Minutes, 7 Feb 1961.
155. P and F S-C, Minutes and memorandum, Nursery Provision: Release of Women Teachers to Schools, 8 Mar 1966; DES Addendum No. 2 to Circular 8/60.
156. West Riding Health Committee, Care of Mothers and Young Children and Nursing Services Sub-Committee, 20 Mar 1967; report of County Medical Officer, Day Care for Children under Five Years of Age.
157. P and F S-C, Minutes and memorandum, Pre-School Playgroups, 15 Apr 1969.

158. P and F S-C, Minutes and memorandum, Nursery Provision and the Admission of Under-School-Age Children to Primary Schools, 9 Dec 1969; P and F S-C, Minutes and memorandum, Urban Programme No. 7, 5 Dec 1972.
159. P and F S-C, Minutes and memorandum, Use of Single Temporary Classrooms for Nursery Units, 7 Mar 1972.
160. Information provided by Mr E. Hepworth, Head of Allocations Section, WR Education Department.
161. P and F S-C, Minutes, 2 Oct 1973.

## CHAPTER VII

1. WRCC, *Triennial Statement 1937–1938–1939* by chairman, 17 Jan 1940.
2. *Ibid.*
3. WRCC, *Statement* by chairman, 16 Jan 1946.
4. *Ibid.*
5. *Ibid.*
6. H Ed S-C, memorandum, 3 Nov 1942.
7. *Ibid.*
8. *Ibid.*
9. S77, Binns to Howlett, 20 July 1943, and Howlett to Binns, 9 Aug 1943.
10. *Ibid.*, Binns to Wilson, 24 Aug 1943.
11. *Ibid.*, Binns to Walker, 3 Sep 1943.
12. H Ed S-C, memorandum, 5 Oct 1943.
13. *Ibid.*, 7 Dec 1943.
14. S77, Binns to Williams, 7 June 1944.
15. *Ibid.*
16. Post-War Ed S-C, Minutes, 21 Nov 1944.
17. PRO, ED 136/290, memorandum on educational reconstruction by W. M. Hyman, undated (1943).
18. *Ibid.*
19. *Ibid.*
20. *Ibid.*
21. *Ibid.*, comments by Board of Education officials on Hyman's memorandum, 1943.
22. *Ibid.*
23. S77, Binns to Wilson, 6 July 1944.
24. WRCC, clerk's file, Holmes to Kenyon, 11 Apr 1945.
25. *Ibid.*
26. *Ibid.*
27. *YP*, 25 Apr 1945.
28. WRCC, clerk's file, Holmes to Kenyon, 11 Apr 1945.
29. H Ed S-C, Minutes, 6 Oct 1942.
30. G77, Binns to Finney, 30 July 1942.
31. E77, Binns to Board of Education, 5 Oct 1943.
32. *Ibid.*
33. *YP*, 29 Sep 1943.
34. *Ibid.*
35. Policy S-C, memorandum, 27 Nov 1951.
36. WREC, *Ten Years of Change*, 1954, p. 134.
37. WRCC, report of Reconstruction Committee, 20 Oct 1943.

38. PRO, ED 136/290, comments by Board of Education officials on Hyman's memorandum, 1943.
39. *Ibid.*, memorandum by W. M. Hyman, undated (1943).
40. E77, Binns to Stockdale, 31 Dec 1942.
41. PRO, ED 136/290, comments by Board of Education officials on Hyman's memorandum, 1943.
42. *Ibid.*, memorandum by W. M. Hyman, undated (1943).
43. WRCC, report of Reconstruction Committee, 20 Oct 1943.
44. WREC, observations on the draft interim report of the Reconstruction Committee, undated (1943).
45. PRO, ED 136/290, memorandum by W. M. Hyman, undated (1943).
46. *Ibid.*
47. *Ibid.*, comments by Board officials on Hyman's memorandum, 1943.
48. *Ibid.*
49. *Ibid.*
50. The term 'grammar school' was not widely applied to West Riding provided secondary schools before the 1930s. This change in name was suggested by the Hadow Committee to differentiate established secondary schools from the senior elementary schools which were projected; H Ed S-C, memorandum, 3 June 1930.
51. WRCC, report of Reconstruction Committee, 20 Oct 1943.
52. *YP*, 13 Mar 1939.
53. PRO, ED 136/290, memorandum by W. M. Hyman, undated (1943).
54. WRCC, report of Reconstruction Committee, 20 Oct 1943.
55. *Ibid.*
56. H Ed S-C, memorandum, 1 Mar 1927.
57. *Ibid.*, memoranda, 7 May and 5 Nov 1935.
58. WRCC, Statement by chairman, 16 Jan 1946.
59. *YP*, 2 Feb 1938.
60. WRCC, Statement by chairman, 16 Jan 1946.
61. T71, Binns to Walker, 30 Dec 1942.
62. *Ibid.*
63. PRO, ED 136/290, memorandum by W. M. Hyman, undated (1943).
64. Post-War Ed S-C, memorandum, 29 Feb 1944.
65. *Ibid.*
66. G77, Binns to Lightfoot, 22 July 1944.
67. *Ibid.*
68. PRO, ED 136/290, memorandum by W. M. Hyman, undated (1943).
69. *Ibid.*, comments by Board officials on Hyman's memorandum, 1943.
70. *Ibid.*
71. T71, walker to Binns, 22 Sep 1942.
72. Binns to Wilson, 13 Sep 1944.
73. E80, Gittins to Wormald, 17 May 1944.
74. G77, Clegg to Parsons, 30 Apr 1946.
75. *Ibid.*, Parsons to Clegg, 21 May 1946.
76. *Ibid.*, Clegg to Clarke, Flemming, Thomson, 6 May 1946.
77. *Ibid.*, Clarke to Clegg, 9 May 1946; Flemming to Clegg, 9 May 1946, and Thomson to Clegg, 28 May 1946.
78. Policy S-C, memorandum, 16 July 1946.
79. *Ibid.*
80. *Ibid.*
81. *YP*, 16 Jan 1947.
82. *Ibid.*
83. *YO*, 30 Apr 1947.
84. *Ibid.*

85. *Ibid.*
86. Policy S-C, Minutes, 22 Apr and 16 Sep 1947.
87. WREC, preface to Development Plan, 1947.
88. *Ibid.*
89. *YP*, 22 May 1947.
90. *Ibid.*
91. Policy S-C, memorandum, 21 Sep 1948.
92. I. G. K. Fenwick, *The Comprehensive School*, 1976, p. 65.
93. Policy S-C, memorandum, 21 Sep 1948.
94. Policy S-C, memorandum, 26 July 1949; copy of letter from Ministry of Education to WREC, 25 Jan 1949.
95. Policy S-C, Minutes, 25 Oct 1949.
96. Policy S-C, memorandum, 27 Nov 1951.
97. *Ibid.*
98. WREC, *Ten Years of Change*, 1954, pp. 3–4.
99. G609/H, Clegg to Rawcliffe, 19 July 1967.
100. WREC, *Ten Years of Change*, 1954, p. 118.
101. U11, Clegg to Hyman, 12 May 1947.
102. P and F S-C, memorandum, 3 Dec 1957.
103. G77, Clegg to Hyman, 2 Feb 1946.
104. G77, Clegg to Brockis, 30 Jan 1948.
105. G77, Clegg to Hyman, 27 Apr 1948.
106. Policy S-C, memorandum, 16 Dec 1947.
107. Mexborough Labour Party to Minister of Education, 9 Oct 1948, copy forwarded to WRCC.
108. *Ibid.*
109. Policy S-C, memorandum, 15 Mar 1949.
110. WREC Minutes, 25 Jan 1949.
111. *YP*, 26 Jan 1949.
112. *YP*, 27 Sep 1950 and 17 May 1951.
113. *YP*, 16 Oct 1950.
114. WREC, *Ten Years of Change*, 1954, p. 17.
115. WREC, joint meeting of HMIs and CCIs, Wakefield, 19 Sep 1951.
116. *Ibid.*
117. At this stage Clegg feared that if bilateral grammar/technical schools were created, the ablest pupils would be consistently channelled into arts and pure science subjects.
118. WREC, memorandum, 27 Sep 1955.
119. *Ibid.*
120. *Ibid.*
121. T80, Deputy Education Officer to Ministry of Education, 18 June 1947.
122. WREC, joint meeting of HMIs and CCIs, Wakefield, 19 Sep 1951.
123. *Ibid.*
124. *TES*, 25 Apr 1952.
125. WREC, *Education 1954–64*, 1964, pp. 175–7.
126. G77, Clegg to Taylor, 15 Apr 1958.
127. P and F S-C, memorandum, 10 Apr 1956.
128. *Ibid.*
129. P and F S-C, memoranda, 3 Dec 1957 and 14 Jan 1958.
130. P and F S-C, Minutes, 14 Jan and 11 Feb 1958.
131. P and F S-C, Minutes, 11 Mar 1958.
132. *Ibid.*, 14 Oct 1958.
133. WREC, Beloe Examinations: meeting of officer representatives of authorities, 21 Sep 1962.
134. SG605, Clegg to Tunn, 4 June 1962.

135. The West Yorkshire and Lindsey Regional Board covered the territory of the following local education authorities: the West Riding, Lindsey, Barnsley, Doncaster, Rotherham and Sheffield.
136. A605, Clegg to Petty, 12 Aug 1963.
137. A605, Clegg to Clayton, 18 Jan 1963.
138. WREC, *Education 1964–74*, 1974, p. 32.
139. WREC, joint meeting of HMIs and CCIs, Wakefield, 19 Sep 1951.
140. P and F S-C, memorandum, 9 June 1953.
141. *YP*, 16 July 1953.
142. P and F S-C, memorandum, 9 Feb 1954.
143. G78A/F, Clegg to Peaker, 19 Jan 1955.
144. Peaker to Barry, 4 Apr 1955, copy forwarded to WREC.
145. P and F S-C, Minutes, 13 Sep 1955.
146. P and F S-C, memorandum, 10 July 1956.
147. P and F S-C, memorandum, 8 Dec 1959.
148. *Ibid.*
149. WREC, *Education 1954–64*, 1964, p. 60.
150. WREC, P and F S-C, memorandum, 8 Oct 1963.
151. WREC, *Education 1954–64*, 1964, p. 60.
152. P and F S-C, memorandum, 12 Jan 1965.
153. *YO*, 23 Feb 1955.
154. *Ibid.*, 23 Mar 1955.
155. P and F S-C, memorandum, 8 July 1958.
156. *Ibid.*
157. *YP*, 9 Jan 1959.
158. *Ibid.*, 22 Jan 1959.
159. WREC, *Education 1954–64*, 1964, p. 51.
160. P and F S-C, memorandum, 8 Dec 1964.
161. P and F S-C, memorandum, 8 July 1958.
162. M77 Co, Clegg to Wright, 20 Aug 1958.
163. Hyman to Clegg, 22 Nov 1958.
164. P and F S-C, memorandum, agendum 8, 9 Dec 1958.
165. P and F S-C, memorandum, agendum 9, 9 Dec 1958.
166. P and F S-C, memorandum, agendum 8, 9 Dec 1958.
167. *Ibid.*
168. P and F S-C, memorandum, agendum 9, 9 Dec 1958.
169. Ministry of Education to WRCC, P/S.450K/187, 7 Aug 1959.
170. P and F S-C, memorandum, 9 June 1959.
171. *Ibid.*
172. 78A/P, Clegg to Cockell, 22 Sep 1959.
173. *Ibid.*, Clegg to Stockdale, 21 Sep 1959.
174. *Ibid.*, Stockdale to Clegg, 9 Nov 1959.
175. *Ibid.*, Cockell to Clegg, 9 Feb 1959.
176. B77 Co, Clegg to Wright, 8 Aug 1958.
177. SG605, Clegg to Fletcher, 15 May 1963.
178. *Ibid.*, 3 May 1963.
179. *Ibid.*, 15 May 1963.
180. P and F S-C, memorandum, 8 Oct 1963.
181. 605, Clegg to Bartlett, 1 Oct 1963.
182. SG605, Clegg to Fletcher, 30 Dec 1963.
183. *Ibid.*
184. DES, Education Survey 8, *Launching Middle Schools*, 1970.
185. 511, Johnson to Clegg, 20 July 1974.

186. P and F S-C, memorandum, 8 Sep 1964.
187. SG605, Clegg to Nicholson, 16 Feb 1965.
188. *Ibid.*, Clegg to Dempster, 9 Nov 1964. A. B. Clegg was a member of the Newsom Committee which reported in 1963. This Committee considered the education of pupils between the ages of thirteen and sixteen of average and less than average ability for the Central Advisory Council for Education.
189. *Ibid.*, Clegg to Monkhouse, 20 Nov 1964.
190. 511/H, Pedley to Clegg, 25 Nov 1963.
191. P and F S-C, memorandum, 8 Dec 1964.
192. P and F S-C, memorandum, 14 Sep 1965.
193. SG605, Clegg to Thomson, 8 May 1969.
194. *Ibid.*
195. P and F S-C, Minutes, 3 July 1973.
196. SG605, Clegg to Dempster, 3 May 1966.
197. 609/H, Hogan to Hewitt, 26 Oct 1966.
198. WREC, Broughton's notes, 18 May 1966.
199. *YP*, 19 May 1966.
200. WREC, Broughton to Crosland, 19 July 1966.
201. *Ibid.*
202. P and F S-C, memorandum, 9 Sep 1969.
203. P and F S-C, Minutes, 9 Dec 1969.
204. P and F S-C, memorandum, 13 Jan 1970.
205. *Ibid.*
206. *Ibid.*, 10 Feb 1970.
207. *Ibid.*
208. P and F S-C, Minutes, 10 Feb 1970.
209. *Ibid.*
210. *YP*, 19 Mar 1970.
211. *Ibid.*
212. *Ibid.*
213. P and F S-C, Minutes, 4 Dec 1973.
214. *Ibid.*, 9 Feb 1971.
215. *Ibid.*, 9 Nov 1971.
216. *Ibid.*, 14 July 1970.
217. *YP*, 12 Jan 1971.
218. P and F S-C, memorandum, 12 Jan 1971.
219. *Ibid.*
220. *Ibid.*
221. P and F S-C, Minutes, 12 Jan 1971.
222. *YP*, 12 and 13 Jan 1971.
223. WREC, *Education 1964–74*, 1974, p. 25.
224. 513/C, Carnegie UK Trust Project, 12 June 1964.
225. 605 Co, Clegg to Miss Sewell, 18 Feb 1963.
226. *Ibid.*
227. P and F S-C, memorandum, 12 Jan 1965.
228. B609/H, office memorandum by J. M. Hogan, 18 Mar 1965.
229. WREC, notes about Minsthorpe and catchment area suggested as background in connection with the visit of the Duke of Edinburgh, undated.
230. R. Lambert, 'What Dartington Will Do', *New Society*, 30 Jan 1969.
231. *Ibid.*
232. WREC, Dartington Hall file, Harvey to Clegg, 30 Jan 1969.
233. *Ibid.*, Clegg to Lambert, 12 Mar 1969.
234. WREC, report, West Riding Dartington Scheme, unsigned and undated (1971).

235. WREC, Dartington Hall file, report, 'The Terrace', Conisbrough, Aug 1971.
236. P and F S-C, Minutes, 11 May 1971.
237. P and F S-C, Minutes, 11 Apr 1972.
238. Policy S-C, memorandum, 25 May 1948.
239. Ibid.
240. TES, 20 Sep 1974, article by A. B. Clegg.
241. Clegg used the expression 'the informal school' in his evidence to the Plowden Committee.
242. M. Golby, 'The West Riding: A Commentary', in The West Riding: Changes in Primary Education (The Open University, E203, Case Study 2), 1976.
243. Ibid.
244. YP, 22 Oct 1953.
245. Golby, op. cit.
246. TES, 27 Sep 1974, article by A. B. Clegg.
247. WREC, Education 1964-74, 1974, p. 12.
248. SG605, Clegg to Young, 25 Nov 1963.

## CHAPTER VIII

1. YCFE, The Reconstruction of Further Education, Sep 1942.
2. Board of Education, Education After the War, 1941.
3. Ministry of Education, Higher Technological Education, 1945, pp. 13-15.
4. YCFE, Minutes of a conference held on 21 Sep 1944.
5. H3, WRCC to Board of Education, 20 Jan 1944; WRCC to WR Members of Parliament, 14 Mar 1944; YCFE, Minutes, 20 Apr 1944, young people's colleges in rural areas, etc.; E80, memorandum on accommodation for young people's colleges and the service of youth, 5 June 1944.
6. 1962/3277, memorandum on further education 1946-7 to 1951-2, 9 Feb 1953.
7. Ibid.
8. Policy S-C, scheme for residential adult college, 15 Oct 1946; Minutes, 15 Oct 1946; G. Allen, HMI, to Chief Education Officer, 4 Dec 1946.
9. G77, S. G. Raybould, Director of Extra-Mural Studies, to Education Officer, 15 Oct 1946; Hyman to Education Officer, undated (about 19 Oct 1946).
10. T80, Haynes to Clegg, proposed residential college, 2 Jan 1947; Education Officer to Ministry of Education, 16 Jan 1947.
11. Policy S-C, Minutes, 18 Mar 1947; Policy S-C, proposed residential adult college Grantley Hall near Ripon, 16 Sep 1947; WREC, Minutes, 15 Oct 1947.
12. Policy S-C, Grantley Adult College, appointment of governing body, 18 Jan 1949; Policy S-C, Minutes, 18 Jan 1949.
13. Policy S-C, scheme for Residential Adult College, 15 Oct 1946.
14. T80, W. E. Williams to Haynes, 9 Dec 1946; T. A. Bennett (Miners' Welfare Assn) to Chief Education Officer, 8 Apr 1947.
15. Special S-C of FE S-C, FE provision in non-vocational classes, 29 June 1954.
16. WREC Minutes, 19 Jan 1955; WREC, oral evidence Mr R. Eyles, CEO Wakefield Metropolitan District Council, sometime AEO for FE, 7 Mar 1977; Colne Valley Guardian, 28 Jan 1955, 'County Further Education'.
17. WREC, Minutes, 19 Jan 1955.
18. YO, 25 Jan 1955, 'County plans wider scope for further education'.
19. P and F S-C, use of day school premises for further education purposes, 7 Mar 1961.

20. P and F S-C, schools and FE linked courses, 10 June 1969; office memorandum FE/1 (undated but 1967), reorganisation of secondary education – implications for FE.
21. H Ed S-C, County Youth Committee report, 7 May 1940.
22. Policy S-C, general report on the youth service, 21 Mar 1948.
23. *Ibid.*
24. Policy S-C, the service of youth, community centres and village halls, 16 Nov 1948.
25. Ministry of Education, *The Youth Service in England and Wales* [Cmnd 929], 1960.
26. WREC, Minutes, 17 Oct 1962.
27. WREC, Minutes, 15 May 1963.
28. P and F S-C, Minutes, 16 June 1964.
29. P and F S-C, full-time youth workers, 10 Feb 1970; P and F S-C, Minutes, 9 Nov 1971.
30. *Ibid.*, 14 June 1960.
31. *Ibid.*, 6 Dec 1960, and memorandum – residential training centre for further education.
32. Bramley Grange College, Minutes of proceedings at the first meeting of the Bramley Grange Residential Training Centre FE Governing Sub-Committee, 19 Mar 1965.
33. Policy S-C, Minutes, 16 Sep 1947; P and F S-C, Minutes, 9 Feb 1965; *ibid.*, 9 Mar 1965; *ibid.*, 3 Oct 1972. In this connection it may be noted that J. M. Hogan had been the first Warden of Aberdovey Outward Bound School.
34. P and F S-C, Minutes, 9 Oct 1956; *ibid.*, 13 Oct 1959; *ibid.*, 7 Mar 1961; *ibid.*, 5 Mar 1967; memorandum – Duke of Edinburgh's Award Scheme, report for the year ended 30 Sep 1967.
35. YCFE, Minutes, 25 July 1946, pp. 426–37.
36. Oral evidence, Mr R. Eyles, 7 Mar 1977.
37. P and F S-C, reorganisation of FE in Harrogate, 5 Dec 1972.
38. P and F S-C, memorandum – Institutions of FE, 6 Feb 1973; oral evidence, Mr R. Eyles, 7 Mar 1977.
39. P and F S-C, Minutes, 15 Apr 1969; *ibid.*, memorandum, policy of 'free trade' for part-time students.
40. P and F S-C, Minutes, 6 Feb 1973; *ibid.*, memorandum, policy of 'free trade' for part-time students, agendum 35a.
41. *Ibid.*, memorandum – discretionary awards for courses at intermediate level, agendum 35b; oral evidence, Mr R. Eyles, 7 Mar 1977.
42. WREC, Minutes, 15 Oct 1941.
43. WREC, Minutes, 19 Jan 1955.
44. PRO, ED 136/554, Butler to Holmes (after meeting with Hudson), 7 Apr 1943.
45. Ministry of Education, Circular 25, 9 Mar 1945.
46. *TES*, 29 Apr 1960, p. 850.
47. P and F S-C, Minutes and memorandum, scheme of development for further education in agriculture, 8 May 1962.
48. Oral evidence, Mr L. C. G. Gilling, Principal of Askham Bryan College of Agriculture and Horticulture, 17 Mar 1977; WREC, Minutes, 18 May 1960.
49. WREC, Minutes, 15 Mar 1967; Oral evidence, Mr L. C. G. Gilling, 17 Mar 1977.
50. WREC, Minutes, 17 Jan 1962.
51. WREC, Minutes, 19 Mar 1969.
52. Policy S-C, Minutes and memorandum, grants to universities, applications for increased grants from the universities of Leeds and Sheffield, 18 Jan 1949.
53. P and F S-C, Minutes, 7 May 1963.
54. Quoted from P. R. Sharp, 'Finance', in Gosden and Taylor (eds) *Studies in the History of a University, op. cit.*, p. 126; Leeds University Central Filing Office, D Finance, memorandum of Sir Charles Morris's conversations with Sir Bernard Kenyon, 17 Dec 1963.
55. P and F S-C, Minutes and memorandum, grants to universities, 1973–4, 6 Feb 1973.
56. G77, Binns to Hyman, 26 Feb and 5 Apr 1945.
57. P and F S-C, county university awards, 8 Nov 1956.

58. *Ibid.*; P and F S-C, Minutes, 4 Dec 1956 and 14 Oct 1958; WRCC, *Triennial Statement 1955–1956–1957*, 1958, p. 7.

59. P and F S-C, Minutes and memorandum, loans to students, with attached memorandum on this subject from the West Riding Treasurer's Department, 9 July 1957.

60. P and F S-C, Minutes and memorandum, county university awards, 10 Mar 1959.

61. P and F S-C, university and comparable awards, 9 May 1961; WRCC, *Triennial Statement 1967–1968–1969*, by chairman, 1970, p. 8.

62. P and F S-C, training college and university awards in the north and south of the West Riding, 8 May 1962.

63. P and F S-C, applications for admission to Oxford and Cambridge from West Riding grammar schools, 13 Jan 1959.

64. 513/K, internal minutes, West Riding scheme for admission to university: progress during the last three years, 14 Oct 1966.

65. WREC, *The Final Ten Years 1964–1974*, 1974, pp. 86–9, gives an interesting account of the scheme.

66. P and F S-C, West Riding scheme for entry to Oxford and Cambridge, 10 Mar 1970.

# Index